ADORATION AND PILGRIMAGE

ADORATION *and* PILGRIMAGE

JAMES DEAN *and* FAIRMOUNT

James F. Hopgood

LUMINARE PRESS
WWW.LUMINAREPRESS.COM

ADORATION AND PILGRIMAGE
Copyright © 2022 by James F. Hopgood

All rights reserved. This book or any portion thereof may not be reproduced or used in any manner whatsoever without the express written permission of the publisher, except for the use of brief quotations in a book review.

Printed in the United States of America

Cover: Photos of James Dean courtesy of David Loehr;
photo of Bank Building by author

Luminare Press
442 Charnelton St.
Eugene, OR 97401
www.luminarepress.com

LCCN: 2022909806

ISBN: 979-8-88679-010-8 (paperback)
ISBN: 979-8-88679-011-5 (hardback)
ISBN: 979-8-88679-012-2 (ebook)

In memory of James Richard Bradham,
an inspiration and true friend.

CONTENTS

Figures . . . xi
Preface and Acknowledgments . . . xiii
   The Cast and Acknowledgments . . . xv

1. Introduction . . . 1
   Another Beginning . . . 3
   About This Effort . . . 7
   Methods . . . 9

2. The Many Faces of James Dean and His Era . . . 17
   Genesis . . . 21
   Life and Death . . . 24
   Yet Another Beginning . . . 28
   The Era, the 1950s . . . 34

3. The Contested Icon: Dean and Fairmount . . . 40
   The Gallery . . . 42
   Fairmount . . . 44
   Local Views . . . 54
   Museum vs. Gallery . . . 60

4. Becoming a Deaner . . . 64
   Interviews . . . 69
      The James Dean Room . . . 69
      Dean of Deanabilia . . . 72
      A Budding Actor . . . 74
      Journey of a Deaner . . . 76
      Existentialist . . . 79

Never Too Young	81
The Navy Vet	81
To Be Part of James Dean's Life	87
Second Generation	91
Dalton's Book	92
Passages to the Self	94
Girl on a Motorcycle	97
Vignettes	99
Little Prince	99
West Coast Woman	100
A Loner	101
East Coast Writer	102
I Had a Dream	102
Obsessed…Now Mellowed	103
Latin American Writer	103
Discussion	104

5. Exploring Semiotics and Meaning ... 107
   Peirce's Semiotic ... 108
   The Porsche ... 113
   The Professor ... 115
   Art, Semiotics, and the Sacred ... 121
   Analysis ... 122
   A Preliminary Conclusion ... 125

6. Artists, Their Art, and the Sacred ... 127
   The Creative Dimension ... 128
   Music and Musicians ... 130
   Plastic Arts ... 136
   Professional Artist: Kenneth Kendall ... 137
      The Meeting ... 138
      Kendall's Art ... 144

	Photography and Photographers	146
	Florist and Amateur Chef	149
	Fetishism	151
	Tattooed	152
	Discussion	154
	A Pause	156
	Further Discussion and a Conclusion	157
7.	**Deaner Pilgrimage and the Role of Fairmount**	160
	Fairmount's Museum Days, the Mecca of Deaner Pilgrimage	166
	The Memorial Service	169
	Semiotics of Pilgrimage	178
	Discussion	183
8.	**Deaners as a Movement: A "Cult" or What?**	187
	What Is This?	189
	Not a Cult?	191
	What Deaners Are Not	193
	Ideology	194
	Conclusions	197
9.	**A Conclusion and Final Thoughts**	200
	The Self and What Is Sought	202
	Community	205
	Fairmount	206
	Charisma	207
	Endnotes	211
	References Cited	219
	Index	231

FIGURES

Figure 4.1. A small sample of Phil Zeigler's Dean memorabilia collection. (Photograph by the author). 86

Figure 5.1. Peirce's Semiotic. 110

Figure 5.2. Triadic Model. 111

Figure 6.1. Kenneth Kendall's painting "Giant" (original in color). (Copyright Kenneth Kendall Estate) 145

Figure 6.2. "El Torero Muerto" by Kenneth Kendall (original in color). (Copyright Kenneth Kendall Estate). 145

Figure 7.1. James Dean Memorial Park, Fairmount, Indiana. (Photo by author). 164

Figure 7.2. Flowers and "gifts" left at Dean's grave during a Festival weekend. (Photograph by author). 167

Figure 7.3. "Nicky Bazooka" addresses the audience during the annual memorial service at the Back Creek Friends Meeting; the late Phil Zeigler, left, and Tom Burghuis, right. (Photograph by author). 172

Figure 7.4. "Nicky Bazooka" places special flowers at Dean's grave following the church memorial service. (Photograph by author). 173

Figure 7.5. Naomi Yamada, a pilgrim from Japan, places her origami cranes on Dean's gravestone in 2005. (Photograph by author). 176

PREFACE AND ACKNOWLEDGMENTS

In order to exist, man must rebel, but rebellion must respect the limits that it discovers in itself—limits where minds meet, and in meeting, begin to exist.

—CAMUS

Why James Dean? Why *this* young actor who died in 1955 at the age of twenty-four? Perhaps a simple question to some yet one with a multitude of possible directions and answers. And there were a series of "whys?" that occurred during this project. What this is *not* is another biography or a hagiography. It is a hagiology. Several chapters are revisions and expansions of previous presentations at professional meetings such as the American Anthropological Association among others. Those were early explorations of those "whys" with suggested or tentative/suggestive answers. For fellow anthropologists I need to indicate my approach is not theoretical but explanatory. I test no theories, only seek explanations. Nor will this be a comparative study of other similar "icons," such as Elvis Presley. There are substantial published materials available (e.g., Doss 1999, 2005) should others wish to undertake such a project. More details on the research methods are found in Chapter 1. Some of the areas explored include issues of charisma, "cult," the role of place and time, the larger cultural frame/context, life history, the creative impulse, the unending/endless/expansive issue of meaning (including the personal and wider levels), and the role of pilgrimage and of community. All these varying observations and explanations coalesce, hopefully providing a deeper understanding of this and similar phenomena.

My research in Fairmount, Indiana, and on the "Deaners" began in 1989 and initially was directed toward (1) interpreting James Dean as a charismatic, saintlike figure (Hopgood 2005b) and (2) the interpretation of the Deaners as a formative or incipient movement with similarities to more mature and ostensibly religious movements along with a first effort on the semiotics (Hopgood, 1997, 2000). I also briefly investigated Japanese interest in Dean (Hopgood 1998a). Here the specific purpose is to concentrate on what has been learned concerning devotion to James Dean. This includes extending analysis, with ethnographic support, deeper into the area of semiotics associated with the Deaners, or more specifically, the meanings sought, experienced, created, or renewed through interaction with the Dean image and in the pilgrimage to Fairmount and elsewhere. Background material on Dean, the genesis of the Dean image, and the Deaners as representing an incipient, acephalous movement with a rudimentary "ideology" or "theology" are discussed as part of the contextualization of this phenomenon.

Most of my research occurred in Fairmount, a small Indiana farming town. It appeared undistinguished at first yet eventually I realized it is imbued with an additional layer of meaning coexisting with its mundane world. Initially, what I observed struck me as an example of Durkheim's sacred and profane, though that particular issue is now of little concern. Like most pilgrimage sites, a round of sacred places associated with the honored person is understood and easily discoverable by simple inquiry.

During that first visit to Fairmount I picked up an expressly prepared visitor's map at the James Dean Gallery, which located the major places associated with Dean when he lived there: his uncle and aunt's farm where he grew up after his mother's death, the high school he attended, the motorcycle shop he frequented, the church he attended, his grave, a memorial erected for him in the cemetery, the local historical museum with its "James Dean Room," the new gallery dedicated to him, and a dozen or so other places. This ordinary looking secular map turned into a guide to special, or as I began to think, *sacred* places and sites.

I learned the sanctification of Fairmount and the enshrinement of James Dean is ongoing. In addition to the various features and sites associated with Dean in Fairmount, on September 30, 1995, the 40th anniversary of his death, a new "James Dean Memorial Park" was dedicated there. Its centerpiece is a bust of Dean by Kenneth Kendall. Since 1995 other projects appeared, including a major expansion of the James Dean Gallery, notable growth and improvements of the James Dean exhibit of the Fairmount Historical Museum, a new monument erected in nearby Marion, a new marker for his mother in Marion's Grant Memorial Park, and the stage from the old Fairmount High School is now rebuilt in Playacres Park.

The Cast and Acknowledgments

Among those in this study who can be thought of as a "case of characters" there are several categories. Front and center are the various types of fans. A very important group for the fans and others are those who knew him in life, such as family, classmates, and teachers. Finally, there are those whose only interest in James Dean are of a financial nature; they are not an important focus of this work, though they are occasionally referred to here. These are not firm categories, but utilitarian signposts for handling the complexity of observed behavior. Those mentioned below are a sampling while many others will be found in the chapters that follow. Some people who were interviewed will appear only with pseudonyms (see list below) while others are simply too well known to be disguised. As part of the project, I interviewed over forty persons and several of them more than once.

Central to the fans category are the "Deaners," who are that category's most serious and involved members. They are central to this study. The term "Deaner" was first suggested to me by David

Loehr of the James Dean Gallery and is a name applied to James Dean when he was a high school student in Fairmount. There is the "just a fan" or casual fan category, who unlike Deaners are most likely to say they liked his movies and have always been fans since seeing those films, "but that's about it." A "just a fan" may visit Fairmount or Cholame, California, where he died, or a few other sites out of curiosity perhaps. In contrast, a Deaner feels a deep need to visit as many of the major sites associated with James Dean and possibly obscure locations in New York and Los Angeles. Many, in fact, return again and again to some of these sites, with Fairmount being the significant one. Deaners are likely heavy collectors of Dean memorabilia. These are only two possible "types" and should not be thought of as somehow fixed. Rather there is a continuum among the fans and Deaners as will become apparent. Many Deaners and fans will be introduced in this book.

Another category that needs mention here are the "look-alikes." There are a number of individuals who attend the annual festival in Fairmount and compete in the "James Dean Look-alike" contest. Some have taken it up as an income source and actively seek employment in the Dean rebel guise while others hope it will somehow help them in an acting career. A few are serious fans or Deaners.

A category of fan that I have generally ignored are those who claim to be, or to have been, in contact with James Dean since his death. Perhaps because of my own disinterest or the difficulty of working with mediums, I decided early on to exclude those fans in any direct way. Early in this project I attempted to contact a medium while in Chicago, but she refused to meet with me. Occasionally I encountered an irrational fan, and I have excluded any input from them.

Among those who knew him in life there are fewer and fewer as time has passed. When I began this project there were many who had known him and were willing to speak with fans about him when he lived in Fairmount. Among them was Adeline Nall (1906-1996), Dean's high school drama and speech teacher who encouraged his ambitions. She maintained contact with him during his years of struggle and at one point moved to New York in an effort to start her own stage career. That effort was short-lived, and she returned to Fairmount to teach. Bob Pulley (1931-2013) was one of Dean's best friends in Fairmount, and like Ms. Nall was sought by fans and interviewers for stories of growing up with Dean. Mr. Pulley served as a pallbearer for Dean's funeral and was one of the few veterans who continued to honor him. Ms. Nall served as the emcee for many years each September 30 at the memorial service for James Dean held at the Back Creek Friends Meeting until her health no longer permitted. The James Dean Gallery maintains an exhibit area dedicated to her.

Those who worked with Dean in New York and Hollywood include many persons in the television and film industry, photographers, and artists. Among those, I interviewed Magnum photographer Dennis Stock and artist Kenneth Kendall, both now deceased.

The family originally included Marcus and Ortense Winslow Sr., Dean's uncle and aunt who took over his upbringing after his mother died in 1940. Their children include Marcus Jr. (b. 1943) and Joan (1926-2021). Both Marcus Sr. and Ortense were central to those sought-out by fans until their deaths in 1976 and 1991. Currently, Marcus Jr. is a central figure in the maintenance of Dean's memory and legacy. He is closely involved with the Fairmount Historical Museum and has loaned many of Dean's personal items and related objects to the museum for display. He is also in charge of the family's financial interest in the franchising of Dean's image as managed by Curtis Management Group. Winton Dean and his second wife, Ethel, were not among the favorites of the fans. Although they benefited from Dean's estate, they apparently contributed little to his legacy. Winton died in 1995 and is buried alongside his second wife, Ethel, in Fairmount's Park Cemetery, not far from his famous son. Winton's first wife, Mildred, is buried in nearby Marion. Other family appear to be largely extraneous in terms of the activities surrounding Dean.

Some of the highly visible participants in events in Fairmount, such as Tom Burghuis, Mark Kinnaman, and Greg Swenson have also contributed to my efforts with this project. One of the most prominent Deaners is David Loehr along with his partner Lenny Prussack. Out of his devotion to James Dean, David has been especially forthcoming with assistance during this project.

In addition to those mentioned, there are others who contributed in various ways to this project. Chris Boehm encouraged me to pursue this project early on and later reminded me on several occasions to publish the results. Since several of the book's chapters began as conference presentations, I want to thank Phyllis Passariello, Walter Randolph Adams, Barbara June Macklin, and others for their comments and suggestions. Thanks also to the Kenneth Kendall Estate and Cindy Cronk Vukovic for permission to reproduce two of his paintings. I also need to thank Sylvia Bongiovanni for sharing her knowledge of the history of the several Dean fan clubs and magazines as well as her personal story. David Dalton also was helpful by sharing his insights regarding many facets of the Dean phenomenon.

In addition I must give my thanks and acknowledgment to those who consented to sitting for taped interviews: Brian Baker, the late "Nicky Bazooka" (Terry Lee Nichols), Tom Burghuis, Joe Bills, Debbie Bottiggi, Sylvia Bongiovanni, Sheri Conover, the late Jim Curran, David Dalton, Dwight Dejaniva, Mary Emmerick, Ken and Anita Grant, Jack Harris, Professor Kurt Hemmer (un-taped), Lisa King, the late Kenneth Kendall, Mark Kinnaman, Don Knudsen, David Loehr, Chris Mathews, Donna McCall, Laura Pardini, Dr. Darryl and Judy Poole, Lenny Prussack, Bob Rees, the late Maxine Rowland, Richard Sassin, Keith Schachtele, Lance Stell, the late Dennis Stock, Greg Swenson, Dr. Robert Trundle, Aleta Vertuno, Luke Williams, the late Kathie Wilson, Mark Winslow Jr., Curt Worl, and the late Phil Zeigler. Then there are those fans who were helpful in informal settings in sharing their thoughts and reactions to James Dean.

The following is a list of pseudonyms used for many of the interviewees and others observed during this project: "Albert," "Angela," "Billy," "Frank," "Fred," "Jane," "Jeff," "Jennifer," "Judy," "Kennick,"

"Lawrence," "Matt," "May," "Oliver," "Sofía," "Tommy," and "Vince." Each will appear in quotations when first appearing in a chapter.

I want to make special note of thanks to David Loehr and Lenny Prussack for their continuous help throughout the project. Their knowledge of the James Dean phenomenon as well as many of the people involved has contributed substantially to my efforts. David opened his archive for me, allowing me to chart many facets of the project. He also provided photographs of James Dean for use in this book from his collection. Finally, and once again, I want to thank my spouse, Esther, for her support and tolerance while I pursued this project.

1

Introduction

*But mortals suppose that gods are born,
wear their own clothes and have a voice and body.*
—FRAGMENTS BY XENOPHANES (CA. 580–CA. 475 BCE)

As if predictors of future events…

October 5, 1955: Two teenage girls were picked up by a local sheriff south of Logansport, Indiana. The girls were on their way to Fairmount, Indiana, to attend James Dean's funeral. They were from River Grove, Illinois, near Chicago, and had taken the train to Logansport, but due to lack of money couldn't continue to Fairmount.

Reserved seating was requested from Hollywood and other places—something unheard of in Fairmount. Henry Ginsberg, producer of *Giant*, attended along with several others representing Warner Bros. Also in attendance was Dean's friend Dennis Stock, a Magnum photographer. Elizabeth Taylor, among other Hollywood friends and associates, along with Edna Ferber, author of *Giant*, sent floral arrangements, as did friends and associates in New York City.

Mr. and Mrs. Marcus Winslow Sr., the uncle and aunt who raised him on their farm, were on their way back to Fairmount from Hollywood when the accident occurred. On the journey back, Mr. Winslow heard on his car radio an announcement of the death of a young movie star on Saturday, September 30. Fearing the worst, he turned off the radio not wanting to know if it was their Jimmy, and they avoided buying or reading newspapers during the remainder of their trip home. Arriving home Monday, October 3, they learned the sad news they most feared.

October 8, 1955: As many arrived in Fairmount for the funeral, one young woman fan who had wandered the streets of Fairmount for two days had disappeared. She was from Brooklyn, New York. Young Dean's tragic death was the subject of conversation throughout the small Indiana town and nearby communities for days. That day, a Saturday, was turning out to be unlike any other day in the memory of Fairmount's people.

The Indiana State Police provided special details, and local civil defense police were assigned to handle the heavy traffic; State Police took up positions at 10:00 a.m. with Fairmount's Auxiliary Police in position by 12:30 p.m.

Dean's body was held at Hunt Funeral Home, but a closed casket was mandatory because of the mangled condition of his body. The family's church, the Back Creek Friends Meeting, was much too small for the anticipated crowd of mourners, family, friends, fans, the curious, and the press. Services were held at Fairmount Friends Church.

Saturday, 2:00 p.m.: The Fairmount Friends Church with a capacity of six hundred pews was filled. Extra chairs were set up where possible, between pews and in the back. With the church filled by 1:00 p.m., a public address system was set up for an anticipated crowd outside the church, but it failed to work. Some took up a spot in the church's nursery while a crowd of an estimated 2,000 persons overflowed around the church, down the street, and along the sidewalks. The burial, initially planned to be in Grant Memorial Park in Marion next to his mother's grave, was changed to Fairmount's Park Cemetery for unannounced reasons. Rev. Xen Harvey and Rev. Dr. James DeWeerd conducted services. Rev. DeWeerd, who knew Dean when he served as a pastor in Fairmount, traveled from Cincinnati to deliver the elegy. Rev. Harvey, who also knew Dean in Fairmount, delivered the eulogy.

An estimated 3,000 people—more people than the total population of Fairmount—attended. This outpouring of public grief for movie stars, rock stars, and other famous personalities is a phenomenon Americans have become accustomed to since the 1950s, but then, coming from this small Indiana town, it was truly remarkable. The finality of the event only marked an episode in a new beginning: An estimated 500 persons waited at the grave site and hundreds more followed the body to Park Cemetery for burial portending a ritual that would be repeated many times over in years to come.

Another Beginning

What is to be made of James Dean in the days since?[1] Opening a copy of the April 19, 2010, edition of *The Nation*, I found a review of the film *Greenberg* that begins with a long description of James Dean, Natalie Wood, and Sal Mineo in a scene from *Rebel Without a Cause*:

> Natalie Wood gazed off-camera, her moonlit eyes glittering with sexual speculation, and wondered aloud what James Dean was like. "Well, you have to get to know him," Sal Mineo replied. His face, turned in the same direction as Natalie's, glowed with similar lust but even greater candor. His words, inadequate to the great subject that had been proposed, emerged in dreamy, indefinite phrases, until at last he hit on the right one: "He's sincere." (Klawans 2010, 34)

Interestingly, this probably would not have been written, and certainly not published, in 1955 when *Rebel Without a Cause* appeared, and the actors' real names are used, not the names of the characters they were playing. So, while it shows how interpretations of the film vary over time (or come out of the closet in this case), in a larger sense Klawans's description demonstrates the "staying power" of James Dean and *Rebel Without a Cause* as archetypical. This is underscored by the actors being identified by their real names rather than their roles.

Then there is a piece in *The Atlantic* online, also from 2010, "Ronald Reagan and James Dean: Rare Video from 1954." A video clip of the episode was included with the short article. The article notes a writer for "Late Night with Jimmy Fallon" on NBC "unearthed the episode" and that "[n]o one has seen this episode in the decades since" (Meroney 2010). This would be surprising to many Deaners who own video copies of the episode. But, while it is true they appeared together in an episode of *General Electric Theater* and that must be of some historical interest, what relevance could this have in 2010? Meroney's short article doesn't provide an answer, but in this era of "icons" it is not surprising that someone would hit upon the idea of pairing the iconic rebel James Dean against the conservative, right-wing icon Ronald Reagan. Dean, in this case, has been made superficially political by contrasting him with Reagan. What is ironic, of course, is that the forces that brought Dean's and Reagan's successes are quite different—though coterminous—the social and cultural unrest beginning in the 1950s and continuing into the 1960s for Dean and the counter and conservative reaction for Reagan (e.g., his anti-student protest, anti-communist, pro-business, and pro-establishment positions).

A short piece from 2011 in *The Chronicle of Higher Education* on director Nicholas Ray features a large photo of Ray and Dean from *Rebel Without a Cause* with smaller photos of Ray with Dennis Hopper and Jane Russell (Tamarin 2011, B23). A search for "James Dean" on YouTube (February 21, 2014) resulted in "about 194,000" hits. Many of those hits are actually misses, (e.g., who is James Dean Bradford?) but estimating a 50 percent hit result is still impressive. Many of the posted videos are film clips from his movies, TV appearances, and documentaries. Some are fan-constructed films and slideshows dedicated to Dean as testimonials and tributes. There are clips of interviews with Dean's family members, those he worked with in film and TV, and fans.

Certainly, adding to Dean's fame was the work of three photographers in particular: Roy Schatt, Dennis Stock, and Sanford Roth.

Some of their photos have become "iconic" and often find their way into advertising and other venues. The importance of photographs and photographers to the story of his rise in the public mind and contribution to Dean's subsequent adoration by many since his death needs attention. Although Hollywood magazines contained countless photographs of him, their lack of endurance pales in comparison with books published by photographers, and three in particular. Schatt, Stock, and Roth each published at least one book of their photographs of Dean and their works were often exhibited.

An art exhibit in New York City during 2014 and early 2015 of the works of Ray Johnson included a piece, collage on cardboard, from 1991-94. The piece is untitled but parenthetically referred to as "Jasper Johns, James Dean with Coca Cola" (*Art News* April 2015, 78). Perhaps Johnson intended to represent Jasper Johns, one of the artists associated with "Pop Art" in the mid-1950s, gazing toward two popular culture "icons."

Among automobile enthusiasts, a piece in the October 2015 issue *Automobile* by St. Antoine recounts Dean's last few days before the tragic September 30, 1955, highway accident. In part, a personal memoir of his visits to Cholame and the site of the crash and a recounting of Dean's final journey, St. Antoine ends his remembrance with:

> ...I always pull over at the intersection itself...I stop, roll down the windows, take a few moments, listen to the birds, the insects, the wind. The setting is largely just as it was six decades ago—the hardscrabble flatland, the gentle hills, the promise of tarmac escaping to the horizon. Never can I linger here without reflecting on time and chance and fate. And why it was that a gifted young man had to die on this quiet road to Cholame (2015, 27).

Meanwhile, in Marion, Indiana, a new memorial was constructed near the site where James Dean was born. Previously, the site was marked only with a bronze star and a rock with a mounted plaque. The centerpiece of the memorial is a six-foot-tall black granite monolith with etchings of the house where he was born, a baby photograph, and an image of Dean from *Rebel Without a Cause*. The rear of the monolith features a brief biography of the actor. The monument is in a parklike setting with three benches flanking the monument. The memorial, designed by David Loehr, was dedicated on September 30, 2015, the 60th anniversary of Dean's death. Even Dean's mother, Mildred Wilson Dean, who is buried in Marion, isn't spared the fame of her son. In 2016 a historic marker was erected near her grave and on the day of her birthday, September 15. The marker notes her influence on her son in the arts followed by a brief bio of Dean.

And, in Lacoste, France, the "Wall of Hope" was erected in 1989 to honor James Dean. It was commissioned by Japanese businessman Seita Onishi and sculpted by Yasuo Mizui. It was the second tribute monument from Onishi. The first was the monument erected in Cholame near the site of the fatal crash site. Onishi originally intended to erect the "Wall of Hope" at Cholame but failed to obtain permission.

Each of these cases demonstrates the continuing evolution of and devotion to James Dean, or better, the evolution and devotion of his image and icon. He is being forever reread and remade. He is not only part of the kitsch world created of the 1950s, but he is to be found at deeper levels of American culture. Nevertheless, the level of popularity in the 1980s and 1990s has not been maintained in the twenty-first century. The decline was apparent by 2005, and in 2007 David Loehr wrote a piece in the *James Dean Gallery Newsletter* about the drop in Dean's public visibility and popularity, noting the decline "won't last forever." He remarks that as long as Dean's films are shown in theaters or on television, new fans will emerge. "The Indiana farm boy presented a screen-presence so powerful, lifelike, and believable it was simply remarkable and unforgettable. Many first-time viewers will become serious fans and admirers of this phenomenal, rare talent" (2007, 3). My interest, however, is not strictly in the history of his popularity but in what his devoted followers seek from and find in him.

About This Effort

Readers of Roland Barthes's *Mythologies* (2012) know well his equation of modern media's and popular culture's products and messages with the mythology in past times. Today we have celebrities instead of gods, goddesses, demigods, heroes, and antiheroes with their legends and epics. Modern folk are exposed to movies, photography, television programs, the internet, and above all ever-present advertising to convey not only images and style, but values. Movies and television, of course, may well be the prime media for conveying today's mythology, and Dean along with many others is among those who have the roles vacated by those of past mythology. Others may note that a favorite avenue along these lines can be found in Lord Raglan's *The Hero: A Study in Tradition, Myth, and Dreams* (1956). Raglan provided twenty-two traits that regularly appear in hero myths, regardless of culture. Certainly, given some latitude for time and variation, Dean would qualify as a Raglan-type hero. And, likewise, turning to Joseph Campbell's *The Hero with a Thousand Faces* (1968) the same exercise is possible.

Many accounts of Dean's life follow those patterns found in Raglan and others, with Dean fitting into the trope or stereotype of the struggling young man of humble origins (in some cases of questionable parentage), a lost mother, abandonment by his father, and a struggle in the big city (NYC). This picture has him as "just like you and me" but one who found the key to success, in part by rebellion against something (the Hollywood system of the time).

While noting the contemporary commonplace comparison of past mythology with its cast of characters and today's media with its cast of celebrities, that is not a purpose here. Given today's current criteria for celebrity status, Dean might not even qualify. For example, he did not have a lavish lifestyle nor great material wealth, which today are markers of celebrity culture. He certainly would not have qualified for an episode of television's "Lifestyles of the Rich and Famous." However, it must be noted that he did achieve some measure of fame and success shortly before his death and given his career direction at the time he would have likely achieved that status. Making comparisons to Raglan's and Campbell's traits for heroes is also possible and would show that Dean qualifies on several of their criteria (see chapter 2).

What follows in chapter 2 is not a biography of James Dean. And it will not be a full account of his celebrity and popularity. Nor can this be a search for the "real" James Dean as this is simply unknowable. About James Dean there are dozens of biographies and hagiographies in book and film form, not to mention articles in numerous magazines, and likewise uncounted accounts of his and others' celebrity status. Dean was barely a movie celebrity before his persona and status began a process of transformation. As a sign and symbol, Dean is multivocal, having many assorted meanings all at the same time (cf. Turner 1969, 52) and while his life and celebrity must be considered, this study is concerned with the fans and followers of James Dean and especially his most devoted, those I refer to as "Deaners." The term "Deaner" was suggested to me early on by David Loehr, who is himself one of the best examples of a Deaner in a number of defining ways. However, the term is not of recent origin. "Deaner" was a nickname for James Dean among his high school classmates in Fairmount, Indiana. The late Bob Pulley, a classmate of Dean's, when telling stories about Dean or responding to questions would often refer to him as "Deaner."

In this project I sought to avoid any notion of either/or regarding questions of a person's religion versus devotion to Dean—though the articulations of an individual's negotiations with received religious training could be of considerable interest—I avoided this issue in my method and analysis. The conflict did arise from time to time when someone I was interviewing or chatting with said something indicating their personal concern with the issue, but most Deaners didn't see it as an issue. For the most part, fans and Deaners kept the question of their religious ideas and their devotion to Dean apart, or at least as two separate domains of devotion. However, this is certainly a concern seen in some other studies of celebrities (e.g., Doss 1999) and is to be expected among Americans generally.

Methods

Regarding field methods, I began working as I would in any other project: observation, followed by participant-observation, and interviews (recorded, semi-structured and unrecorded conversational). For the most part I conducted this project from 1989 to 2005, but with occasional fieldwork and visits since. Truthfully, it is difficult to put an end date to this project. Observation and participation were carried out at public and private events in Fairmount along with "backstage" events among fans and Deaners. This was for the most part a "weekend" project although there were occasional midweek visits. Still, I did take time to attend many of the regular and special events: the James Dean Festival weekend, the annual September 30 memorial service, the birthday parties in February, and other non-regular events. I also conducted some taped interviews in other locations in Indiana, Ohio, and Kentucky as well as visiting Cholame, California, and the Griffith Observatory in Los Angeles. I made observations in several locations in Japan and Beijing and conducted one interview while in the People's Republic of China.

My research included watching films made by fans and Deaners as well as commercial films made for TV or theater. In terms of print material there is a vast quantity of books, magazines, and articles related to James Dean and his fans. I also was allowed to access David Loehr's archives at the James Dean Gallery. The various creations of Dean fans are also an invaluable source that includes books, paintings, drawings, and other creative works.

I realized with this project I was entering a domain thought of by many as "popular culture." I had no knowledge of scholarly work in that area; at best I was a participant. In fact, there were seemingly several industries devoted to popular culture, and the more I looked the more I found: there were professional popular culture associations and many journals devoted to popular culture. In speaking with several colleagues, I was told, yes, there is scholarship in that area, but no theory or methods of its own—popular culture studies are derivative. Whatever the case, I was determined to proceed as an anthropologist thinking that with the tools, concepts, and paradigms of sociocultural anthropology along with a bit of philosophy I could study any aspect of whatever culture. Regarding popular culture I am reminded of Matthew Shirts' warning: "Social analysts who ignore the specific content of popular culture by reducing it to a mere prop of economic and political arrangements make a serious mistake" (1989, 123). Early on I realized what I was studying could be approached from several different interpretative perspectives, and that will be reflected in the chapters/essays that follow.

When I began this project in 1989, I wondered if any anthropologist had studied the James Dean phenomenon. The only reference I found was in Weston La Barre's *The Ghost Dance: The Origins of Religion*. In his discussion of "crises cults," as one example among many of responses to the deaths of heroes and leaders of these cults, followers refused to believe in their leaders' deaths (1970, 270). In Dean's case La Barre notes pulp literature stories that Dean hadn't actually died in the car crash; instead, he was in "seclusion" where plastic surgeons were working to restore his face and body. Though accurate for pulp stories of the mid- to late 1950s, and one that occasionally reappears, this notion was never widely believed by his fans.

So I began the project in an exploratory way and with a few expectations, not at all sure what I would find. Along the way there were surprises, with some beyond the obvious ones that any anthropologist expects in the field. One early and surprising dimension of the research I discovered was the breadth and depth of interest in James Dean. It seemed everywhere I looked I saw James Dean: in various genres of magazines, books, movies, TV shows, ads and commercials, even comic books, and of course on the internet. He could be seen in shopping mall shops of all kinds and on restaurant walls. And in all sorts of forms and every conceivable type of object: mugs, plates, clocks, cigarette lighters, posters, paintings, murals, calendars, cookie jars, life-size stand-up figures, and so on. It is certainly the case that after Dean's death in 1955 and on into the 1960s, he was a "godsend" to teen magazine publishers, but why now with magazines on the decline? So, this was the 1980s and '90s—a period I now regard in many ways as a generational phenomenon of those who grew up in the 1950s and early 1960s.

I wondered if perhaps the video revolution of the 1980s drove much of the new and renewed interest in Dean. In the 1950s through much of the 1970s, fans and potential fans had to look for Dean's films to be shown on TV or at film festivals and revivals. With the 1980s, everything ever filmed, it seemed, became available on video. In Dean's case this not only meant his three major films, but films where he had bit parts, a host of early and mid-1950s TV appearances, a number of documentary films (from the 1950s to the present), and eventually through fan networks, an amazing variety of clips from, it seemed, every TV show where he was the topic of coverage. You could now watch James Dean anytime. Changing social mores of the 1970s and '80s also could be behind the interest of some in James Dean: a focus on Dean's androgyny may stem in part from the increased emphasis in US society on gender equality and greater social acceptance of homosexuality. While the media and its technology are certainly a factor in promoting anyone or anything, it remains something of a crapshoot as to who or what will catch on, much more so as to who or what will endure.

Moving into the 1990s another factor is the decentralization of culture often noted in reference to globalization, though in this case it is not world cultures, but the internal ones. Given the internet and worldwide web, the mechanisms available through globalization make possible relatively easy access to just about anything and the creation of networks of any kind. What are your values?

Does anyone else out there share them? Well, just log on to such-and-such website, and you will find others who share your values, or something like them. Create a network of like-minded people, share ideas, photos, videos, whatever, instantly. The structure of a common American culture crumbled and with its subsequent reclusterings of fragments and ever-diverging strands then reappear in clusters of common interests and passions.

Like all signs, symbols, and "icons" of long-standing, today's are subject to change in order to fit changing times. So, was Dean's resurrection in the 1980s a mere fragment of a conservative backlash and a reach into nostalgia? Yes and no. If popular culture is any measure, the 1980s were a time of '50s nostalgia expressed in part by the Reagan era of national hubris and increased economic inequality. Loss of jobs overseas, major changes in the labor force with a shift to services, high-tech work, and nonunion employment created a climate of national longing. This longing for good old Americana was a natural response to American decline. This is part of the story, but I must leave it to the historians and return more directly to the subject at hand.

Simple visibility or greater availability are not sufficient explanations for Dean's popularity, not to mention his adoration. I learned early on that the fans, including those I'm calling Deaners, were not only composed of original fans from the 1950s and the 1960s (which was expected), but from yesterday and every decade in between. This unexpected "realization" set the tone for much of the research and posed many questions to be addressed. The extensive publicity he received during the 1950s simply is not sufficient to explain the continuing interest and adoration he receives.

Elsewhere I explored the devotion and adulation of James Dean as an example of the creation of the *sacred* (Hopgood 2005a, xv-xvii; 2005b, 124-125) or, as some may prefer, a "religious" manifestation. In large measure the US is a secular society—even among the religious, secularism is a significant component of their lives, and very few are given over to an all-encompassing religious life.

In such a society, where do people go for transcendence, the spiritual, inspiration, "enchantment," or guidance if church or temple as usual is unfulfilling? And while many Deaners resist the idea that they "worship" James Dean, I must reply that they are simply ignoring their own behavior. They are tapping the sacred impulse in their devotion. Given that the contemporary North American religion scene can be described as "combinative," referring to the mixing or recombining of religious practices and beliefs from various denominations and traditions, the present case should not be surprising. Another trait of American religious belief is the increase in the percentage of people who do not claim any specific religious affiliation (Kosmin, Mayer, and Keyson 2001, 10-11, 16-18), yet maintain some sort of belief in God or simply consider themselves "religious" or "spiritual" (Baylor Religion Survey 2006, 12). These trends in the United States are further supported by a Pew Research study on the "millennial" generation (Pew Research Center 2010) and as recently as 2021 by the Public Religion Research Institute (PRRI Staff 2021). Although this point will not be pursued here, it is possible to view the Dean phenomenon as an example of American "civil religion" (*cf.* Demerath 1974).

Where the root (or roots) of religion and the belief in the sacred and supernatural is to be found is a matter for other studies. Is it innate as Thomas Hobbes suggested long ago (1950, 85ff), as among many others since? Or is it a creation purely of individuals within society, as many others see it? For purposes here it doesn't matter. The impulse may be innate, but the manifestation and elaboration surrounding that impulse derive from the socio-cultural settings and individuals who participate in the milieu. Despite these problems, it is best to simply accept as useful the notion of "sacred" as a human creation, innate or otherwise. But where does fandom cross into that domain? I argue that persons doing or participating in seemingly secular activities may pass into the sacred. In American society the two areas are considered different and largely separate, so if an act appears to be sacred but is done in a secular event or setting, then what is its meaning? One way out of this dilemma is to argue that in such cases the use of a sacred-style act is a way of adding/giving additional weight/importance to the subject or content of the secular event. This is quite common in American culture as seen, for example, in prayer before sports events, taking oaths in court, etc.; again American "civil religion". It can also be argued that, like other human creations, what is sacred is simply a matter of agreement. But how is agreement expressed? Does it have to be voted into existence, or can it arise from human action? For example, how to reconcile the tension of the Durkheimian "sacred and profane" (Hopgood 1992, 412-413). Dean was for me a secular figure, but as I began observing the ways he was honored and adored, I realized I was dealing with the sacred, and at other times perhaps something quite near that domain—the liminal "betwixt and between." When an individual or a group of persons behave toward something or someone in a sacred manner, that is where the issue will rest.

Eventually I began moving from the discovery phase to a focus on meaning (with some help via semiotics). I decided that was where some issues could best be addressed. What goes on "between" James Dean and the Deaner? What is the nature or content of this interaction? What is the Deaner "getting from this transaction"? Durkheim's notion of collective representations (= symbols) doesn't go deep enough to deal with questions of meaning; collective representations certainly play a major role but are only part of the picture. In the present study, collective representations would refer to those from the larger society and can be viewed as providing a larger context. The issue(s) of semiotics applied at the individual level—i.e., what individuals do with those symbols—goes unaddressed. In attempting to address questions of meaning, I turned initially to Milton Singer and Charles Sanders Peirce, and then to various commentators on the Peircean semiotic (chapter 5).

The next issue was to explore the nature and extent of the entanglement and enchantment. A Deaner's "involvement" or "obsession" with Dean is not limited to a relatively passive activity such as only watching his films, reading books about him, or viewing his photos. This may be followed by pilgrimages to Fairmount and other sites. But this affective "involvement" may also lead to action (agency) in the form of a creative activity. To my surprise I found that many paint, sculpt, draw, write poems or prose, make films, write plays, create public displays, and even do flower arrangements out of their love and devotion to James Dean. In the same vein, others decide to pursue acting or other performance arts. Still others are obsessed with collecting Dean relics and memorabilia. Consequently, one of the issues is to model this seemingly dialectical and emotionally dialogical interaction in an explicit manner. This interaction is best modeled as a triadic relation, rather than a dialectical one. As a triad, the result of the interaction is allowed for the human actor and her interaction. Specifically, the content or result of the interaction is the third part of the triad, with Dean as perceived and what the Deaner brings to the interaction and the result that she leaves with. Since this interaction is ongoing and subject to modification, the initial and subsequent content is subject to change with subsequent events and interaction, including interactions with others and media.

A final point here about semiotics: the term "icon" and problems with its use. James Dean is often described as an *icon*. The problem today is the explosion in the popular media's usage of the term "icon" creates a dilemma of significance and meaning. It has a long history of usage in semiotics, of course. Stemming from the Greek *eikōn* meaning "image" followed by its historical usage and reference to paintings of religious figures or images of the Eastern Orthodox Church.

Today there are more and more "icons" being named throughout many domains of life and work. Anthropologist Margaret Mead is an American icon, according to Lutkehaus (2008). Elvis, the Rolling Stones, and The Beatles (among many others) are icons of rock and roll music. There are local icons (surfer Duke Kahanamoku of

Hawaii), national sports icons (Babe Ruth), painters (Frida Kahlo), and today (2021) *everyone* knows Oprah is an icon. It appears there are icons everywhere and that anyone who was the "first," the "best," the "greatest," a benchmark, is now an icon. So those who in the past might have been termed heroes, founders, famous leaders, legends, etc. are now candidates for icon status.

But, of course, icons are not limited to people (living and dead), but include buildings (the White House), monuments (the St. Louis Gateway Arch), automobiles (Ford Model T), and other things (the US flag) and places (Silicon Valley). Even Spam, from Hormel, gets the "icon" treatment (Ryan 2010, 98). In recent years icons have appeared throughout the landscape: in software, *Icon Magazine*, Icon shoes, Icon comics, Hotel Icon, and on and on. There are iconic advertisements (the Hathaway Shirt man) and commercials (the Geico Gecko). Many of these are temporary icons, of course, which will simply disappear to be replaced by the next icon. In any case, what or who is referred to as an icon comes and goes as does all fashion. For all these reasons and concerns, the term "icon" will be limited and usually placed inside quotation marks. (The only exception will be where the term is needed in the discussion of semiotics and will appear in *italics*.)

2

The Many Faces of James Dean and His Era

But no matter how long I may contemplate an image, I shall never find anything in it but what I have put there.

—JEAN-PAUL SARTRE

So, what sort of James Dean do you want? How about a "macho" Dean? Then, go to Neibaur (1989, 178-184). There we find one version of the "tough guy" and "antihero," but with a difference. A "tough guy" off-screen and in his films, yet mixed with passion for others, compassion, romanticism, love, and sensitivity. The image of Dean as a "tough guy" is there if that's what the viewer seeks. Brett Farmer underscores that view and finds Dean's and (young) Brando's film images expressed through "male angst, aggression, and violence" along with "sensitive, vulnerable, tender, passive, fragile, weak" characteristics, all of which challenge traditional images of masculinity (2000, 227-228).

A different slant on the issue of "macho" men in film is found in Cohan's *Masked Men* (1997). If a fan is looking for a different take on Dean (and Clift and Brando), Cohan's scattered comments on the Dean, Clift, Brando trio point to the tension between heterosexuality and homosexuality in their performances. Perhaps an exploration of Dean's sexuality is sought. If so, there's John Gilmore's *Live Fast-Die Young: Remembering the Short Life of James Dean*

(1997) or Paul Alexander's *Boulevard of Broken Dreams: The Life, Times, and Legend of James Dean* (1974), and a recent film, *Joshua Tree, 1951: A Portrait of James Dean* (Mishry 2012).

Or maybe a more rounded image? A recent short article in *Christophorus*, a magazine devoted to things Porsche, manages to hit just about all the "buttons" of the Dean persona in less than two pages, accompanied by three photos of Dean in his 550 Spyder. Consider these characteristics: "unconventional," "melancholy look," "rough manners," "lived fast and died tragically," "a legend," "defiant and simultaneously passionate," "a conflicted character," "an elemental force," "[he] runs riot; he lives fast, unyieldingly, obstinately," "restlessness," "thirst for life," "misunderstood, wounded, abandoned," and "His journey out of darkness [his life in Indiana] becomes a struggle against an overwhelming magnitude of teenage angst" (Daun 2015, 38-39). After that run-through on Dean, Porsche is introduced to complete the connection. Porsche had become a "status symbol for individualists" due to its newness along with its spartan, sporty and uncompromising nature. Dean had selected this "deeply emotional anti-mainstream car" for his next race on September 30. And, on that day, he "is full of vitality and high spirits" as he drives toward Salinas with his race number "130" and "Little Bastard" freshly painted on the car. The crash later that day is "banal, unnecessary, fatal." The "rebel with the wild heart" dies, but "his legend lives on" (Daun 2015, 39). So ends this brief article that hits most of the "buttons" except for talent and the sexual. He must be charismatic too, though that label isn't mentioned. This brief piece manages to perpetuate the Dean story along with his image and the Porsche connection: two interconnected "icons" that remain so today.

Others may prefer the hero image, and there are many authors who borrow from that genre. Here, this can best be approached via the "myth of the hero" demonstrated by Lord Raglan (1956, 171, 174-175) and Orrin E. Klapp (1962). Other scholars, such as Joseph Campbell (1968) and Clyde Kluckhohn (1960), should also be noted here. Raglan and Kluckhohn each find a similar pattern when considering hero mythology, though the many details differ. Raglan limits his coverage to examples from Western traditions and with most of those from antiquity. The most recent case he considers is Robin Hood. The Dean legend cannot contain all twenty-two traits of Raglan's pattern. Part of the lack of match is due to Dean belonging to the modern era where, for example, heroes usually are not literally of royal birth, marry a princess, become king, etc. Nevertheless, several of Raglan's traits can be "stretched" to fit: the circumstances of Dean's conception as unusual (according to some), he is spirited away (after his mother's death), and he is reared by foster parents in a foreign country (leaves California and is reared by an aunt and uncle in Indiana). On reaching manhood he returns to his future kingdom (back to California and Hollywood, via NYC). Then after a victory over the king, a giant, dragon, or wild beast (after his successes in TV and on stage), he becomes king (he becomes a star). For a time, he reigns uneventfully (making three major films with plans for more), prescribes laws (establishes a style/persona of life and performance). Next, he meets with a mysterious death (the circumstances of his death in a car accident are mysterious). He has one or more holy sepulchers (his place of burial and several sacred sites). His children, if any, do not succeed him; i.e., he leaves no successors (though many attempted to become the "next" James Dean, it never happens).

Finally, his body is not buried (for a short time, some believed Dean was not buried in his grave in Fairmount, though this is no longer believed).

In contrast to Raglan and others who wished to define the hero as one type and in terms of various traits, sociologist Orrin Klapp takes a social type approach and seeks to subdivide the hero-type in American popular culture into subtypes more in keeping with the modern era. These subtypes are winners, splendid performers, heroes of social acceptability, independent spirits, and group servants (1962, 27-28). He places Brando and Dean in the "independent spirits" category, along with Abe Lincoln, Frank Lloyd Wright, Ben Franklin, and Teddy Roosevelt, among others. Not bad company. By placing Dean in this category, Klapp hit upon several aspects of the Dean persona: individualist, lone wolf, self-made man, rebel, and a bohemian because his "way of life reflects *creativity*" (1962, 44).

If one prefers a *liminal* James Dean, first consider his role as Jim Stark in *Rebel Without a Cause*. In *Rebel* he finds himself between the gang (wildness and anti-civilization forces) and respectable society (the status quo, traditional family, respectability). He is confronted by the meaninglessness and hypocrisy of middle-class life and the dangers of the gang. Dean, as Stark, mediates among these conflicting forces, which pull him in both directions. He can be viewed as a rebel or in rebellion in attempting to find his own place within this struggle. In *East of Eden* the same dynamic is at play. The mediation is between his father's ideas about "the good" and Dean's character's rebellious nature and the truth about his mother. In his actual life, Dean can be viewed as negotiating between his rural Indiana, Quaker upbringing, and its values versus the world of the actor and Hollywood star.

Such classifications of character types can continue *ad infinitum* but fail to answer questions regarding the depth of influence from and/or adoration of the hero by his or her followers. Many Deaners certainly refer to Dean as their "hero," though it's doubtful any have in mind Klapp's or other scholars' definitions of the hero or hero types. Deaners think of qualities such as daring and courage, originality, charisma, and talent; for them, Dean becomes an "ideal type."

James Dean's image as a "rebel" is the most widely accepted among fans, Deaners, and the public, and certainly is the most visible one. A survey conducted by *Netflix* on September 30, 2005, found that among the streaming service's subscribers, 57 percent chose *Rebel Without a Cause* as their favorite film. Some of the older Deaners sometimes attempt to separate Dean from that image, noting that it was only his film role. Nevertheless, today Dean and this rebel image are practically inseparable. This image of Dean, or others based on it, in the red jacket, white T-shirt, blue jeans, and boots constitutes a general sign or symbol in its use in media.

To begin: take a closer examination of images of Dean in his role as Jim Stark in *Rebel Without a Cause*. There are certain photographs and stills from the film in his guise from the film, specifically, the red jacket, white T-shirt, boots, and blue jeans (note the red, white, and blue) that have come to represent: (1) the role he played in the film, (2) James Dean the person, and (3) certain conceptions of the rebel as a type of which there are many variations, *tokens*, or aspects. (In Peircean semiotic terms, this image, in a collective sense, would perhaps provide an exceptional case study.)

Certainly, the reading of Dean's films has gone much deeper, including into what Marchand calls "unintended consequences" (1982, 177). About *Rebel Without a Cause*, Marchand writes that it was intended as "a 'lesson' movie for parents: be careful and understanding, or this [rebellion] could happen to you." Instead, the young "made the movie theirs." Young rebels sprung up after seeing the film and "adopted James Dean as an expression of contempt for the satiated and challenge-less life of the middle-aged suburban America."

For some they were simply rebelling against authority and control—it was that simple. "Jeff" related a story to me about getting his parents to finally take him to see a double billing of *East of Eden* and *Rebel Without a Cause*. Jeff said he had hoped his parents would see and understand what he (Jeff) was rebelling against. Being only thirteen years old at the time, he now says, he was a bit too optimistic, and after seeing the films his father just didn't "get it" and instead was upset. I asked him if there were other sources of this "rebellion," and he replied that was only one of many, but that incident fueled his feelings: "I got sick and tired of everyone telling me what to do or not to do, what to wear, and how to look."

Genesis

Discussion of the Dean image should not be considered complete without some coverage of its genesis. A fortuitous series of events combined to play roles in the creation of Dean's career, persona, image, and legend. Certainly, a significant and foundational part of Dean's early life is the loss of his mother at an early age and subsequently being returned to Indiana to be raised by an uncle and aunt. This plays a part in the legend as well.

Other events that are of some significance are:

1. He benefits from encouragement by his high school speech and drama teacher, Adeline Nall.

2. His father, Winton Dean, lived in Los Angeles, which permitted him to move there in 1949 after graduation from high school. However, his father wanted no part of his son's desires for an acting career. Dean did enroll in the pre-law program at Santa Monica City College to please his father, and later a brief time at UCLA. But he pursued drama projects while at the college. He only lived with his father and stepmother a year before rooming with William "Bill" Bast, a fortunate connection for Dean, whom he met in 1950. Bill knew people in the movie and television business and often introduced Dean to new contacts. Bast later wrote the first book-length biography on Dean (1956).

3. Having dropped out of college, Dean sought acting jobs and did land a few bit parts. Significantly he also began taking acting classes with James Whitmore, who advised him to go to New York City if he was serious about acting. There were more opportunities there for stage work as well as in television. Rogers Brackett also advised Dean to pursue his career in NYC, and Brackett had already helped Dean get bit parts in film and television. (The story goes that they had met when Dean was working as a parking-lot attendant at CBS studios.)

4. In 1951 in New York, Dean contacted Rogers Brackett. Brackett had numerous connections in television, radio, and film, and Dean became a Brackett protégé. At one point Dean moved

in with Brackett. Brackett introduced him to Jane Deacy, who became Dean's agent. Deacy's introduction was only one of many that helped the young Dean in his budding career.

5. In 1952 Dean had the good fortune of being accepted to study at the Actors Studio, associated with the Method style of acting and with two of Dean's favorite actors: Montgomery Clift and Marlon Brando.

6. Another important step for the young actor was becoming friends with photographer Roy Schatt in 1954. Schatt began photographing and teaching Dean photography. Schatt is perhaps best known for the "Torn Sweater" series of photographs, and one known as "The Photographer" (Schatt 1982, 7-23, 48-49). They are among the many "iconic" Dean photos. Phil Stern also took a series of photos of Dean in 1955, including another "sweater series" (Stern 1993).

7. Magnum photographer Dennis Stock was the second of three major photographers who contributed to the Dean image. Stock was assigned to do a photographic essay on Dean for *Life* magazine in 1955. Stock is responsible for several additional "iconic" Dean photographs, including the famous Times Square shot in the rain, numerous other photographs of Dean in New York, and a series of photographs of Dean in Fairmount that figure importantly in the Dean mystique (Stock 1978, 1987, 2005). The 2015 film *Life* is a biographical take on the Stock and Dean relationship (Corbijin 2015).

8. Sanford Roth, another established photographer, is assigned to cover Dean by Warner Bros. in 1955. Roth may be best known for the final photographs taken of Dean on September 30, 1955, but he is responsible for several famous shots of Dean, such as photographs on the set of *Giant*, at the Roth home, at an auto racetrack, and with his Porsche (Roth 1983). Seita Ohnishi, a Japanese businessman and Dean fan, purchased all

of Roth's photographs of Dean. He also erected a monument to Dean in Cholame, California.

9. His first significant film roles were in major films with three of the best film directors of the 1950s. All three films were shot in color and two in wide-screen format, with excellent musical scores and solid stories and casts.

10. He entered the scene during a period of considerable change and growth in both television and film. It was also a period of increased challenges to censorship in literature and in the arts (including the "code" applied to film) and the emergence of youth-oriented film for the teenage market.

11. A personal story that included tragedy (death of his mother, abandonment by his father), a struggle to find self-fulfillment and an early, tragic death.

Life and Death

Who was James Dean?[2] Today many will vaguely remember Dean as a movie actor of the 1950s. Some may remember one or more of his three major film roles. At the time of his death on September 30, 1955, only the first, *East of Eden*, was in release. For other people, Dean may only be linked to Marilyn Monroe, Elvis Presley, and other American "icons" representative or symbolic of a near-mythical 1950s. Deaners, however, find in James Dean profound meanings well beyond the simple facts of his life and accomplishments.

James Byron Dean was born in Marion, Indiana, on February 8, 1931, to Winton and Mildred (*neé* Wilson) Dean. His mother's favorite poet, Lord Byron, provided the middle name for her son. He was an only child. His father was a dental technician at the local Veterans Administration Hospital. When the future Hollywood star was five years old, his father was transferred to Santa Monica, California. Four years later his mother died. The young Dean was given over to Uncle Marcus and Aunt Ortense Winslow (Winton's brother-in-law and sister) just outside Fairmount, Indiana. There he was raised with their two children, Joan and Marcus Jr., on the family farm.

One can only speculate about the young Dean's first nine years and what influences stayed with him throughout his brief life, but many believe he acquired his interest in the arts from his mother during those years. For the next nine years, he flourished under a variety of influences emanating from life on the Winslow farm, the Fairmount schools, and the ambiance of a small, rural Quaker community. Outside of the family, among those who significantly influenced the young Dean was Adeline Nall, his high school speech and drama teacher. Certainly, an important influence was Rev. James DeWeerd. He was a Wesleyan pastor in Fairmount, where he lived with his aged mother in the early post-World War II years. He was highly educated and introduced Dean to the fine arts, classical music, philosophy, auto racing, and even bullfighting. Some claim DeWeerd also introduced Dean to homosexuality (Hyams and Hyams 1992, 18-21), while others find this notion unsupportable (Gehring 2005, 71-73). According to Gehring, DeWeerd was "the worldliest person James had ever met" (2005, 58), which probably explains Dean's attraction to the man. It was DeWeerd who delivered a eulogy at Dean's funeral and since often reread at the annual memorial service in Fairmount.

According to his teachers and classmates, Dean was always interested in the arts, including theater, drawing, and painting. Although short in stature, he also participated in sports such as basketball and baseball, a trait others later employed in his "boy next door" image.

Following graduation from Fairmount High, Dean moved to California and, for a very brief time, lived with his father and stepmother. He tried pre-law for a while at Santa Monica Junior College and UCLA, mainly to please his father. However, acting still interested him, and he soon began seeking roles, including school plays. Near the end of 1950, Dean acquired an agent and appeared in a Pepsi-Cola commercial. The next year he appeared in an episode of *Family Theater*, a religious television program, in which he played John the Apostle. This small role spawned the first Dean fan club, organized by female students of the Immaculate Heart High School in Los Angeles, called the "Immaculate Heart James Dean Appreciation Society." This was a small manifestation of the adoration that would follow.

Dean briefly studied with actor James Whitmore in his Hollywood acting school, where he was introduced to "method acting." But Dean was dissatisfied with his progress, Hollywood's artificiality, and with the few bit parts he was getting in films. Taking Whitmore's advice, he moved to New York in 1951 where he believed he could better develop his talents. After all, Whitmore had told him that if he was serious about acting, he had to go to New York. There, with the aid of director friend Rogers Brackett, who had befriended and aided Dean in Hollywood, he obtained an agent and received bit parts in television shows. Eventually he landed a major part in *See the Jaguar (1952)*, his first Broadway play. The play was not a success, but it was a major breakthrough for James Dean with more and better roles to follow. He was twenty-one years old. Dean began reinventing himself in New York City, developing that persona for which he is best known.

A major goal of young, aspiring actors to stage and screen in the 1950s was to study at the Actors Studio, regarded by many as the best acting school in the country. There they would study "the Method" style of acting[3] under Lee Strasberg. Auditions were very competitive, and very few applicants were successful in their bids to study there. In 1952, Dean auditioned, and out of more than one hundred other applicants, was one of fifteen accepted. Although the experience was not entirely satisfactory for either Dean or Strasberg, Dean's association with the Actors Studio was a major boost to his career.

More television roles followed in which Dean was often cast as a disturbed or misunderstood youth. In 1954 he landed a major role in *The Immoralist*, at the time a highly controversial play in its treatment of homosexuality. The play opened on Broadway on February 8 with

Dean receiving excellent reviews for his performance. On February 23, Dean gave his final performance in the play; still he received the "Daniel Blum Theatre World Award for Most Promising Personalities" for that performance. His abrupt departure was for Hollywood and an assured role in *East of Eden* for Warner Bros. Based on John Steinbeck's novel and to be directed by Elia Kazan, another Actors Studio alumnus, this film would secure Dean's place in film history and in the hearts of millions of moviegoers.

Before *Eden* was released, Hollywood hype and pulp magazines were announcing that James Dean was a star. In fact, Dean was already at work on more television roles and was being courted for the lead in a film called *Rebel Without a Cause*, a role he accepted shortly before *East of Eden*'s premiere in March 1955. *Eden* received excellent reviews from the critics, with Dean and his performance being generally applauded by the movie-loving public. For his performance in *Eden*, he received a posthumous Academy Award nomination for Best Actor; the film received four nominations, with only Jo Van Fleet winning Best Supporting Actress. He was also nominated for Best Actor in *Giant*, his second posthumous nomination. George Stevens received the Oscar for Best Director, while the film garnered ten nominations. *Rebel* received three nominations with no wins. No matter: Dean had three major films with three major directors behind him as a fitting tribute.

Dean had become a "hot property" in Hollywood, and his third and final film, *Giant*, was in production before he finished work on *Rebel*. Finishing *Rebel* in May 1955, he spent a weekend indulging one of his other loves—racing his Porsche Speedster in Sports Car Club races—an activity seemingly suited to his fast-paced life. He then joined the cast and crew of *Giant* on location in Marfa, Texas, in June. Then back to Hollywood in July, where work on *Giant* continued in the studio. Dean finished his work on the film on September 17. Days later he took delivery of a new Porsche 550 Spyder in great anticipation of the forthcoming races in Salinas. He had the car prepared for the race with the assigned number of "130" painted on the car. His own motto, "Little Bastard," was painted on the car's rear boot. On September 30, on his way to the races and driving the new Spyder, Dean was killed in a two-car accident near Cholame. He was twenty-four years old. This is, for purposes here, where the story begins. The move from celebrity status—a brief eighteen months or so—to "icon" and symbol now began.

Yet Another Beginning

Now, the question shifts: Who *is* James Dean? With his tragic death the question of who James Dean *was* became increasingly layered with speculation and fantasy. In a real sense, he is "frozen in time," and as pointed out by Eylon and Allison (2005), impressions of people are resistant to change after they die. Apparently, that is not entirely the case with those who become the subject of adoration and who died so young with great promise. At times a remaking has been the case. What followed in the wake of his death was variously described as disbelief, hysteria, and "cultic" behavior. Warner Bros. was swamped with thousands of letters requesting his photograph, his autograph, anything he had touched. *Time* magazine in late summer 1956 reported that "a weird new phenomenon is loose in the land; a teenage craze for a boyish Hollywood actor named James Dean, who has been dead for 11 months" (Hoberman 2006, 46). Yet, this was only a sample of what was to follow.

Recognizing a major selling point, Hollywood, and movie star pulp magazines, such as *Motion Picture, Modern Screen,* and *Photoplay,* couldn't publish enough about him for his "crazed fans" and an increasingly curious public.[4] Any magazine with his photo on the cover would sell. Beginning as early as February 1956 special pulp magazines devoted exclusively to Dean appeared along with dozens of articles in every print media including the most popular national magazines of the era, *Life, Look,* and *Esquire* as well as intellectual fare such as *Saturday Review* and *Evergreen Review.* He was also a subject of discussion in *The New Statesman, Daedalus, Dissent, Esquire, Time, Cosmopolitan, Colliers,* and *Coronet.* James

Dean was everywhere, and in fact, it seemed never ending.[5] Beyond the popular print media, those who chose to write about Dean in some fashion included a string of well-known poets: Frank O'Hara and Phillip Whalen, writers Norman Mailer ("The White Negro" of 1957) and John Dos Passos (*Midcentury: A Contemporary Chronicle* from 1961), and critics Robert Brustein and Daniel Boorstin.

Another genre of pulp magazine featured pieces with titles such as "The God of a Weird and Morbid Cult," "Did James Dean Commit Suicide?" "Exposed! The Amazing James Dean Hoax!" "Dean: Object of Passion Mania," "James Dean Tells His Life Story!" "Elvis and Jimmy Made Natalie Wood," "Money from the Grave," "James Dean's Black Madonna," "Jimmy Dean's Hidden Heartbreak," and "The Truth About Those James Dean Whispers." There was something for every taste. These magazines, generally referred to as "scandal magazines," had titles like *Exposed*, *Hush-Hush*, *Inside Story*, *The Lowdown*, *Rave*, *Suppressed*, *Whisper*, *Hollywood Love & Tragedy*, and *Uncensored*. There were also several "one-shot" 25-cent magazines published in 1956 devoted entirely to Dean with inviting story titles such as "The Strange Mystery That Lives On," "Jimmy's Moods," "The Star They'll Never Forget," "The Lonely One," and "Jimmy Dean is Not Dead." Despite his lack of involvement in the emerging music scene, Dean made it into some of the early issues of pulp magazines devoted to rock and roll music such as *Dig* and *Disco Review*. He was viewed as a spiritual ancestor. Merchandising of collectible items closely followed magazine publishing. Pieces were offered, from Dean's Porsche to various "lifelike" Dean busts, figurines, photos, pens, posters, masks, medallions, etc. It appeared to be never ending.

Following his death, reruns of television programs in which he appeared were featured by the major networks. Programs such as *The Steve Allen Show* and *The Ed Sullivan Show* featured special tributes and coverage of Dean's life, family, friends, and films. His three films were rereleased and recycled. *The James Dean Story*, a documentary by Robert Altman and George W. George, was released in 1957, the first of many. Hollywood began turning out films aimed at teenagers with Dean-like characters and "rebel" story lines. In addition to receiving a posthumous nomination for an Academy Award as best actor for his role in *Giant*, he also received numerous other awards.

Soon after his death, a new trend began (even a type of continued adoration) that has continued on and off to the present day: the "next James Dean" or the "new James Dean." Led, of course, by the movie magazines of the day, it appeared there was a major search underway by the studios to find the next Dean. Perhaps there was such a search, but it mattered little. Some observers have confined their work to compiling a list of the "nexts" (Riese 1991, 362-363) while at least one other writer chronicled the history of this "search." The latter resulted in a book *The Next James Dean: Clones and Near Misses, 1955-1975* (Russo 2003). One of the earliest "nominations" (or nods) went to Sal Mineo, a Dean co-star in *Rebel* and *Giant*. Mineo was followed by many other heirs such as Dennis Hopper (also in *Rebel* and *Giant*), Nick Adams (in *Rebel*), Elvis Presley, Paul Newman (who got several movie roles scheduled for Dean), and on to more recent times with Mickey Rourke, Sean Penn, Matt Dillon, Brad Pitt, Johnny Depp, River Phoenix, Leonardo DiCaprio, Luke Perry, and Jason Priestley. Along with the heirs were copies such as Michael Parks (TV's *Along Came Bronson*) and Christopher Jones. Somewhere in between were Dean Stockwell and Martin Sheen. However, none was able to capture Dean's charisma.

It often seems mandatory for a celebrity to somehow be compared to Dean, in this case self-compared: consider "LOL: Justin Bieber Thinks He's James Dean" with a photo of Bieber from his *Instagram* page in a white T-shirt, looking moody and dangling a cigarette from his lips (Beck 2014). Then there were those who portrayed Dean in a film and, at another level, the impersonators and "look-alikes." Only a few females have been considered "female James Deans"—Brigitte Bardot, Christina Ricci, and the Japanese androgynous female performer Daichi Mao, known as the "Japanese James Dean" (Robertson 1998, 79-81).

Nor were foreign actors immune to this phenomenon: Roger Nimier and Cyril Collard, both candidates for the "French James Dean," and Zbigniew Cybulski the "Polish James Dean." In some cases, such as that of Japanese actor Yujiro Ishihara, the reason why would be lost on an American fan. Additional progenies were spawned with the "James Dean of _____." Among those selected was Chet Baker as the "James Dean of jazz," who along with Bud Shank released their take on Leith Stevens's score for *The James Dean Story*. Then there are the German tennis star Boris Becker, who believed at one time he was James Dean reincarnated, and ballet dancer-choreographer Rudolf Nureyev, who was described as "part James Dean, part Mick Jagger, part Lord Byron, a blend of fierce sexual authority and the vulnerability of a waif" (Kaye 1991, 125). Of course, much if not all of this was advertising hype along with some genuine effort at comparison (generally in the physical looks or lifestyle areas). All considered, it is perhaps no more than an example of the "myth of the eternal return."

Even in Mexico Dean had an impact, though much less so and never as a major "icon" there. Mexican actor and comedian Cantinflas "acknowledged the ambivalent nature of masculinity and thereby conveyed some of the emotional introspection of James Dean" (Pilcher 2001, xvii). Cantinflas is an acknowledged Mexican cultural hero referred to as the *"pelado,"* meaning the ambiguous one. He had a multifaceted appeal to several social strata of Mexican society. Beyond the case of Cantinflas, "disaffected youths" in reference to Dean's best-known film were referred to as *"rebeldes sin causa"* during the 1950s and 1960s (Pilcher 2001, 188). Eric Zalov in his exploration of Mexican counterculture and the role of rock and roll and Elvis Presley gives credit not only to Elvis but likewise to James Dean and Marlon Brando (1999, 28). He notes that the rise of youth culture in Mexico and the undermining of traditional *"buenas costumbres,"* referring to family values and proper upbringing, along with other factors can be attributed to "the irreverent, raucous spirit of the new youth culture, embodied in such mass cultural male icons as Marlon Brando, James Dean, and Elvis Presley" (1999, 28). He further notes they "immediately overshadowed the official heroes of the Revolution... [leading to] a different vision of heroic masculinity: the youthful gallant outcast who rode a motorcycle, raced cars, or strummed his electric guitar" (1999, 28-29). But, according to Zalov, the appeal of the Brando and Dean connected with different audiences: motorcycle-riding Brando of *The Wild One* appealed to working-class youths, and Dean's appeal was with upper-class kids (1999, 39).

Not only was Dean followed by others in life as a "next James Dean," he was also followed in death by the next "cult." Elvis Presley was hopeful of following in Dean's footsteps to become a "rebel up on the screen" and the "James Dean of rock and roll" (Halberstam 1993, 457, 486). He did, of course, become more popular than Dean and, since his death, has become the object of great adoration (Doss 1999, 2005). There is also the case of Jim Morrison, who died at age twenty-seven in 1971. Often compared to Dean (Dalton 1991), he has become the target of considerable affection and devotion. His grave in Paris is the goal of many pilgrimages. Nevertheless, he has not received the same degree of attention nor level of continuing devotion.

When River Phoenix died at age twenty-three with a promising movie career ahead of him, there was considerable speculation that he would become the next "cult" figure. Yet, the predicted cult following never materialized. Perhaps it was Kurt Cobain who was selected next for continuing fandom, and like Morrison, has a following. There are memorabilia, clubs, tributes, and continuing interests in their music. Perhaps it is the manner of their deaths—due to drug overdoses—that has failed to sufficiently echo the romantic notion of a fallen hero. Marilyn Monroe presents a conflicting case in that the circumstance of her death remains unclear, yet she remains one of the most celebrated "icons." In any case, from American popular culture Presley is a prime example of one who has moved from celebrity to enduring symbol. Perhaps

Michael Jackson will likewise assume a similar mantle. In any case, there are a host of candidates for such status not just from popular culture, but from the larger field of celebrity.

Less than a year after Dean's death, in May 1956, Fairmount friends and relatives established the James Dean Memorial Foundation to provide financial assistance to young actors and actresses through grants. A five-week summer course in theater was held in the Fairmount High School. The foundation also planned to establish fellowships and scholarships at colleges and universities.[6] Dean's high school drama teacher, Adeline Nall, established a scholarship trust in his memory to award promising local drama and speech students. A Dean friend, Arthur Lowe Jr., established the James Dean Memorial Fund at the Actors Studio. Lowe contributed $1,000 and others also contributed to the fund, which helped many members and lasted for over a decade (Riese 1991, 269).

James Dean memorial car "runs" were organized to annually retrace the route Dean traveled to Cholame on September 30, 1955. Various James Dean fan clubs were established, some by serious fans and others by strictly commercial interests. According to one source, by 1957 there were 3.8 million dues-paying fans in the various clubs in the United States alone (Beath and Wheeldon 2005, 81). Of course, many of these "clubs" lacked a grass-roots origin and were the creations of movie studios, magazines, and other entrepreneurs. But others did begin at the local level (Tysl 1965, 650-656). Writing in 1965, Tysl regarded the local-level clubs as concerned with "togetherness" and "their existence…ephemeral and sporadic" (1965, 651-652).[7] What was more telling of the building devotion was the continuing pilgrimages of fans to Fairmount and the annual memorial services in Fairmount on the anniversary of his death. John Wayne may continue to be America's favorite film star (Inglis 2010, 190); Dean's case is something else.

While his impact on society at large is impossible to measure, there are lasting traces in many areas. Consider an article from the online edition of *Milenio* in Monterrey, Mexico (Encinas 2008). The article concerns issues of "*tribus urbanas*" ("urban tribes") among the youth of Monterrey and other Mexican cities. Encinas begins his article with: "History repeats itself. In the 20th century the *rebels without a cause* and the Hippy movement were reason for alarm" (author's translation, emphases added). Although Dean has never been a major "icon" in Mexico (as noted above), that phrase (and Dean's connection to it) has found its way into Mexican discourse (Zalov 1999, 37ff).

The Era, the 1950s

There is something to be said for the 1950s: it was certainly a time of significant new beginnings. Reading about the 1950s today leaves a strong impression of contradictory forces pulling at some vague center. Efforts to link major subsequent events of the 1960s to the 1950s seem banal and only beg the question of what happened in the 1940s, the 1930s, and so on. Nevertheless, in the present case, several Deaners I've spoken with or interviewed linked Dean's status to other developments of the '50s and often gave Dean some credit for events of the '60s and later. Dean's success as an actor is typically tied to the earlier successes of Montgomery Clift, Marlon Brando, and "method acting" generally.

The emerging culture of the 1950s included significant threads such as the Beat movement with its new realism and breaking down barriers. There was Jack Kerouac and *On the Road* (1955), Alan Ginsberg[8] and *Howl* (1955), and a host of other Beat writers challenging the status quo, not only in literature but with issues of lifestyle and society at large. Despite continuing misogynism in arts and literature there was an emerging new feminism, a period of breakthroughs in the arts with abstract expressionism of Jackson Pollock and Willem de Kooning. Significant changes in theater and film styles and industry have been noted by many (e.g., Morin 2005; Kouvaros 2010). Other movements in the air included French existentialism[9], which was also influential in Beat literature. Dean was perhaps existential without being an existentialist, but in any case, he became a Beat "icon."

ADORATION AND PILGRIMAGE

I visited the Beat Museum in San Francisco in 2008. Most of the ground level is given over to a Beat bookstore with the museum's exhibits located upstairs. Walking up the stairs the visitor is greeted with photos of several well-known figures of the 1950s with labels at each: "What Elvis was to music…what Brando and Dean were to movies…Jack Kerouac and the Beats were to literature." Such expressions and sentiments are reflected in Halberstam's *The Fifties* when he notes that Brando "was the first in a tradition of new American rebels that would include James Dean and Jack Kerouac" (1993, 269). Even clothing styles changed, leading to a prole or "rebel style" that represented anti-conformity (Boyer 2006). Conformity and consumerism were out; it was a time to be "hip" and "cool." Certainly, much of the "rebellion" was against the perceived growth of conformity, the growth of "Levittowns" and suburbs, bureaucratization of life, or basically any threat to individuality. Halberstam also notes the "dissidence of Brando and the other rebels was social rather than political" (1993, 269). Ginsberg, the Beat poet *par excellence*, referring to the early 1950s as viewed from NYC, wrote: "It was the beginning of the 'American Century,' the beginning of hyper-militarism, of the Atomic Era and the Age of Advertising, of Orwellian double-think public language" (1993, 8).

Marchand, writing of the 1950s, summarizes the impact of a series of developments. He refers to the emergence of a "mystique" that combined elements of Marlon Brando's role in *The Wild One*, James Dean's in *Rebel Without a Cause*, J. D. Salinger's Holden Caulfield in *Catcher in the Rye*, the rebels of *Blackboard Jungle*, and the driving energy of aggressive sexuality of the new heroes of rock 'n' roll into a new image (1982, 179).

His insightful view of a mystique that influenced many artists of the '50s and later continues with the observation that it "emphasized a hunter for authenticity and sensitivity." Emotionally, this mystique "ranged from moody insecurity to fierce independence with nuances of sexuality, pain, and violence." Furthermore, the expression of these sentiments "expressed a contempt for hypocrisy and conventionality and used body language to convey emotion (1982, 179)." Another development especially in post-World War II was the emergence of "cool," though its initial emergence predates the 1950s with Lester Young and African American blues and jazz (Dinerstein 2017), not with James Dean.

Many other developments and events of the 1950s, including aspects of popular culture, contributed to an atmosphere of change. Consider *Mad* magazine: there was something totally irreverent about *Mad*. Practically any topic could be a target for its special style of humor. Holland Cotter (2009), writing a review in the *New York Times* for an art exhibit of works by Basil Wolverton (an artist primarily associated with *Mad*), notes that

> [the] magazine's appearance was, in its cultish way, a transformational event in American pop culture. Suddenly humor no longer meant comfy titters on an "Ozzie and Harriet" laugh track. It was an assaultive form of anarchy, like The Creature from the Black Lagoon, out of who-knew-what murky social and psychological depths.

Perhaps *Mad* was a harbinger of a future liberalism and cultural criticism.

Despite the "dullness" of the Eisenhower era, it has been noted often enough that the 1950s were also a time of increasing prosperity and a growing middle class. Yet it was also a time of considerable violence and racial strife in the United States, extreme anti-communism in the form of McCarthyism and its "witch-hunts," the execution of the Rosenbergs, and continuing repression of minorities. It was a time of the Cold War, the Civil Air Patrol, and "duck and cover" exercises, but also a time of actual war in Korea (and the beginnings of one in Vietnam) threats of using "the bomb," and the rise of "middlebrow culture" (Jacoby 2008, 103ff.). The civil rights movement may have been in its infancy, but the groundwork was being laid. Angst was everywhere, and there was great fear of contracting polio and spending one's life in an iron lung or of dying in a nuclear attack. In Salinger's *The Catcher in the Rye* and Holden Caulfield's flight from phonies and search for authenticity, it was clearly a time for antihero heroes.

Likewise, others have noted the transitional nature (again) of the '50s: "the '50s were rather more complex than the '60s would allow—an interval relatively quiet among decades greatly calamitous, though haunted by what it remembered, and what it darkly anticipated" (Rubinfien 2009, 170). Many viewed the forthcoming 1960s in terms of an emptiness of modern life.

Many social and cultural critics and commentators have given Dean some of the credit, deserved or not, for the restlessness and rebelliousness of the 1950s and the counterculture of the 1960s. Rifkin notes that Dean in his role in *Rebel Without a Cause* "became the archetype of alienated youth for a generation…as they readied themselves for the 1960s" (2009, 389). It is doubtful any of 1950s youth "readied themselves" for anything in particular, let alone the counterculture. While this statement sounds a bit teleological, it is likely Rifkin only means the youth of the 1950s participated in creating an atmosphere that contributed to the 1960s' counterculture. Tom Hayden, one of the founders of the Students for a Democratic Society (SDS), wrote:

> Dismissing the establishment as absurd, disaffected young people adopted a lifestyle eventually labeled the "counterculture." This was, in its way, an outgrowth of the earlier fascination with James Dean, Jack Kerouac, the blues culture, and the experimentation with mind-altering drugs by Aldous Huxley's disciples (1988, 202).

Earlier in his memoir Hayden notes the influence Dean and others had on his development (1988, 17-18). In any case it is of note that Dean continued, and continues, to receive credit for such developments well after his death and to be a target of blame for what was wrong with the country. Malcolm Boyd, advertising guru turned Episcopal priest and author of *Christ and Celebrity Gods* (1958), targeted not only secular films and Hollywood celebrities, but religious films as well. Some figures, like Dean, were viewed as "cult" figures by Boyd (1958, 8-9).

The conservative reaction to the "rebellious" 1950s and 1960s took many forms and directions. It was often directed against "race" music, "jungle" music, "overly sexual" rock and roll music, and their performers (Jezer 1982, 278-280). Even comic books were targeted by psychiatrists and a subcommittee of the US Senate as encouraging delinquency (Jezer 1982, 239-240). In fact, a US Senate subcommittee began an investigation of juvenile delinquency in 1953 that included comic books, movies, television, and radio broadcast as likely culprits, overlooking poverty, poor schools, and broken families (Gilbert 1986, 143ff). As Gilbert notes, the creation of the subcommittee "fueled the energy and hopes of reformers and cultural censors: here, after all, was a major federal investigatory body that appeared to agree that media caused delinquency" (1986, 143). Teenagers were taking over, or so it appeared to many observers beginning in the mid-1950s (Marwick 1998, 45ff). And, Dean, primarily for his role in *Rebel Without a Cause*, was seen as encouraging juvenile delinquency, especially among middle-class kids. It is often noted that rock and roll and James Dean "entered national consciousness" at the same time (e.g., Whitehead 2001, 168). Both, according to Whitehead, "expressed a changing state of mind that their audiences did not completely understand but embraced intuitively" (2001, 168). In writing about Kerouac's *On the Road* and the era of the early to mid-1950s, O'Hagan notes that three films *The Wild One* (1953), *Rebel Without a Cause* (1955), and *The Blackboard Jungle* (1955) "…married uncertainty about the old, pre-war order to new feelings about sex; they braided fresh notions of freedom with antisocial frolics, wrapping them inside the brand-new rock 'n' roll and the teenager" (2013, 15).

The cultural and religious conservatives of the day, however, could do little to stem the ever-shifting tides of change and their efforts at suppression accelerated in the 1960s. Such efforts did little as evidenced by the rise of the "New Left," the Civil Rights Movement, the Free Speech Movement, and the Students for a Democratic Society (SDS), among others. Many leaders of the New Left had found inspiration in Dean's image and persona, though they now turned to sociologists, philosophers, and leaders like C. Wright Mills, Herbert Marcuse, John Kennedy, and Che Guevara (Hayden 1988, 76-78, 201-202).

As for Dean, he and his first two films appeared at a pivotal point in the emerging cultural movements in the 1950s that granted him considerable stature—credit and blame—in subsequent events. His status as a popular symbol for various sectors of the population was established, while for many others he was much more than mere symbol.

3

The Contested Icon: Dean and Fairmount

"Well, I'm certainly not going through life with one hand tied behind my back."
—ATTRIBUTED TO JAMES DEAN

After an evening hanging out with David Loehr, Lenny Prussack, and others at the Dean gallery, I began the drive back to my motel in Anderson around nine o'clock. The road connecting Fairmount to Interstate 69, a nearly straight shot, was lightly traveled at that time of night. The recently resurfaced road was smooth, and its posted speed limit of fifty-five mph felt inappropriate. I was startled when my radar detector sounded. State police are rarely seen on this road at night. But a state trooper had me at a speed of sixty-eight mph. At the time I thought it was just one of those cases of being on the wrong road at the wrong speed. Later I learned of David's and Lenny's legal problems due to accusations of child molestation involving a fifteen- or sixteen-year-old boy. I put my encounter together with the loose accusations of drug use and local concerns with "outsiders," and began to wonder. I was a bit concerned after the trooper took the passenger seat in my car, but afterward he spoke with me at some length—after noting my out-of-state license—about what I was doing in the area. At the time I only thought he was killing time or perhaps just curious. On the other hand, maybe because of the upcoming trial law enforcement was keeping a watch on the coming and going of folks around Fairmount, especially those from out of state.

The above quotation from David Dalton's *James Dean: The Mutant King* (1974, 150-151) is often cited by those who hold the belief that Dean was gay or bisexual. The exact origin of the quotation appears lost.[10] Nonetheless, the quotation is often repeated and together with other claims about his sexuality created considerable discomfort for the Winslow family, others who knew Dean during his Fairmount days, and many fans. Those not accepting of this view have been in the forefront of many efforts to convince the public that Dean was heterosexual. Perhaps no place else does one find this dichotomy in such pronounced relief as in Fairmount. As a symbol, Dean is multivocal, having many meanings at the same time (cf. Turner 1969, 52), a point that will become increasingly apparent here.

The struggle for control of the image of James Dean in the small Indiana town of Fairmount exposes several characteristics tied to his image. On one side is the Fairmount Historical Museum (hereafter the "Museum"), representing local people and a local view, and on the other side—challenging the Museum's version—is the James Dean Gallery (hereafter the "Gallery") and, to many Fairmount natives, its foreign and unwanted view. The tension created was not chosen by the Gallery. In semiotic terms it is the *interpretant* that is at issue. Although the Gallery has gone through some difficult times—the recession, including a closing in 2006, and the pandemic—its founder and his partner have persevered living and working in Fairmount. Loehr set up exhibits for a time in the Kruse Museum Complex in Auburn, Indiana, for example. But the Gallery in Fairmount began a process of rebuilding its exhibits in 2008, although only after selling much of its collection to settle debts. Today, Loehr continues rebuilding the collection and setting up new exhibits.

This "struggle" for control of the Dean image and legacy dates back at least to the time of his death. At his funeral the Rev. Xen Harvey noted in his eulogy that "Jimmy's life was as normal and natural as any other boy's, contradicting various newspapers' statements that his aloof personality resulted from lack of love at home" (*The Fairmount News*, October 13, 1955, 1). The Rev. Dr. James A. DeWeerd, who also delivered a eulogy, is reported in the same newspaper to have been Jimmy's "hero" during his high school days and to know the "inner" James Dean "better…than anyone else." Dean had a "deeply religious nature," DeWeerd was reported to have said. He was also reported to have said, "We could [always] reach an understanding through religion."

Referring to his performance in *East of Eden*, one local report noted: "Homefolks who saw the movie were heard to comment that many of the mannerisms Jimmy used were just like he did 'at home.'" The article in the local paper goes on to cite Dean's many high school activities in sports, theater, speech, and art, and to say that when he came home for a visit he would include speaking with high school classes and attending school events (The Fairmount News, October 7, 1955, 1).

The Museum presents Fairmount, its history and famous people, in a way considered accurate and favorable. Much like other small-town museums, its two floors of exhibits tend to be of local interest such as Native American artifacts, old items associated with the town's history, and so on. But James Dean is given the majority of floor space and dominates the gift shop.

The Gallery

After all, James Dean is the local kid who made good and made it big, thus fulfilling the American dream. For the Museum, the very image of Fairmount and its people is at stake in controlling Dean's story and image. The Museum claims legitimization and priority in its position as having the "authentic" representation of Dean in its exhibits, which is proudly proclaimed in brochures and on billboards. Complicating the Museum's efforts to control the presentation and representation of Dean was the presence of the James Dean Gallery, established in 1988, by David Loehr and his partner, Lenny Prussack. They came from New York City and as a couple have been together since about 1979 and were married in 2010. The Gallery's closure in 2006 certainly may be seen as a victory by locals and their viewpoint, but that is not the whole story, and in any case, the Gallery reopened in Fairmount.

Loehr had been coming to Fairmount for several years and pitched in to help with the Museum's efforts to set up displays. But for many, the establishment of the Gallery was an "invasion" from the "big city," bringing with it "evils" many local people associate with cities and representing an "outsider" or "foreign" view. And, unlike the Museum, people from out of town often hung out there. It seems David and Lenny became symbols of undesirable "big city" ways, or at least what some locals thought were "big city" ways. In another sense, the Gallery represented a challenge to the integrity of the Museum's and local version of Dean. Several dimensions of the contested Dean image came to the fore, including one at the center of the struggle: the issue of Dean's sexuality.

In the small rural Indiana town of Fairmount, a struggle over the meaning and control of James Dean's image is an undercurrent in the business of promoting Dean to the outside world. Many townsfolk and "the family" are concerned with what visitors and the outside world think of their famous hometown boy. This tension between two conflicting images of Dean also feeds fans and Deaners with basic reactions from belief to disbelief, outrage, or indifference.

Yet, despite the commerce and business issues, many local people don't want the "wrong" image of James Dean presented or perpetuated. They are eager to correct any errors as they see them about Dean. But what is Fairmount like, and how is the "debate" over James Dean contested there? Certainly, the issue is not new to observers of communities and especially those undergoing change, yet each case has its unique issues. There is more here than just "insiders" vs. "outsiders," nor is there such a clear-cut division.

Fairmount

Fairmount is much like any other small Indiana town or for that matter any other small Midwestern town. What makes Fairmount unique is its association with James Dean. This is where James Dean grew up and is now known as his hometown. Bill Bast, Dean's first biographer and former roommate, wrote that Fairmount "is a peaceful, wholesome little farm town near Marion" (Bast 1956, 78). Bast hitchhiked there with Dean and Liz Sheridan in 1952, and much of his description still applies today. Fairmount's economy has varied since its founding in the nineteenth century, though the surrounding rich farmlands have always played a major part in the local economy. Located in southern Grant County in central Indiana, Fairmount boasted a population of 5,300 in 1900. That followed the town's greatest growth with the gas boom of 1887, when natural gas was discovered in Fairmount and nearby Marion. The boom reached its peak in 1894 and was depleted by 1897, taking with it most of the previous ten years' growth of businesses and population. Today, with an estimated population of 3,957 (2021), Fairmount is increasingly becoming a "bedroom community" with a decreasing number of local businesses and employment opportunities. Most of the employed work in Marion, Gas City, Anderson, or another nearby town in manufacturing and retail businesses. Among the largest employers are the General Motors metal fabricating plant in Marion, Wal-Mart's distribution center in Gas City, American Woodmark in Gas City, and Marion General Hospital. Other employment opportunities exist in manufacturing, large-box supermarkets, and distribution centers in Marion, Gas City, and Upland. The city proudly proclaims it's "Where Cool Was Born."

A strong Quaker presence contributed to Fairmount's antislavery role before and during the Civil War (Carr 2006, 157), but it has never been a community of much racial or ethnic variety. It is approximately

98.3 percent Caucasian. Fairmount has a half dozen or so Protestant churches, including Quaker Meeting, Wesleyan, Methodist, and other mainstream denominations. The Fairmount Historical Museum boasts the town is the "Home of Distinguished People." But the town's and the Museum's claim to fame is James Dean and the annual festival in his name. But Fairmount remains a quiet, comfortable small town where most days—and nights—there is little going on.

It is the nature of ethnographic research to learn much more than is initially thought to be necessary for the questions under study. Despite my focus on the Deaners and their adoration of Dean, I have recorded a good bit of information since 1989 on Fairmount's social environment and the interaction of some of the major players in this struggle and debate about Dean. The major players were either associated with the Fairmount Historical Museum Inc., or the James Dean Gallery. This "debate" or "struggle" concerns two disparate versions of the same image: Dean the multifaceted, many-layered image and a symbol of the larger world *versus* Dean the local kid who hit the big time and the image of the American dream. Deaners and fans are often caught between the two images of James Dean, and that tension feeds their involvement and commitment, yet there is a middle ground.

There is also a third player in this game: "James Dean Inc.," which means for most purposes the legal heirs to the Dean legacy and is often referred to as "the family" and the "James Dean Foundation." Their interests are handled by Curtis Management Worldwide of Indianapolis.[11] A trustee and *de facto* head of "James Dean, Inc." is one of Dean's cousins, Marcus Winslow Jr. Since the deaths of Winton Dean, Marcus Winslow Sr., and his wife, Ortense, only Marcus Jr. and his sister, Joan, constitute the "family." Marcus Jr. and his family live on the family farm just outside Fairmount, the same farm where Dean lived for nine years. Marcus was eleven years old with Dean died. Dean Inc. as such has no office or other public visibility in Fairmount, and its activities are largely outside public view. The views of "the family," however, are extremely influential in all matters relating to public homage and adoration of Dean and basically to any matters concerning Dean. That influence, it should be noted, reaches far beyond Fairmount and Grant County, where actions may be launched to control presentation of Dean's image.

I spoke with Marcus Winslow Jr., Dean's cousin, about "James Dean Inc." and Curtis Management (interview, July 13, 1991) and why it was created in 1984. Speaking for the family[12], Winslow noted that in the 1970s they began to see photographs of Dean on many commercial items such as posters and T-shirts, and it didn't seem right that "total strangers were making money" off Dean while the family "had no say-so in the things going on." Nor was the family "benefiting." Winslow also stated that they "had mixed feelings on commercializing…[and] wondered if it was right to try to make money off him…but, on the other hand, was it right to just look the other way…?" Concerning what was being produced, Winslow noted that "if you sit back and don't do [anything], they're going to project Jimmy the way they want. If you don't do something about it, you're more or less saying it's OK. And that's not right. We were just as concerned—matter of fact, that was our main concern—… to be sure that the T-shirts and things were positive…" He also continued with his concerns by noting young kids who look up to Dean, and so the family didn't "want the wrong things being projected on him in an unfavorable way." Regarding the results of the relationship with Curtis Management, Winslow stated that they have "made money off it, but that wasn't our main intent."

One of Winslow's roles as a trustee is to consider proposals from merchandisers for the use of Dean's image, likeness, name, and quotations. Proposals are made to Curtis Management, followed by consultation with Winslow, unless Curtis knows it would be turned down. One example I uncovered of how this process can work involved a figurine of Dean in his ubiquitous "rebel" pose. The original photograph on which the figurine was based has Dean holding a cigarette in his right hand, but the figurine as approved by Curtis Management and James Dean Inc., was without the cigarette.

Apparently, it was felt being true to the original photograph would be a bad influence on young people, so the figurine was sanitized. In the 2007 interview, I asked Mr. Winslow for an example of licensing requests that have been turned down. He thought for a moment and said he couldn't think of any at the time but gave me an example of what would be rejected: a T-shirt with a Dean photograph and a saying like "Live fast and die young" (interview, May 10, 2007). For the fiftieth anniversary in 2005, Mr. Winslow was one of the producers of a new documentary about Dean, titled *James Dean, Forever Young: Rebel, Outcast, Hero, Legend* (Sheridan 2005).

Winslow is often filmed for documentaries and guested on TV programs. One TV appearance of interest was on CNN's "Larry King Live" on January 12, 2004, titled "James Dean: The Man, The Legend." In addition to Mr. Winslow, his sister, Joan (neé Winslow) Peacock, Martin Landau, Liz "Dizzy" Sheridan, Jane Withers, Mark Rydell, and Frank Mazzola were guests. Near the end of the program, author David Dalton was interviewed from a different location. Interestingly, the issue of Dean's sexuality was not mentioned for discussion until after Winslow and his sister's departure.

The Museum is a typical small town history museum in most ways. It displays items of local geology and prehistory, antique clothing from local people, items associated with the town's history, and generally lots of local stuff from local people. The Museum's motto is "Fairmount—Home of Distinguished People." But what makes Fairmount's Museum different is the "James Dean Exhibit," currently housed in three of the Museum's eleven rooms. The Museum has exhibited items associated with James Dean since the late 1970s, at first in a previous, smaller location, and since 1983 in its current location. The Museum Board also sponsors Fairmount's annual "Museum Days," recently renamed the "James Dean Festival," which it began in 1975 to honor Fairmount's "favorite sons." Among these are *Garfield* creator Jim Davis, CBS correspondent Phil Jones, and Truman presidential historian James Houston. "Museum Days" is a typical autumn festival similar to hundreds of others seen throughout the Midwest with parades, carnival rides, shows, and so on. What distinguishes "Museum Days" for most people, however, is its association with James Dean, Fairmount's "favorite son." In fact, many people simply refer to the event as "Jimmy Dean Days" or the "Festival." It has grown from a three-day event to nearly four days and is always held on the last full weekend in September, which sometimes overlaps with another significant event: the annual memorial service held for Dean each September 30.

The Museum is very much a local creation, operated by, supported by, and representing local people. The Museum presents Fairmount, its history, and famous people, in a way considered accurate and favorable by the people associated with the Museum and presumably by others who help support its activities. The Museum also provides visitors with brief histories of Fairmount, Dean, and other topics written by a local historian, who was also an influential member of the Museum community for many years. The Museum maintains a website, which highlights its collection of James Dean artifacts.

For the Museum, the very image of Fairmount and its people is at stake in controlling Dean's story and image. Dean is the local kid who made it big, thus fulfilling the American dream. In the Museum's various brochures, handouts, web page, and billboards it claims to have the "Authentic James Dean Exhibit" and the place to see "James Dean Artifacts." Most of what is exhibited, and certainly the items that justify the claim of "authentic," are on loan from the family. The Museum has Dean's acting awards, two of his motorcycles, his racing trophies, his bongos, many items of clothing, and numerous personal items from his days in Fairmount, New York, and later. They also exhibit dozens of photos of Dean, his family, and his career and activities. Some paintings done by fans are on the walls along with a few posters. Examples of Dean memorabilia are also on display. There are several scrapbook collections of letters, poems, and news clippings available for browsing. The Museum also sells Dean memorabilia in its gift shop.

The Museum's control of the Dean story and image was to some degree challenged in 1988 when David Loehr and his partner, Lenny Prussack, from New York City opened the James Dean Gallery. Prior to this, the Museum had no local institutional competition. Some stores in town sold James Dean memorabilia, but none offered exhibits, tours, programs, and a website. Now those representing an outside image of Dean were there in the flesh, on the ground, in Fairmount. At the time, Loehr had the largest known collection of Dean memorabilia in the world (Loehr and Bills 1999), and he came to Fairmount with a dream of presenting that collection for all to see and enjoy. Loehr is known as the "dean of Deanabilia," a name given him by David Dalton.

It's not clear if all the Museum people initially viewed the Gallery in a negative way, although I did encounter some who had been apprehensive about its opening in Fairmount, perhaps providing unwanted competition and bringing in an unwanted "element." (There were rumors from the start of drugs being brought in.) Before starting the Gallery, Loehr first visited Fairmount on Mother's Day 1979. This was followed by many subsequent visits. He got to know many residents, including people associated with the Museum, and helped out with the Museum's operations. After it became apparent the Gallery was going to be more than just a small shop selling memorabilia but rather a serious operation with exhibits and activities, several key people associated with the Museum "cooled" toward Loehr.

For many, the Gallery was seen as a positive contribution and another draw that would bring more visitors and business to Fairmount. After all, the Gallery only had memorabilia that occupied one room in a Victorian house built in 1903, and it didn't have the "authentic" stuff.

Then the Gallery began expanding its displays and exhibits from one room to the full first floor of the house, broadening the scope of the exhibits, and generally enhancing the overall appearance of the Gallery's building and location. Next, the Gallery began offering additional activities, some in association with the Museum's festival and others at different times of the year. It also began to attract national and international news coverage and appeared to some to be taking center stage. Tension between Gallery and Museum only increased when during a Festival weekend a board member of the Museum accused Loehr of stealing her car and contacted local police. They investigated and later discovered she had forgotten where she had parked the car.

Unlike the Museum, the Gallery stayed open year-round and soon became the focal point and "hangout" for most visiting Deaners and fans, especially the younger crowd. This was a role not filled by the Museum. Among the events the Gallery began sponsoring were dances, rockabilly concerts, and a Dean fans day and weekend in July—without seeking support or approval of the Museum people. In 2004 the Gallery moved from Fairmount to a new location and a new purpose-built building just off Interstate 69 in nearby Gas City. Unfortunately, this move was to be short-lived, lasting only 20 months. Loehr is most adamant that the move to the Gas City exit location was not motivated by negative apperception by anyone in Fairmount. He mentioned his concerns with such issues as long-term preservation of the collection and water and fire hazards in the original location.

For some people in Fairmount, rumors about parties, drinking, and drugs only reinforced long-held beliefs about people from "big cities." These developments along with some particular revelations, however, put the image and the very future of the Gallery on trial. Put simply, for a while the Gallery came to epitomize all that is wrong with "big city ways" in the minds of many Fairmount natives. The fact they were from New York City said it all for some of the local people. A story in 1991 from the *Wall Street Journal* by Laura Castro pointed to several tensions between the Museum people and the Gallery owner, which only increased stress among the parties and among the fans. A book regarded as notorious by most in the community and many fans as well, *Boulevard of*

Broken Dreams, appeared in 1994. Written by Paul Alexander, who ingratiated himself with many Deaners, members of the family, and the community in 1992, the book presented Dean as gay, and while it didn't present any additional information on the issue, it presented the stories in a graphic way as never before. Alexander also reproduced in his book a certain infamous, nude photograph allegedly of Dean. This event caused quite a stir among the Deaners, fans, family, and friends.

The reaction to Alexander's book was often muted and circumspect. Others attempted to ignore the issue, wishing it would simply go away. In the August/September 1994 issue of the *WRDI*, editor Sylvia Bongiovanni notes having received "many letters, expressing, to say the least, anger and dissatisfaction over the book..." The "book" being Alexander's. Bongiovanni notes that books "in extremely bad taste" are not usually even given a mention in the *WRDI*, but Alexander's book requires an exception, and she selected excerpts from a couple of letters for inclusion in the issue. The uproar among many fans and Deaners had to do, of course, with Alexander's explicit claims of Dean's homosexuality and an additional claim that Dean dated women only for cover. Also singled out for condemnation was Alexander's explicit descriptions of Dean's supposed homosexual encounters. Bongiovanni laments the fact that she gave assistance to Alexander while he was working on the book.

A number of issues later covered include additional reactions (*WRDI*, August/September 1996, 12). One fan wrote noting that he believed Dean to be bisexual and said, "If we're going to admire him, we have to take the *good* with the *bad*." Responses to this letter appeared in the October/November 1996 (p.29) issue and included parts of three letters selected by the editor. Again all condemned Alexander's book, and one writer even condemned Hyams' and Hyams' *James Dean: Little Boy Lost* (1992) for "describ[ing] Jim's most intimate experiences..." An anonymous writer denounced the very suggestion that Dean was bisexual and cited those in

Fairmount who knew Dean and "the women he loved." And, he adds, "They all say the same thing, Dean was a normal, heterosexual male." The final shot at Alexander in the *WRDI* came in the October/December 1997 issue (p. 8) with this: "I will never believe the trash written [about Dean]" and those "so-called writers" have been "unkind to our Jim, and I for one resent it." Following the book's publication, I spoke with several Deaners who consented to be interviewed by Alexander. Their general reaction was disgust. Still, others regarded the matter as a nonissue[13], while others were comfortable with the notion of Dean's sexual ambivalence.

That there was some "concern" with the issue of Dean's sexuality among Fairmount natives first occurred to me on my second visit to Fairmount on October 21, 1989. I was still exploring the possibility of doing research on this Dean phenomenon. The trip included another visit to the Gallery as I was hoping to meet David Loehr, but he was not there at the time. I spoke with a local woman in her fifties who was working in the gift shop. Business was slow, so we began a conversation about Dean. Among other stories, she told me she had known him and had gotten his autograph when he last visited Fairmount in February 1955. In speaking with her about some of the items on sale in the gift shop, she made a reference to David Dalton's *James Dean: The Mutant King*. She thought it was a "pretty good book" until she got to the part about Dean's alleged homosexuality. That is what makes the book "trash," she said. She gave a brief laugh, stopped herself, and asked, "You're not David Dalton, are you?"

Perhaps worst of all for Gallery-Museum-Fairmount relations, it became widely known in Fairmount that Loehr and Prussack were a couple. When charges of "sex with an underage person" involving a fifteen-year-old boy were brought against the two men in early 1993, some critics felt justified in their previous concerns. The charges soon became the talk of Fairmount. Not unexpectedly, the charges and the trial nourished local prejudices and cooled some relations between the Gallery people and the townspeople. A few fans even turned their backs on them. Both men maintained their innocence throughout the trial but were convicted. They believe the boy was manipulated by local police looking for an excuse to get them because of their gay lifestyle and other suspicions. Their defense attorney, David Payne of Fairmount, is reported as believing "antigay bias played a significant role in their convictions. [Payne] says it was impossible to select a panel of jurors that was free of prejudice against gays" (Gowen 1996, 88). During this period harassment by locals of Loehr and Prussack naturally increased. The Museum people began to tell visitors not to go to the Gallery because of those accusations. Someone carved "Fag" on their truck, they received harassing phone calls and letters, and youths shouted obscenities from drive-bys of the Gallery. Jeff Kovaleski, city editor for the *Marion Chronicle-Tribune*, is quoted as saying regarding the charges: Fairmount is "a dinky little town and they were all honked off…There was a lot of 'Let's run them out of town on a rail' kind of stuff" (Gowen 1996, 88).

When Loehr and Prussack were found guilty and sentenced, the future of the Gallery seemed in doubt. Prussack received a shorter sentence and was released in 1995. I spoke with him shortly after his release about how people were behaving toward him, and he related some of his negative experiences. Prussack and others also filled in for Loehr at the Gallery and maintained close contact with Loehr via phone on work at the Gallery and other projects. The Gallery survived, and when Loehr finished his sentence in 1996, he was more determined than ever to see his work flourish. But, these events, and certain subsequent ones, may have set the stage for Loehr's eventual decision to move the Gallery.

And what of the kid who accused him? As months and then years passed after Loehr's return, stories of the plaintiff's activities occasionally made their way to the Gallery, usually through secondhand sources. The personal problems he faced before the accusations—drug and alcohol use and problems with his stepfather and other family members—continued, eventually leading to institutionalization. Some overtures of regret were made by the young man, and in April 2005, at age twenty-seven, visited the Gallery and spoke with Loehr. Loehr informed me he apologized for what he had done to them and claimed the police had threatened him with jail on underage drinking and drug charges if he didn't help them prosecute the two men.

Local Views

But what are those local, hometown views of James Dean[14]? What values and world views do they present? There are some tendencies to reveal the "real James Dean" in these narratives—as if memories of his youth in Fairmount can somehow reveal an underlying truth. Those seeking this truth are not only representatives of the media, but fans and Deaners. Many Fairmount natives are willing to discuss what they remember about "Jimmy," "Jim," or "Deaner." Much of what is told fits the "just like you and me" and "hometown boy" image. Phyllis Cox, who knew Dean in his Fairmount days, was quoted on a broadcast of *CBS News Sunday Morning* (October 15, 2000) saying, "I know these people are always saying that Jim was kind of weird and all this, but there's nothing weird about him. He was just like the rest of us." The CBS program was hosted by Phil Jones, also one of Fairmount's famous native sons.

Jim Grindle, who knew Dean in Fairmount, says "he was a nice kid. Everyone kind of liked him. He was kind of quiet, shy. He was all through school" (Driscoll 2005a, 12). Then after visiting with him in February 1955, Grindle says, "I don't think he was any different than he was in high school. Maybe a little more mature" (Driscoll 2005a, 12). Grindle also recalled the times he and other friends played basketball and ice-skated on the pond at the Winslow farm with Dean. Another childhood friend recalls that Dean "was real nice right away, and everyone liked him, and he was just part of the family" (Driscoll 2005b, 13). Dean was a "gifted athlete and enjoyed parts of farming…The kid could do anything that he set his mind to…It seems…that it came very easy to him" (Driscoll 2005b, 14). In his talk at the 2003 memorial service, Grindle has added that Dean was "no rebel."

The late Bob Pulley (along with other childhood friends) often recalled Dean's propensity for speeding around town and the countryside on his Czech Whizzer motorbike. Mildred Carter, wife of the late owner of a motorcycle shop in Fairmount, notes that Dean "liked to lay down on [the motorcycle] and ride it as fast as he could" (Kipp 2005, 32). Pulley relates how Dean played practical jokes on people: "He wasn't different than any other boy. We were all that way. I can't say that he was any different than any other kid in school" (Driscoll 2005c, 17). After hanging out with Dean on his final visit home in 1955, Pulley said, "He hadn't changed a bit… He was the same ol' Jim he was when he left here" (Driscoll 2005c, 17). And Pulley in an interview for *Cool: James Dean, 50 Years Later* (Cline and Kiefer 2005), says of Dean's role in *Rebel Without a Cause*, "That wasn't Jim Dean… He got into trouble in school" like many boys did, but "he wasn't anything like [the character] he played in *Rebel Without a Cause*." In another interview, Pulley disputes the characterization of his friend as "living on the edge…reckless and all this" (Hauge 2000).

That he was unchanged from his experiences after leaving Fairmount is repeated by others. Harrold Rust, another childhood friend, visited Dean in Hollywood in 1955 and found him to be the "same guy he'd known" in Fairmount. Rust states: "He wasn't anything like his movies portrayed him to be—like he was raised in the Bowery or something" (Driscoll 2005d, 18, 20). Wilma (Smith) Brookshire, a member of Dean's graduating class of 1949, recalls that "[p]eople talk about him being a loner. I don't think that he was. I think he was in the group. He was a very talented child. He acted, even when he wasn't acting" (Driscoll 2005e, 23). Another class member, Barbara Jane (Middleton) Jackson, says, "He could do anything and everything…To me, he was a very special person." She joked about some of the class members getting together and wondering what he would look like now: "We laugh and say, 'He'd look like we do'" (Driscoll 2005e, 23). To underscore the hometown boy image, there's a photo accompanying the article of Dean in his high school letterman sweater. The caption notes that he "was a member of several sports teams…He wasn't among the biggest or strongest players, but his energy and drive won him acclaim." Marcus Winslow Jr., Dean's cousin and "guardian of the Dean legacy," knew him as "someone like an older brother…[He] help[ed] Dad on the farm" (Driscoll 2005f, 24). Winslow also notes that Dean "was interested in sports… [He was] a good baseball player…He was good in track…a star basketball player…" (Cline and Kiefer 2005). Winslow's older sister, Joan, was also interviewed by Driscoll (2005g, 28), something she rarely agrees to do. Joan was fourteen years old when little Jimmy moved in with the family. She recalls that Dean made friends "easily and quickly, and always had a gaggle of them over at the family farmhouse for fun and games." She also notes several times in the interview that Jimmy was a "very persistent person…[who] knew how to get what he wanted… [and] he'd always get to do whatever he wanted." That the movie star Dean is remembered as being the same person who lived in Fairmount is underscored by Jerry Payne, who knew Dean slightly (he was about eight years younger): "It was awfully hard for me to realize that he'd made such an impact with his acting, because he was doing just all the things that we saw him do while he was around town" (Driscoll 2005h, 38). And, later: "It's hard for us to think of him other than the person we knew, because to me, he did the same thing[s] in everyday Fairmount life as he did on the screen" (Driscoll 2005h, 38).

The image of Dean's father, Winton Dean, apparently also needs defending after his depiction as a distant, uncaring father—perhaps not even the boy's father—in the biographical film *James Dean* by Mark Rydell (2001). However, the theme of estrangement between the son and father is a theme that frequently comes up in biographies and hagiographies (e.g., Dalton 1974, 59; Hyams and Hyams 1992, 12, 28-29). Mark Winslow Jr., in an interview for *Cool: James Dean, 50 Years Later* (Cline and Kiefer 2005), defends Winton: "…a lot of books and magazines have tried to make out that him and his Dad didn't have a good relationship...[but] that's just not true. Actually, his Dad because of his love of Jimmy gave him up." Winslow also notes in the interview that because of the doctor and hospital bills associated with his wife's cancer, Winton didn't have any money left. Elsewhere he states that Winton knew that having him raised on the Winslow farm was "the best thing for Jimmy" (Hauge 2000). In an interview I asked Winslow if Winton had ever expressed any regrets about sending the boy to Fairmount, and Winslow didn't know if Winton had ever said as much, but he expressed the belief that Winton did regret that decision or at least regretted having to make the decision.

The image of Fairmount's Jimmy Dean is consistent with a kind of collective self-image. It's clear that "leveling" is occurring with the "just like you and me" rhetoric. Whatever happened to him after leaving Fairmount and whatever changes occurred in his views did not change the boy they knew. As James Cory put it, "Fairmount has become a symbol of a symbol" (1987, 31), and that judgment is borne out by the countless lamentations about what he was "really like."

Certainly, the most contentious issues regarding Dean are those surrounding questions of his sexuality. Many Fairmount people have long fought the notion that Dean was gay—in fact, going back to the mid-1950s following his death—since such a view does not fit well with the Museum's nor most local people's image of their "favorite son." Some who attended high school with Dean insist he was not gay, but the stories survive and mainly because, it is believed, of "outsiders" who didn't know him. Nevertheless, the story is told of the large bronze bust of Dean by Kenneth Kendall being stolen in 1959 after being erected on a plinth in Fairmount's Park Cemetery in 1957. It was supposedly stolen by local veterans upset that Dean had declared himself a homosexual to avoid being drafted. Although it is not in fact known who stole the bust nor what happened to it, the family supports a somewhat different story of how it came to be that Dean declared himself a homosexual to the draft board: it was something that was done by actors on a regular basis in those days to avoid the draft (of course, to a veteran such an excuse is beside the point).[15] Dean's acting career was beginning to take off, and he didn't want his progress stymied. In *James Dean: American Legend* (Hauge 2000), narrator Anthony Michael Hall states: "At the suggestion of a few close friends...[Dean] filled out his draft forms and claimed he was a homosexual, an automatic exclusion at the time." He did this because he was "determined to escape the draft," and this was often done by New York actors "seeking to preserve their careers." Dean's declaration to the draft board coincided with the time when he was performing a role as a homosexual Arab boy in *The Immoralist* on Broadway. He was also in line for the role of Cal in *East of Eden*, a consideration that could have motivated his declaration to the draft board.[16]

The stories of Dean's homosexuality are regularly countered with stories of his various girlfriends from New York to Hollywood. Among others, his public dates with Terry Moore, Ursula Andress, and most importantly Pier Angeli are standard fare. But his relationships with women in New York also provide fuel for those who believe, or want to believe, Dean was strictly heterosexual. In contrast, William Bast, who roomed with Dean in the early 1950s in New York, depicts a sexually experimental and sexually ambivalent Dean in his teleplay *James Dean: Portrait of a Friend* (Bast 1975, 1976) as well in his more recent book, *Surviving James Dean* (2006).

Questions about Dean's sexuality won't go away. The story of Dean being introduced to homosexuality by the Rev. James DeWeerd was first reported in Hyams and Hyams (1992, 18-20). While serving as a pastor in Fairmount, DeWeerd is said to have had a major influence on Dean.[17] He was highly educated and introduced the young Dean to the arts and philosophy, but also to auto racing and bullfighting. In any case, this story is countered in *James Dean: American Legend* (Hauge 2000). While noting that DeWeerd was Jimmy's "mentor," the narrator states that the stories about DeWeerd are steeped in "rumor and half-truths." It is generally agreed that DeWeerd was a liberal thinker and that he exposed Jimmy to "the finer things of life" and to a philosophy of "personal immortality," but the line is drawn in Fairmount when it comes to homosexuality (or bisexuality). Composer Leonard Rosenman, a friend of Dean's, is brought in to discount the story. Even if this late-breaking story involving DeWeerd is discounted, as Gehring indicates, "the sexual liaison with [Rogers] Brackett is a given in the Dean literature…" (2005, 113), and for many Deaners it is accepted as truth.

Bob Pulley, a frequently interviewed Dean chum in Fairmount, tells the story of Dean's last visit to Fairmount in February 1955. They went out on the town one evening "to party" (Cline and Kiefer 2005), and Pulley relied on his authority as one of Dean's friends to say Dean was a "good man of character," "Jim wasn't any different than any other boy," and "he was just a normal boy [and I want to] set people straight" on that (Cline and Kiefer 2005). Mark Winslow Jr. also refers to Dean as a "very normal kid" when he lived in Fairmount (Cline and Kiefer 2005).

The suggestion that Dean was gay or bisexual, along with his manifestation as a "rebel," are the two most frequently disputed characterizations by locals. Dean wasn't a "rebel," it was just a role he played. In fact, the general thesis of the film *James Dean: American Legend* (Hauge 2000) appears to be that all of Dean's outrageousness, provocative statements, and nonconformity were just part of a "persona" he developed. Dean was playing that role as a way of developing his acting skills. Mark Winslow put it summarily regarding Dean's portrayal in *Rebel Without a Cause*: "[he] was not really that way" (Hauge 2000). Although Loehr may be accused of promoting the rebel image of Dean, he doesn't believe Dean was anything like that while he lived in Fairmount (interview May 10, 2007). Perhaps the change came later.

Stories of Dean's "death wish" or his "fascination with death" began to appear in many pulp magazines shortly after Dean's death, and he is often quoted as saying "live fast, die young, and have a good-looking corpse," a quotation he picked up from the Nick Ray film *Knock on Any Door* (1949). His fascination with bullfighting, fast cars, auto racing, and motorcycles contributes to the reckless image. The stories of his very strong attachment to his mother and her desire for him to excel in the arts and, in some cases, connecting his "death wish" to a desire to join his dead mother was another favorite theme. In the Hauge film and many other sources, however, any notion of a death wish or of suicide is summarily dismissed: Dean had a bright career ahead of him, and he had just signed a major contract for nine films with Warner Bros. Likewise, the suggestion that Dean and his father, Winton, were estranged is likewise dismissed by Winslow.

The Museum has a story to tell: there is much, much more to Fairmount than being the home of James Dean. He is only part of a larger story of what is special about Fairmount, and as part of that story, their version of James Dean conforms to an image of what is good about Fairmount, and perhaps by extension about small towns throughout the Midwest. It won't do for Dean to deviate from the story line. The struggle over Dean's public image is manifest in several ways, but in this case, and at the core, it is a contested view of Dean as the "kid next door," the kid "just like us," and the local boy who "made good" and fulfilled the American dream. The Museum portrays the human Dean and Fairmount native who made it "big "in the outside world. That is the view cherished by many of the town's people.

Museum vs. Gallery

The Gallery, in contrast, honors a Dean who was more than a mere human and whose accomplishments are extraordinary, if not sublime. In the Gallery's exhibits, Dean's image is ever-present in all forms. The Gallery continues to provide a home for true pilgrims, where friends meet and share their lives, and a place of real fellowship, if not worship, and a true "hangout."

But what makes this case of interest is not that it confirms what we already know about conflict over differing world views, although that may be comforting, but that it demonstrates efforts to control a cherished local symbol by the people of a small town and its museum over another, similar institution, run by someone from the "outside." And this struggle has a contested Dean image at the center—primarily the issue of Dean's sexuality. This is not a struggle in which the Gallery owner wished to engage—to champion one side or the other—but a struggle in which the Gallery's position was, in effect, predetermined.

Given the nature of symbols and especially of one like Dean, exclusivity cannot be established and maintained by any one group or viewpoint. Even legal endeavors to control the presentation of images are only partly successful. Dean belongs to everyone, and what people find in his image is as varied as their interests. Dean is not only a symbol of the small-town boy who made good, thus fulfilling the American dream, but a symbol for many others, including many gays and lesbians (Golding 1988). For the Museum and many people of Fairmount, what is perceived as the public view of Dean is, by extension, how Fairmount is viewed. The Museum finds its self-image and that of Fairmount bound up with the larger public image of Dean, over which it has little control, except perhaps in Fairmount and Grant County. The Museum's claims of legitimization and priority in having the "authentic" representation of James Dean in its exhibits are an interesting marketing ploy but they gloss this larger issue. Given that James Dean has become "the symbol" *sine qua non* for Fairmount, it becomes clear why many of the town's people reacted negatively to suggestions regarding his sexuality. This view represented the "outside world" of Hollywood and New York and of those who didn't "really" know him. When that world moved in, the threat seemed greater.

How has the Gallery recovered from the role chosen for it? In 1999 the Museum and "Rebel Rebel" still sponsored some events jointly, such as the "James Dean Birthday Weekend" in February. But relations were still often uneasy, a kind of carryover from the near past.

On a visit in 1999 I learned of other incidents by Museum personnel that were offensive to the Gallery's owner. Not only were those unnamed persons telling of Loehr's and Prussack's legal difficulties, but the Museum had produced a scrapbook of newspaper clippings that followed the trial. This was made available for visitors to view and read. Loehr took this as an attempt to take business away from the Gallery. Eventually Marcus Winslow interceded, and the problem was resolved. Other problems over many years were rumors that the Gallery folks sold drugs, a rumor that was traced to one of the women at the Museum. A more serious problem arose in June 2000 when the Museum erected several new signs at key locations on Main Street (where the Gallery is located), including one directly across the street from the Gallery, and at other locations directing traffic directly to the Museum and away from the Gallery. This appeared to be an intentional effort to direct traffic and visitors away from the Gallery. These signs read: "James Dean Museum" and "James Dean Artifacts." According to Loehr (personal communication, October 14, 2000), during the months of June, July, and August attendance at the Gallery dropped by 50 percent, and gift shop sales dropped 40 percent compared to the same months of the previous year. His efforts to have these signs removed initially failed. Those developments, together with previous efforts by Museum personnel to discourage visitors from visiting the Gallery, could only add to Loehr's dismay and frustration. Once again, thanks to an intercession by Marcus Winslow, most of the signs were removed.

In some cases, this disregard of the Gallery seemed to spill over into press coverage. Phil Jones, another of Fairmount's "famous sons," did a segment in Fairmount during the "big weekend" in September 2000. His program, *CBS News Sunday Morning*, was broadcast on October 16, 2000. Jones avoided any mention of the Gallery, but he did show the Museum and interviewed a key Museum figure. For Loehr, this was bewildering, but he would only say, "Well, at least it [the program] gave Jimmy some exposure." Those were problems that existed before the Gallery's move to Gas City, but they clearly illustrate the sorts of problems and issues confronted by Loehr. It is difficult not to link such issues with the decision to move, but Loehr denies they contributed to his decision.

Since the closing of the new Gallery in Gas City and Loehr being forced to sell much of his collection, he and Prussack are doing well. Despite the ebb and flow of economic times (and those effects on visitors) and a pandemic, they continue to maintain the Gallery's and Prussack's business: "Shirts by Lenny" and his antique shop. Loehr continues to rebuild his Dean collection, publishes "The James Dean Gallery Newsletter," maintains contacts with fans and Deaners, and works with the community on various projects. Both men say relations with the people of Fairmount and the Museum continue to improve.

In recent years, the Fairmount Historical Museum made notable strides in expanding and improving the quality of its displays and gift shop reflecting its major focus on James Dean. In 2022 the Museum's Board of Directors in a major move voted to change the name of the Museum to "The James Dean Museum" (Accessed June 10, 2022, https://www.thejamesdeanmuseum.com/). In making this change to "better reflect" its holdings the board acknowledged the generosity of the Winslow family for providing Dean items amounting to "the world's largest collection of [his] personal belongings." Not included in the announcement was the Museum's ongoing plan to move the exhibits to a large vacant building on N. Main Street. Fairmount citizens and longtime fans have seen the difficulties and back and forth of both Gallery and Museum for many years. Perhaps another new chapter is now beginning.

4

Becoming a Deaner

[A]dolescence isn't something we should look away from, a shameful churning in dirty hormones. It's the crucible of our identity, the answer to everything that comes later, and we need to look long and hard at it, no matter how gross or painful it might sometimes feel.

—SAM ANDERSON

How does it happen that a person becomes devoted to James Dean? How do you get to be a Deaner? There is no contract to sign, no membership fee, no initiation, exam, public confession, or conversion rite. There is no organized proselytizing or concerted efforts to find new fans and Deaners.[18] Nothing marks becoming a Deaner, at least outwardly, with the possible exception of an occasional tattoo, T-shirt, or red jacket. How, then, does it happen? Initially it may be Dean's appeal and charisma, whether on screen, poster, or photograph, that sparks the interest. But a budding Deaner does not stop there. It is only a beginning of a process of discovery, of Dean and self.

The process is somewhat varied, but there are several underlying similarities and consistencies. For older Deaners, Dean is part of his era: Kerouac and the Beats, bebop, modern jazz, hot rods and fast cars, early rock and roll, perhaps a mythologized past, and so on, yet they continue to make him over in their image and to contemporize him. Younger Deaners come with a different frame. She may have grown up in a small Midwestern town, attended a certain church with her parents, attended certain public schools, and so on. None of those experiences prescribed becoming a Deaner—probably just the opposite. Perhaps he's just a fantasy, a ghost. But once the quest begins, they seek and sometimes find answers sought, new directions, more questions, or even disappointment. But what do they get out of this "relationship," this quest?

Some Deaners seek a kind of new self, or at least one that seems "new," to break free from where or what they feel is their situation or circumstances. Some Deaners seek a sort of salvation: From the "Who am I?" to "I'm not doomed—it's okay, I can be like this." "I can be who I am." They seek liberation and deliverance and a justification, e.g., "This is how I am and it's okay. Dean was like this, too." They seek a guide, a role model, but also a redeemer (again, it's okay). Dean is not just a role model for many, of course, there's too much adoration to leave it at that. He may become a savior, a saint, a nonconformist saint, a gay saint (whatever is needed).

But, in a larger societal sense, is this just another response to modernity or post-modernity and its perceived ills? Is this a return to a past of myth, heroes, and gods with a search for the magical and enchantment? Do these rebels seek not rebellion but something solid, sure, and maybe eternal? This quest is about the self: "What can I become?" "Can I do that?" The Jimmy they seek brings strength to go beyond one's usual bounds. "I can try to be more, achieve more….After all, I'm much like him (in this or that way)."

Underlying the devotion of a Deaner or a fan is perhaps the question of cost-to-benefit: what is the benefit to the person from her actions (including expenditures of time and funds) in honoring Dean? What does she gain from this devotion? To a large extent that is what this effort is about.

These dynamics do not reduce to a model of a game, unless the Deaner is competing with another competitor. Introducing a game model would require several different models or it would exclude many players. Consider this brief range in Deaners:

1. The solitary Deaner
2. The collector Deaner
3. The social Deaner
4. A combination of 2 and 3 Deaner
5. A combination of 1 and 2 Deaner

Not only is this oversimplified, but it ignores one of the most important issues: the depth or degree of devotion. Perhaps a higher degree of devotion may be found in number 1, but that is highly problematic from a research perspective. The private devotee is the most difficult to locate, much less measure. How to measure depth of feeling and emotion associated with devotion, unfortunately, is beyond the scope of this project.

There are two "domains" to consider: his films and his actual life, both of which contain a multitude of characteristics and traits. For a Deaner the movies are not enough. Anything approaching a "real" connection requires digging into Dean himself or, correctly stated, how he is remembered, spoken, and written about, and where he lived and performed. His talent as an actor will be a factor, but so will his interests and ambitions. The exploration goes deeper: where he grew up, how he grew up, what his early years were like, and so on. The fascination with Dean's performances can lead to another question: what is that "magic" and where does it come from? The quest for more and still more may be endless, digging deeper and deeper, leading to reading "all the books" seeking a still deeper insight. As will be shown the first positive reaction to Dean is often in one of his films, or the initial reaction may come from other possible stimuli such as a book, magazine, photograph, and so on.

But first: who are, and are not, Deaners? They are not just fans. There is a continuum, which I won't attempt to quantify, from the curious to the fans to the Deaners. Of course, there are cases where the journey of becoming a fan or even a Deaner may have begun out of curiosity. A Deaner may or may not be a collector of memorabilia. She may collect a few items, attempt to amass a vast number, or focus on specific types of items. She may attend events in Fairmount every year, only occasionally, or rarely. Some have never made the pilgrimage to Fairmount or any Dean site, others attempt to visit each at least once, including Cholame, specific locations in New York and Los Angeles, Marfa, and Mendocino.

Another distinction between a fan and a Deaner is provided by the range or depth of their views of Dean. Some fans have latched on to the rebel image of Dean and not much more. A Deaner in contrast has a much more complex and nuanced view of Dean.

We Remember Dean International (WRDI) testimonials reviewed contained eighty-nine statements giving the circumstances on initially becoming a Dean devotee and a vast majority (75 percent) credited seeing one of his movies as doing the trick (and usually *Rebel*). Another 8 percent experienced an initial attraction/excitement when seeing a documentary on him. Only 9 percent turned to Dean after reading a book about him. Interestingly, about 9 percent stated it was seeing a photograph of him that got their interest. Also, among the testimonials, age at becoming a fan averaged fourteen, with the oldest stating an age of twenty-five and the youngest claiming to have been three years old! Others simply stated the occasion as "in 1954," "since high school," and "for ten years," or when "I saw him on TV."

Among 166 letters written to David Loehr from 1987 to 2005, writers expressed a wide range of sentiments and themes related to their "feelings" about Dean. In some letters, of course, an assortment of themes and sentiments were mentioned. Expressions of love, passion, enchantment, obsession, or having "deep feelings" for him were stated by 12.5 percent. Explicit expressions of devotion or worship were mentioned by 8.75 percent of the writers with terms such as "idol," "worship," and "apostle." The desire to acquire a specific, rare object to somehow "get closer" to him was sometimes stated, e.g., something that belonged to Dean or was touched by him. In the context of worship and devotion, some writers mentioned having a personal "shrine," "cult," "James Dean room," or "wall of photos." Admiration of and personal influences from Dean accounted for another 16.5 percent including the notion that Dean helps them with their personal problems. Finally, and closely related to "influence" and "personal identification," 15 percent of those writers mentioned Dean as a "great actor," "gifted," "remarkable," "inspiration," "role model," "guide," "like me," "my whole life is based on Dean," or "we would have been friends." Turning to specific interviews with Deaners is more helpful and insightful.

Illustrating how a passive event, like seeing a photograph, may stimulate a change of direction, a young woman whom I interviewed spoke of her initial attraction to Dean via a photograph or poster in an older sister's room. She was very young and fell in love with the image in the poster, becoming a Dean fan. Or, as Deaner Pamela DesBarres told David Dalton:

> I'd just turned nine, and I was trying to fall asleep on my mother's lap in our '49 Ford when news came on the radio that James Dean had died. I asked my mother who that was. It was just so sad and mysterious that from that day on I became obsessed with him. For a long time I carried around a picture of his tombstone in my wallet. I bought Bill Bast's book [*James Dean, A Biography*] about him and took it to high school with me every day where all the boys compared pretty unfavorably with Jimmy. That's how I got into rock stars, and most of them didn't match up too well either I can tell you (Dalton 2001, 3).

One lady wrote in *The Dean Zine* "I've been a Dean fan since I was 12 years old. I will be 32 next month. Jimmy forever changed my life and my attitude—to be brave, to always try to learn and experience as much as I can, and to try to be the best that I can be. He was so special and I'm so glad that I discovered him at so young an age" (2004, 13).

The role of community in the process is not always apparent, and today the ease of being connected via the internet, while allowing for more connections and affiliations, does not necessarily lead to increased group solidarity (Conley 2009, 161-167), only its illusion, perhaps. Those seeking more face-to-face interaction and perhaps an authentic self find the internet lacking and look elsewhere. There is something "solid" about an actual place where the fan can see where his idol lived. All these folks initially have just one connection—James Dean—and it may remain there, but many build additional points of connection that sometimes lead to long-term friendships. Those who return repeatedly often build local networks of friends, though not all expand their web into locals but remain linked only to other fans and Deaners.

Preexisting networks do not play a significant role, though a few were influenced by a friend or family member. Among some of the older Deaners who started their adoration in the mid-1950s, schoolmates often played a supporting role, though not necessarily as fellow fans. Groups of young mates, neither a fan nor a Deaner among them, make the trip to Fairmount for no other reason than curiosity or perhaps in the hopes of finding some excitement. Likewise, friends often accompany a Deaner friend to the festivities in Fairmount for no other reason than to "see what goes on," "meet people," or "for a change of scenery."

Interviews

The James Dean Room

My first formal interview with a Deaner was Maxine Rowland (1932-2020). She was recommended by David Loehr, among others. For this interview I arranged to visit her at her Xenia, Ohio, home, located in a modest middle-class neighborhood. We had met previously while lunching at The Crossroads, a restaurant near Fairmount and a favorite of locals. This was during the Festival weekend, and we were part of a large group of fans and Deaners.

Inside her home and passing through the living room, I noticed a sizeable number of Catholic religious items. Bob, her husband, was at home but not well, and I never met him. She was to mention several times that he wasn't a Dean fan. She was born in Virginia, married when she was fifteen, and had two children. She was employed as a seamstress.

Turning to how she initially became a fan, she said she recalled seeing some of Dean's early TV programs and reading stories about him in magazines, but it was the 1970s "before I really got to be a big fan or anything." She began keeping a scrapbook of articles she found about Dean. After learning about Fairmount, she convinced her husband to make a visit there. The first time was in July 1973, and they had some difficulty finding the grave. Still, she got her son to take her back on September 30 of that year. That was before they had established the Fairmount Historical Museum, she noted. Asking her about the September visit since there was no festival then, she noted there wasn't much going on, but a few people did come to visit his grave. After she read Dalton's *James Dean: The Mutant King* in 1974 she wanted to know more, but eventually began discounting and disagreeing with Dalton's book. On a return visit to Fairmount, she asked around, seeking someone who had known Dean and eventually being directed to an older man who recalled some stories but suggested she pay a visit to the Winslows at their farm. Although she was reluctant, the man encouraged her, saying the Winslows will be "tickled to death to see you."

Once at the farm she was warmly greeted by Ortense, Dean's aunt, invited in, and made to feel at home. While Maxine was there, Ortense brought out some of the family photo albums and other mementos to show her. Marcus Sr. was there but was in and out. Maxine said she spent about two hours there and that included a visit to "Jimmy's bedroom…it was still just like it was [when Dean lived there]—she showed me his motorcycle jacket and let me try it on and all his boots that he wore in *Giant* and his bongo drums… she showed all that stuff."

ADORATION AND PILGRIMAGE

After that visit, Maxine continued to visit nearly every year, sometimes several times, and during those visits she added to her growing list of friends and acquaintances, including members of the Winslow family, other fans, and those involved with the Museum. In 1978, she met Bill Lewis and Sylvia Bongiovanni, who were starting the new *WRDI* fan club, and she became the twelfth person to join.

When asked about her collecting, she again mentioned her first scrapbook and how she had rediscovered some of the first clippings she had from 1956 and, asking if I would like to see it, took me to what she called her "James Dean Room." She showed some of her recent photos from Fairmount as well as her first scrapbook, then items about other Hollywood stars as well as numerous clippings and photos of Dean. She had a rubbing of Dean's grave monument from 1973 as well as a framed photo of it on the wall. I also noticed a photo of John F. Kennedy on the wall next to one of Dean and asked for the connection. Her reply was that he was one of her heroes and added, "I've got a whole cabinet drawer full of stuff on him in the other bedroom…" The walls of the Dean room had two and three rows of framed photos. The several bookcases and stands in the room contained books, tapes, her numerous albums, and various small items. Two of the cases had vases with fresh flowers.

Maxine had photos from each of her visits to Fairmount organized by date and event. Other items she collected on those visits were also included with the photos, so everything appeared to be in chronological order. Her collection included photos she took of Dean's bedroom in the Winslow home, a photo of her in one of Dean's motorcycle jackets, photos of flowers she placed on the grave, and photos taken during her first viewing of *Rebel* in 1974. Only later did she see *Eden*. Her collection also included photos of every place in Fairmount associated with Dean. As this progressed it became clear her collection was comprehensive of the events she attended, and she knew nearly everyone in attendance.

Regarding why she is a serious Dean fan and following a statement about how much she likes his acting—"he put his whole self into it"—she expressed her deeper feelings. "...I think it's just something you feel inside and to me, it's something I can't explain... You just can't explain it to someone that doesn't understand." She expanded on the difficulty of explanation by relating one of the ways she deals with "hard times" by corresponding with friends or calling Marietta Canty, the African American actress who played the Crawford family maid in *Rebel*. Maxine had connected with her via Sylvia Bongiovanni, co-founder of the James Dean fan club at that time. When feeling "down" sometimes, she could "talk to her and, why, she picks you up just like that. She just had a way about her, and I think a lot of it is just corresponding with the fans...we have that connection in common."

Dean of Deanabilia

Among the more serious Deaners is David Loehr, and from my first interview with him in 1989[19], as well as subsequent interviews and interaction, I learned of his serious quest. He describes himself as being "obsessed" with James Dean. His initial interest in Dean came in 1974 when an old friend gave him a Christmas gift of a copy of Dalton's *James Dean: The Mutant King*. The friend had inscribed inside the book that there was much in the book that reminded him of David, thereby making a connection between the two. For David that marked the beginning of his "obsession" with Dean, although at first, he didn't find much in common with the actor. After reading the book, he saw *East of Eden* on the big screen in a movie theater and "was just knocked out..." Later he saw Dean's other films and *The James Dean Story* all on the big screen: "So I was fortunate to see them all the first time in a theater, instead of on TV, with commercials." Before Dean, his interests and enthusiasm were for the Rolling Stones followed by David Bowie.

Then he began collecting in 1975 with a few items but not with any particular plan in mind; he "wasn't deeply into it yet." As time passed, he continued to collect Dean memorabilia including books. And, as he learned more about the person James Dean, he began to find more similarities with himself, and his feelings of a connection increased. His "identification" with Dean developed, without the realization of a "connection" or "similarities" with him. He gradually realized their "lives were so similar," and he came to "identify" increasingly with him. He came to feel his life was to be "intertwined" with Dean. He said it was like his "whole life led to Dean."

Among those similarities in Dalton's book between himself and Dean were several important life events. Both lost a parent at the age of nine and were raised by a relative or relatives—in David's case it was his father who died and a grandmother who raised him. He also grew up on a farm as was the case with Dean. David noted that identification with Dean is "often more of a feeling you can't really explain." David also noted that after high school he moved to New York City to attend art school and had a few bit parts in films or other performances, while Dean had left for Los Angeles and began pursuing acting there before moving to New York with the same goal. David could also cite both having interests in the arts. David also traveled back and forth between California, where his sister and her family lived, and New York, with occasional trips back to Massachusetts. While at those locations, he often worked doing set designs, helping to restore a house, playing and performing in the rock-psychedelic band/theater group Magic Tramps, lived in a hippie-type commune, and worked for and traveled with other music groups. While in New York, he fell in with the Andy Warhol crew. In 1982, David began the "James Dean Walking Tour" in New York, which visited Dean's known haunts and apartments during the actor's time there.

Regarding his collecting, David once mentioned he had always been a collector and an organizer and cataloger/indexer, so when he began collecting Dean items it was only natural for him to repeat those functions. His collecting of Dean memorabilia began slowly, but soon picked up and "just kept snowballing, I didn't plan on doing it—it just happened." And to make the long story short, he eventually had the largest known collection of Dean memorabilia, leading David Dalton to crown him the "Dean of Deanabilia."[20] Eventually, his collecting and feelings of connection with Dean led him to visit Fairmount many times and then to establish the James Dean Gallery.

A Budding Actor

"Lawrence" was twenty-seven and a former winner of the Dean "Look-alike" contest in Fairmount when I interviewed him in 1998. He was a resident of a southern US state at the time and noted that Dean was not as popular in the South as Elvis and Marilyn. Lawrence was supporting himself as a pipe fitter. He has a younger brother and a sister. Both his parents were still living as were his grandparents and one great-grandmother.

He became a Dean fan in 1985 after seeing *East of Eden* on TV and thinking, "This man has magic" expressing "sensitivity" and "vulnerability." He continued: "I knew then that I had to follow him, so I bought all of…his films on video [and] all the books that I could find." Among the books, he found *The Mutant King* to be "the most interesting," he said, adding, "It's like the 'Dean bible.'" He was not a serious collector, and his interests in Dean were very personal.

I asked about Dean's effect on him, and he noted that *Rebel* symbolized his "life in high school" dealing with the tough types (like "Goon" and "Buzz") and, if lucky, a "Judy." He also spoke about his efforts with looking like James Dean and getting into the look-alike contest. Lawrence noticed after having his long hair cut short that there was some resemblance with Dean. He prides himself on being a Dean fan for eight or ten years before ever thinking of participating in the look-alike contest. He had made his first trip to Fairmount in 1986 but didn't return until 1993. That was when he finally entered the contest. He was critical of those who became Dean fans only because someone told them they have some physical resemblance to him. He was already a Dean fan and still in high school when some of his mates noted his resemblance. He mentioned that in the school's senior yearbook he was featured in the classic Dean "rebel" pose beside a photo with Dean in the same pose. The associated caption noted something to the effect that many students had noticed his "striking resemblance to his idol."

Lawrence is multitalented and writes poetry, acts, and draws. He credits Dean with his efforts in those areas, saying he wanted to

> break through and make my mark in the Jimmy Dean thing somehow—if it's a book of poetry, if it's a book of artwork, if it's a comic, if it's one-in-a-million break of getting to act out something using his character, but some way or another that is a dream in its own that I would like to accomplish before I die.

Lawrence regards Dean as an "intellectual" and not "just a rebel." He admits emulating Dean but still wants to go his own path. Lawrence wants to focus on acting but lacking any professional credits his goal remains out of reach. He has experience from roles in local theater back home, but that has not helped. He said he would like a "Jimmy Dean part" but does not expect that to happen. So, he seeks any role and will use his "own style," though he expressed some fear of falling back on Dean mannerisms and other parts of his acting style because he has been studying for a long time. He still gets inspiration from Dean when he thinks about how the actor came from a small town about the size of his own hometown and "made it, he's nationwide, he's worldwide."

Answering a question about his post-high school experiences, he mentioned attending art school in Kansas City for a year before deciding to try something else. Having seen some of his artwork, I suggested maybe he should keep it up. In his reply, he said he has "the rest of his life to do art and poetry" but felt that acting had a built-in limit as to how long they will want you.

I learned some time later that Lawrence had moved to California, no doubt to seek acting jobs. He also began attending college again and had gotten married. In 2006 I read a piece about a short nine-minute film about Dean's love affair with actress Pier Angeli written and directed by Lawrence. The film won an award in a local college film festival.

Journey of a Deaner ———————————————
Interviewing twenty-two-year-old "Vince" in David Loehr's and Lenny Prussack's kitchen, I asked about his first trip to Fairmount. He grew up in an upper-Midwestern state and had been in Fairmount for two years at the time of the interview. Vince and three of his college friends were on their way to the West Coast, but their actual plans were vague and shifting and they were away about two months. Three of the group, including Vince, had dropped out of college, and all were living at home before the trip. Vince said he had seen something on the news about events in Fairmount, and he suggested they visit there since it was not far out of the way. He knew who James Dean was but did not have much interest in him at the time. Their visit was a week after September's Museum Days. They arrived late, about nine o'clock he thought. They did not see much that evening—played some pool and walked around some—and ended up sleeping in a church parking lot in their van. The next morning, they walked to the Gallery, but since they were short on money, Vince was the only one who toured it: "I was the only one that was really into it, so they sat on the steps outside." He didn't stay long because the other guys were waiting. On this first trip to Fairmount, they also visited Dean's grave, and Vince said he was taken aback by all the flowers and other "stuff" at the grave that were still there from the festival events and memorial service. They drove past the Winslow farm but did not stop, nor did they visit the Museum or any other sites. It was off to California.

Nevertheless, Vince was impressed with the place and said, "I knew from the first time being here—like I told them [his friends]—this is where I want to stay…This is where I want to live. And that was like the first day." He was not impressed with the town, he was impressed with the Gallery and Luke, whom he had met at the Gallery; he thought he might like to work there, too. He found Luke to be "very, very nice," and he liked his looks and Australian accent. This was the beginning for Vince, and his interest in Dean continued to grow during and after their trip west. He bought a used copy of Dalton's *James Dean: The Mutant King* for $1.50 and read it during the trip, finishing it shortly before returning home. Back home he enrolled for a summer session at college and got a job at a local movie theater. He found a copy of Alexander's *Boulevard of Broken Dreams* in the library to read and his interest in Dean continued to grow. But Vince said by July he was feeling very tired and got fired from his job. He said, "I was just kind of really tired of being home—like, I don't want to stay here anymore, what's the point, I thought. I'll just go to Fairmount." His only other option was to move in with a sister, her husband, and child in Massachusetts, but he thought that would be "too complicated."

A hometown friend journeyed to Fairmount with Vince, and they stayed at a motel in Marion, about ten miles away. Before leaving home, Vince had called the Gallery and spoken with David Loehr. David told him to be sure to come by the Gallery when they arrived in Fairmount. This turned out to be opportune as David invited Vince and his buddy to have dinner with the Gallery group at a Pizza Hut in Marion, and from there Vince began to build a network of new friends. Besides David and Lenny Prussack, there were two other regulars. But his hope of getting work at the Gallery did not pan out right away. After spending two weeks unsuccessfully looking for a job in the area, Vince returned home, but he stayed connected with his new friends and eventually got an offer to move in with one of them in Fairmount.

Back in Fairmount he sought employment again and again without success. But one day he was hanging out at the Gallery when David asked if he wanted a job, and he jumped at the chance. He thought David had learned of his desire to work there from one of his new friends. At first he worked in Lenny's operation in the basement, but eventually he got the chance to work in the Gallery's gift shop.

I asked him about his two years there, his experiences, and what he had learned. "I think I'm a lot stronger than I thought I was maybe. I can do things myself...[even if] it's hard I'm going to do it. And, having my own bills and having all that sucks at times because I don't have any money ever, but they're my own and I never had that before." Besides learning to take care of himself, he also expressed a change in attitude. "I think my mind has opened up to a whole new thing, and that's why it's just like so amazing that Dave and Lenny are here...I don't think I would have got that if it would have been the typical kind of, you know, married couple [running the Gallery] ..." Vince considered the environment of the Gallery a different world from Fairmount. When he is in the Gallery, he explained, "It's like I can breathe; you can kind of be yourself, relax, and I don't have to have my guard up. I don't have to play or be fake and that kind of stuff, and they never expected that of me. They've actually encouraged me to kind of be more of who I am, and I think I really didn't know who I wanted to be until I got here."

With Vince it's possible to follow the progression from a mere curious interest in James Dean through a series of episodes that piqued his interest in Dean and expanded his network of friends and life experiences, leading to self-growth and close friendships, along with further exploration of Dean and depth of involvement with other fans and Deaners. All those possible influences cannot be measured. It is apparent that Vince, in his quest to find himself, found James Dean of help, as well as his friendships with Lenny, David, and others. The role played by the Gallery's environment and the ambiance it created was significant in this case, as is clear from speaking with Vince. Where did these experiences lead Vince? The introspection that he exercised there was beneficial in expanding his awareness and viewpoint:

> I've had this moment [in Fairmount], and it's been the best thing I've ever done in my life, but it's time for me to do something else. And that comes from being in Fairmount

and seeing just how small people can be... I hope to expand, I guess, somebody's mind or way of living or way of thinking. That's kind of my goal.

Later he states his belief that the presence of Dean fans in Fairmount has been beneficial to the people there in expanding their

> images of people other than straight, white, Christian people.... The people that come here, to a certain degree, have been positive influences in making people think, and that's what I want to do. I want to make people think maybe twice about what they may think or about what their stereotypes [are] or what they've grown up believing or someone has put on them—just think for yourself.

When we discussed his future plans, he spoke of going into public relations and specifically to do something for gay rights "because I feel more passion about that as opposed to other things." Later in our talk he admitted he also had an interest in acting. He had acted in high school plays but had not pursued it afterward. Still, "the little narcissistic part of me wants to be recognized for something—for doing something."

Over the next few years, I learned that Vince had returned to college in his hometown, graduated, but remained unsure of what he wanted to do. When I saw him again in 2001, he was thinking of moving to California but seemed tentative about any specific plans. In 2003 I learned he was in Los Angeles and doing some film work. Lenny said Vince was "doing OK." I next saw him at the opening of the new James Dean Gallery in 2004. He was still living and working in LA and trying to get into acting.

Existentialist

Vince's gradual move into Dean is in contrast with the case of "Kenrick," a college professor from a large Midwestern city. I met him at the 2004 opening of the new Gallery through "May," a former interviewee. Over lunch I learned a good deal about his interest in Dean. He explained that when twelve or thirteen he had seen *East of Eden* on a black-and-white TV. He emphasized watching it alone, and this was one of the first times, if not the first time, he watched a movie alone. How this came about is not particularly important, but basically no one else in the family wanted to watch the film and instead watched something else on the color TV. This would have been in the early 1980s. He was overcome by Dean in that film. He said it may have been partly because he was going through adolescence and partly because he felt alone as the family had recently moved. He also mentioned that he saw Dean as the older brother he did not have, as he's the eldest of three sons. From what he said he did not have family problems growing up. He asked his parents about Dean, whom they remembered and could relate to, and eventually he was given a copy of David Dalton's *The Mutant King*.

He credits Dean with "turning him around" and considers Dean the major influence in his life. Before this encounter with Dean he was having problems in school, but afterward he got interested in many things. He credits Dean and what he learned about Dean from Dalton's book with influencing him in many, many ways including his interests in literature, drama, the arts, and philosophy. He said his interest in existentialism comes from reading in Dalton's book that Dean read existentialist philosophers. He also said Dean is always with him in whatever he does. He earned his PhD and now teaches, in addition to some of the standard ones, courses on existentialism and literature of the 1950s (including the literature of the Beats). I must note that he often uses examples or cases that involve homosexuality. He also linked his own liberal ideas about race and sexuality to Dean. I do not know how he and May met, perhaps at the college where he teaches. They were leaving to return home about three o'clock in the afternoon, so I did not get a chance for a longer interview. Kenrick is the first Deaner I have spoken with or interviewed whose inspiration from Dean has led to this particular career line and interests. He seemed to want to link all his intellectual interests and choices as well as many of his social attitudes back to that initial encounter with Dean in *East of Eden*.

Never Too Young

"Billy," one of the youngest I interviewed, was a fourteen-year-old eighth grader at the time. He was from Indiana and said he had been a Dean fan for nearly six years and had been attending the festival for about seven years. He said he visited the Gallery in 1988, and the experience started him in the direction of collecting Dean memorabilia and learning more about him. He found a lot of information in a local library and "really got hooked." His favorite Dean film is *Rebel*. One of his ambitions is to create a collection of Dean memorabilia second only to David Loehr's, but he's also interested in acting and has joined the drama club at school. When asked about the ways Dean has affected him, Billy said, "He's inspired me mostly in sculpting and arts and stuff." He apparently draws a great deal and sometimes tries to draw Dean. When asked about his family's reaction to his interest in Dean, he said, "Sometimes my mother and father, they think [I'm] blowing him out of proportion and stuff but sometimes don't think I do." He collects books on Dean, and his favorite is His Life–A to Z [*The Unabridged James Dean: His Life and Legacy from A to Z*]. But when he read Dalton's *James Dean: The Mutant King* he finally "got it" and was "hooked" on Dean.

The Navy Vet

Phil Zeigler (1931-2020) stands in contrast to many Deaners, yet he is a prime example of strong lasting commitment. David Loehr mentioned to me that Phil was among the first "serious fans," but some time passed before I could set up an interview. He stood out among the fans with his cowboy hat and 1950 Merc. He was a regular in Fairmount even before he moved there in 1996 after retiring from his career as an optician in York, PA. After high school Phil attended college for a year, then served in the US Navy from 1951 to 1955, and later learned his profession under the GI Bill. He married in October 1955, not long after first seeing *Rebel*. Like many Deaners, Phil visited a number of sites associated with Dean outside of Fairmount, including the crash site near Cholame (which he found too emotional). He also visited several locations in Hollywood, such as Griffith Observatory and Warner Bros., where he visited some of the back lot locations where *Giant* and *Rebel* were filmed. Phil was active with the various Dean clubs over the years and also contributed commentary and poems to their publications.

My first interview with him was in 1990 at the Gallery. Before I could pose my first question, in clear anticipation of what I would ask, he began:

> I'm the same age as Jimmy if he would be living. He graduated the same year from high school, 1949. I saw his first movie in York, Pennsylvania, in March 1955—*East of Eden*. And, when I walked out of the movie house, I was stunned. He mesmerized me. I thought to myself, I can relate to this guy right off. The movie, I mean, the way he and his old man hit it off, that's the way my dad and I were. We just couldn't hit it off together.

Then, he continued with a story from 1948 of wanting a leather jacket that was on sale and his father's reaction. After considerable "harassment" by his father and intercession by his mother, his father finally consented and even contributed five dollars toward the purchase. His father had objected because "only hoods wear those and...motorcycle guys."[21] Phil showed a photo of the jacket and said he wore it all the time until it wore out in 1966.

Later he continued to explain his reaction to James Dean: "I thought to myself, here's a guy I can relate to—what an actor! I mean, I just—was in a daze really. It just—there was something there and to this day, I can't explain it. It's charisma, I guess."

When *Rebel* came out, he said he couldn't wait to see it. When he read about Dean's death, it "shattered" him, he said. Phil was twenty-four years old at the time, and "a guy like [Dean] has an effect on me. I thought to myself 'Are you going nuts or what?' Wacky, over this guy." Seeing *Rebel* "just blew" his mind. But, he also thought, "Everything in this cockeyed world is just all used up." With Dean gone, he thought there would be no more movies, but then he learned that *Giant* would be coming out. The theaters were also running double reelers and showing *Eden* and *Rebel*. "Over and over again, I went to see his movies."

Later in the interview I asked him about Dean's continuing inspiration. He responded by citing what he and others see in Dean, but mainly in his films: an independent guy who wanted to be himself and not dominated by a father; a self-thinker. He spoke of *Rebel* as his favorite Dean film "because he fought with his old man in that—but I mean, we used—when I was a kid, we used to do stuff like he did with those cars, you know?" In a clarification, Phil explained they didn't steal cars, but they did do a lot of dangerous driving such as drag racing on a certain highway outside of town.

In the 1998 interview, conducted at his new residence near Fairmount, I returned to the question of Dean's impact or inspiration in his life. He indicated his interest in auto racing and said he attended some races in California while he was in the Navy and wondered if his and Dean's paths ever crossed there. When Phil was in high school, he liked acting and got a part in the junior play. During his senior year, he was selected to help direct the play. He explained he didn't like to tell others about his early interests in acting since they might draw the wrong conclusion (i.e., drawing a "parallel" with Dean). He also related how he first came across a copy of Dalton's *The Mutant King* in a local bookstore: "I grabbed that thing, and I read that thing through twice because I—and then I made up my mind that someday I was coming to Fairmount. I wanted to see where my hero—or my idol, whatever you want to call it—where he lived and grew up." Dalton's book only amplified his interests in things Dean. More books followed along with several documentaries, all of which fed his desire to make a trip to Fairmount.

After his stint in the Navy, a new chapter in Phil's life would begin. He married his first wife in October 1955, eventually fathering three children. When their first son came along, he wanted to name him James Dean, but his wife objected. They eventually agreed to call him Mark Anthony with Dean's cousin Marcus Winslow as a namesake.

After seeing *Giant* his feelings toward Dean only strengthened, and he felt Dean was "a man for all seasons." He said, paraphrasing Martin Sheen, "There were two pillars in the '50s—Elvis and Jimmy. Elvis changed the music and Jimmy changed our lives." And he's still doing that. He illustrated this point with a story about his youngest daughter. When she was about fifteen years old, she watched *Rebel* on TV. That was in 1977, and she didn't know Dean was dead. After watching the film, she said things like: "Daddy, he is cool" and "I really like him, and he's cute." The next morning Phil saw she had written a letter addressed to James Dean at Warner Bros. Studio. When she came into breakfast, he explained to her that Dean was dead. She was devastated and couldn't believe he was dead. However, her interest in Dean continued, and soon after a poster of him appeared in her room.

In August of that year Phil asked her if she would like to go to Fairmount. She became excited and said, "Oh, Daddy, I would love that." Phil became emotional in telling of the first visit:

> We went to the cemetery, and this was a traumatic thing for me. It really was, I mean, I had never been there before, and here was somebody that I—I mean, I'm not ashamed to say it—I loved that guy. I mean, he was everything that I thought that I was. I mean, he was. And I sat down there, and I said a little prayer. I mean, it just came out—I couldn't help it, I cried. And I got myself together then, and I felt different. It wasn't

as much—I don't know what word to use—the admiration is still there but being there broke some of the spell.

He continued: "To me this was hallowed ground. Here was my shadow. Let's face it, every guy that ever saw him thought that he was talking right to you. That's the way I felt."

They continued the Fairmount tour by visiting the Museum. At that time it was on the second floor above an auto parts store on Main Street. It had to be opened for their visit by Mrs. Ann Warr. There weren't many Dean-related items to see back then, he explained, but he was grateful to Mrs. Warr for opening the Museum.

Phil's next visit was in 1983. It was during that visit that he first met several of Dean's relatives, including his cousin Joanne and Ortense Winslow, Dean's aunt, who along with her late husband, Marcus, raised Dean after his mother died. Among others, he met Adeline Nall, Dean's high school drama teacher. Also on this trip, Phil was treated to seeing Dean's old bedroom suite. On a return visit in 1984, Phil was to meet Marcus Winslow Jr. and his wife, Mary Lou. From these meetings, Phil built strong friendships with the members of the Winslow family, and especially Marcus Jr. About these friendships, Phil said:

> All these good people that I've met, you know, through him [Jimmy]. I'm not placing him above God—I would never do that—I just thank the good Lord that I had the privilege of coming out here, you know? I'm not a religious fanatic—I never was—but I've met so many nice people out here—they are just great.

To my questions about his collecting, Phil told of his divorce in 1976 and what happened to the collection he started in 1955. He said she refused to let him retrieve his collection of Dean memorabilia and rock and roll record collection, and that he learned later she had torn up his magazine collection. So, Phil began collecting again and, with some difficulty, found some of those '50s magazines. He continued collecting (Fig. 4.1) and later remarried.

Figure 4.1. A small sample of Phil Zeigler's Dean memorabilia collection. (Photograph by the author).

Phil's involvement with the fans and other Deaners extended beyond merely attending events in Fairmount. He often contributed news and poems he had written to the various club newsletters like the *Deanzine* and would often read one of his poems for the memorial service or at Dean's burial site. After Adeline Nall's death in 1996, Phil became more deeply involved in the annual memorial service, and along with Tom Burghuis he served as a co-emcee for the service. After moving to Fairmount in 1996, Phil had taken a part-time job, joined the local American Legion Post, volunteered at the Museum, and joined the Back Creek Friends Meeting—the same church that the Winslow family attended. He began renting a small house on the edge of the Winslow farm. It was the same house where Winton Dean, father of James Dean, had lived after returning from California and until his death. Asked about his decision to move there, he said: "People think I moved out here just because of James Dean. Well, it's not only that, I mean, the area, I just like it out here. I think the people are more outgoing in this section of the country than they are back east." His only complaint was the difficulty of getting seafood in Fairmount, especially his favorite, haddock. Phil's ashes are buried in Fairmount's Park Cemetery.

To Be Part of James Dean's Life

"Oliver" was in his mid-forties when I conducted his interview on September 30, 1994; he was the person with the most complicated history interviewed, yet he was open and articulate. He was visiting Fairmount for the sixteenth or seventeenth time; he wasn't sure which. Six or seven of those times were during the Festival. From a large urban East Coast region, Oliver explained that he came from a classic "dysfunctional family" and was the oldest of five siblings and a cousin. His parents fought frequently, and he described his father as a "violent alcoholic" and his mother as being at fault for maintaining the relationship. There were "beatings and violence" in the home with the consequent "stress and tension." Back then he didn't understand why it was like that, and he grew up thinking he was "flawed" and to blame for his own unhappiness. Eventually, his father committed suicide. Outside the turmoil of immediate family, an aunt provided him some solace. It was she who first told him about "this amazing person James Dean, who had changed her life when she was a young girl."

Beginning in the fourth grade, the "reality of movies" became Oliver's escape when he realized this was a way of dealing with the family situation and his stress. Eventually he saw *Eden* at age eleven on television, and from that film he began to understand that pain like he was feeling could be expressed and not hidden. He saw Dean's character in *Eden* was in the same kind of pain familiar to him but was not covering it up, and he realized there were others "out there" like him. Eventually he saw both *Eden* and *Rebel* as a double billing at a theater where you could stay all day for the repeat showings. He came to view acting as a way to transcend the pain he felt, and from those two films he saw "someone who was releasing the very feelings that I was told were shameful and not to be recognized in any formal way."

By junior high, Oliver was passionate about movies and began acting in school plays while his interests also broadened to including writing and drawing. They were "all ways to try to come to grips with the reality that I lived," he said. Dean's increasing impact was being felt in his own efforts and in the hope for something better. Speaking to Dean's impact, he cited the experience of sitting in a dark theater and, alluding to his Catholic background, likened it to being "able to sort of sit at an altar and heal myself. I could grieve, I could cry, I could release an enormous amount of joy"—which was not allowed in the home environment. But, sitting in the dark theater "among strangers who were experiencing a similar situation" was like being in church.

I broadened my inquiry by asking about obsession with Dean. Oliver said that he was obsessed with Dean for "awhile" and that he "identified with Dean on a very tragic level." "I truly believed that he had the right answer to die at twenty-four," he said, stating that he had crashed a car once and had attempted suicide more than once. "Yes, I was obsessed." After reading Dalton's *The Mutant King* around 1975, he became even more obsessed as he learned about Dean's background and origins. It was Dalton's book that led him to make his first trip to Fairmount. Like many he wanted to discover what if anything could explain Dean's growth there. He thought "maybe it has some secrets" that would help him with his problems.

This first visit was in midsummer, and he spent several weeks getting to know the town and several of its citizens, including some of the Museum people, one of whom told him Dean was "nothing special.…He was like everyone else," an expression of Quakerism, he thought. He also learned from the townspeople about Dean being an athlete and his other activities. Oliver was struck by Fairmount's appearance because it looked just like photos of Dean taken by Stock during their visit to Fairmount. But Oliver experienced several negative reactions that led him to conclude that Dean's "specialness was that he had to escape from [Fairmount] and...to go someplace where what he had, his gifts, would be respected."

By the 1970s Oliver was studying acting and working in New York City. He was beginning to get parts in off-Broadway plays. He was spotted by a Columbia Pictures scout and eventually brought to Hollywood along with others to be future stars, which he said was a "fiasco" that turned out to be a publicity stunt, and eventually he and others selected were dropped. However, Oliver continued his efforts, working his way through hard times and managing to get small roles in television shows and low-budget movies during the 1980s and '90s. He expressed the belief that he didn't "fit any of the slots" wanted. He wasn't "good-looking enough" for leading roles or "unattractive enough to be a character actor." And blaming himself he said, "I was much too articulate about what I wanted to do and what my intentions were." He said he was ready to do something like *On the Waterfront,* not the parts offered.

During the 1980s he corresponded with David Dalton and stated in one of those letters that his goal was to be a part of James Dean's life. He expressed doubt about knowing what he meant at the time, yet in a way he did become part of his life. With the second edition of Dalton's book, Oliver was thanked in the acknowledgments. So, seeing that, he said he had become part of Dean's life—only in a peripheral way—but there it was. Oliver recognized this as fulfillment of sorts and said:

> I was going to say a justification of my struggle to—because my struggle to be an actor like James Dean was fraught with dead-ends and pain and rejections, and I thought that was how I would get into his life because, certainly, when I became a star, I would say it was because of James Dean, as a lot of people have said.

Despite his struggle as an actor, Oliver had been writing, and through a friend he began writing a weekly column in a rock and roll magazine. A "wonderful thing" for him was that his first article was on Bruce Springsteen, whom he had met previously when working in a bookstore. In one of their conversations, Oliver learned that Springsteen was not only a Dean fan but that Dalton's *Mutant King* was "his bible" and that he had carried the book with him on tour. His second piece for the magazine was "Rebel Without a Band" and put forth the argument that James Dean was the first rock and roll star in that he "personifies a rock 'n' roll star." He continued writing for the magazine for two and a half years, writing numerous articles.

Around the time Oliver decided to stop pursuing acting due to the abuse and cruelty actors face, the president of a record company offered him a job working for one of the major music business groups. He accepted the position but decided afterward he didn't want that kind of job. Later, another contact suggested he write a book about his early experiences of coming to Hollywood. Despite a promise from his contact to publish, it was not published. Unfortunately the book rights were owned by the record company. Oliver needed to find a new job, and a commercial production company eventually hired him as casting director.

From there other opportunities came along, including an offer, again from that same sponsor and record company, for Oliver to write a screenplay related to James Dean for $25,000. Oliver returned to Fairmount for three weeks to work on the play, bringing with him a fellow with a video camera. They filmed fourteen hours of video, including the Festival and a car show, while Oliver tried working on the script. Finally, he decided that the only story that "made any sense" was his own story but set in Fairmount. The story has a main character (based on him) plus two close friends, a boy and girl. It takes place during the Festival, and the three kids all want to be like James Dean and to leave Fairmount for the wider world. They go through the things Oliver went through. Two of the kids get out of Fairmount, but the other doesn't and dies tragically. That character's story is his, Oliver said, except that—unlike the character—he didn't die. The sponsor liked the story, which Oliver titled "Free, Like James Dean." Oliver continued to work on that script and others for two years, until his sponsor was fired by the record company, leaving his projects, book, and play in limbo.

Second Generation

It was common when speaking or interviewing a fan or Deaner that they would mention their parents as perhaps "liking" Dean when they were younger, but only a few told of a parent or parents being serious fans. When I interviewed twenty-four-year-old "Fred" from an upper Midwest city, he mentioned he's a "second generation" fan. He explained that his dad, who graduated high school in 1955, was very aware of Dean and felt he "was really influenced" by the actor. He noted that his dad has copies of some of Dean's movies and a "James Dean scrapbook" and that his sisters sometimes bought posters of Dean for their dad. His mother thinks Fred's "a little obsessive" with his collecting, but otherwise she's OK with the Dean thing. Fred has four older sisters, but none of them are Dean fans.

Fred continued his story, recounting a time in seventh grade when he came home from football practice and decided to "sneak" a viewing of one of those movies since no one was at home. The film was *Rebel*. Once it was playing, his reaction was surprise:

> I just sit there, and I was struck—the movie was amazing and that's what started it...my room was posters, everything. Took my dad's posters...and put them on the bed—got them all up [on the wall] and that started it—and it just ballooned in high school. I mean, any time I could watch a movie or do anything—any school project I associated James Dean to it somehow. Had to write a paper or whatever.

He went on to tell me of his first trip to Fairmount at age sixteen and how he continued to make the trip sometimes two or three times a month. He's made friends with David and Lenny and has sometimes helped in the Gallery. His dad gave him *his* own '49 Merc on his twenty-first birthday, explaining that his dad "bought and restored the Mercury because he liked James Dean, and now it's mine." Fred has also managed to visit all the Dean sites except those in New York City but plans to do New York eventually.

When I probed about Dean's influence on him, he first said how much he likes all of Dean's movies and all three characters he played. Then he added, "I'm interested in Dean as a person—I mean, I think the best character he ever played was himself. He was just amazing....I don't know how he knew he was going to make it [in Hollywood], but he did—just the energy he created...I'm mystified with it."

Returning to Dean's influence on him, he noted being turned on to the arts and exploring old movies and the history of movies. He noted that he had watched all of Elia Kazan's and Nick Ray's films because of James Dean. As we continued the interview and discussed some of Dean's interests, I mentioned he had taken up sculpting, and Fred said, "I took a sculpting class last semester at the local community college." I asked if that was because of Dean's interest, and he responded, "Yeah, basically...I'm going back for Sculpting II this year...I would have never gone on and done that without his influence, I'm sure." Finally, about Dean's influence, he said: "I can't think of a day in the last ten years that I haven't thought of James Dean...."

Dalton's Book

Kathie Wilson (1951-1999), from Topeka, Kansas, recalled first becoming aware of Dean when watching *Rebel* on TV, and she "fell in love with the man." She couldn't recall her age at the time but thought she was in junior high school, maybe thirteen. At first, she didn't see much or find any books on him, but she recalls seeing a poster of Dean walking down a street in New York, and she "fell in love with that poster." Her story of becoming a Deaner, though not unique, is one that illustrates a long process with interruptions. Some years later (after a failed marriage and after her son had a serious motorcycle accident—more on this later), she found a copy of Beath's *The Death of James Dean* and then Dalton's *The Mutant King*. These books revived her earlier interest, but it was Dalton's book, she explained, that really got her hooked and is still her favorite. It was there that she learned the most about Dean, and it created her desire to travel to Fairmount. She referred to it as the "bible" to Dean fans.

The interview with her was in 1993. At the time, she worked as a supervisor for Yellow Freight. I asked if during her teen years she shared her feelings about Dean with her girlfriends. Her response was that it was "just kind of a private thing."

> I remember, you know, we shared the songs then, growing up, of course, rock 'n' roll was the big thing, too, and the Beatles and the Rolling Stones and all that, oh yeah. Girlfriends: [I] shared all that with girlfriends, but James Dean was always kind of a private thing with me.

We spoke about some of the other books and films, her collecting, and activities in Fairmount and with other Deaners and fans. She made her first trip to Fairmount in 1989 and many years since. She met Maxine Rowland early on, and they became very good friends and stayed in touch. She made many other new friends on her visits to Fairmount and remarked that she "writes more letters than I ever have." *Rebel* remained her favorite Dean film, with *Eden* second and *Giant* being her least favorite. She said about Dean in *Giant*: "His acting was fabulous, but I don't care for Rock Hudson and some of that." She also had been on the "James Dean Walking Tour" conducted by David Loehr in New York City.

Her son's motorcycle accident in 1987 resulted in major injuries including a severe head injury. He remained in a coma for two and a half months and went through another year of therapy. He was up and around again by the end of 1988 and wanted to visit a bookstore. That was when she spotted Beath's book, which led her to Dalton's, known as the "James Dean bible." Those books led her to come to Fairmount and visiting there helped her "regain trust in people.... You feel like it's a second home....I love to come back and see the people—it's like a family reunion every year."

Returning to Dean's impact on her, she noted that "after reading the books, it almost brought some normalcy [to her life]." She continued: "Almost a comfort to me, I guess, to be able to take my mind off everything and concentrate on Dean and his life." Overall, learning about Dean's life and visiting Fairmount helped her deal with the trauma she was experiencing. When she's alone, that's really when she thinks most about Dean and Fairmount.

Passages to the Self

After the annual memorial service at the Back Creek Friends Church for James Dean in September 1994, about a hundred of us walked in pilgrimage fashion from the church three-quarters of a mile or so to Fairmount's Park Cemetery. The procession was led, as in the years since 1980, by the venerable, mysterious, motorcycle-riding, leather-clad Deaner "Nicky Bazooka." After the multifarious rituals at Dean's graveside, Bazooka fired up his cycle and roared out of the cemetery in the proverbial "cloud of dust" (it's so *Deanesque*). Unfortunately, Nicky died in 2004 and with him, that tradition.

As the ceremony began winding down, reporters and film crews selected this or that person from the crowd for on-the-spot interviews. I listened in. An interview already in progress caught my ear. A woman is speaking about how, in 1955, she was walking along a downtown Chicago street in the very intense heat of a summer day. "May" spotted an air-conditioned theater and decided to seek relief from the heat by taking in a movie. On the marquee was *East of Eden*. It meant little to her just then. She was just seeking the cool, dark comfort of the theater. The film was James Dean's first major film, and at that time his second and third films had not been released. May's chance encounter with James Dean on the screen in a Chicago theater was a momentous one for her.[22] She watched James Dean on the screen and saw herself. May used the metaphor of "the mirror" during her on-camera interview. The next day I located her and arranged for an interview (Hopgood 1998b).

May was twenty years old when she wandered into that theater seeking relief from the heat and discovered herself on the screen in the image of James Dean as "Cal Trask." She said, "I came out a totally different person. I had never seen anything like him." I asked about her life at the time. She explained she had a terrible relationship with her father, which she said the relationship between Cal and his father in the film "mirrored." About men and boys, she said the boys in her south Chicago neighborhood were "idiots," and the men in "gray-flannel suits" she met "frightened [her] to death." Dean, she said again, was "my mirror image." But Dean, as Cal, was able to scream back while she couldn't. Dean, as her "mirror image" would understand her, and "he wouldn't fall into either category" of neighborhood boy or "gray-flannel suit." This "*wasn't* love," she said, "*he was me.*" When she learned of Dean's death in September 1955, she traveled to Fairmount for the funeral services. She was among the first "Deaners." She did not return there until 1980 for the twenty-fifth anniversary of Dean's death, and she has visited a couple of times since then.

In 1957, May moved to Greenwich Village in New York, in part, because of Dean's example, hoping to pursue writing. She fell in with the young artistic types, including many "Dean wannabe" actors. She took one of the actors in for six weeks but, laughing, she said he later left her for a man with a bigger apartment. From there it was on to San Francisco. She worked near City Lights Books and "made that whole [Beat][23] scene." Eventually she completed her college education, returned to Chicago, and taught high school English for twenty-three years, eventually taking early retirement.

May has now "gone back and picked up" where she left off in her writing. She has taken up playwriting and has performed a few of these onstage. I asked her about those twenty-three years teaching and if Dean played any part. She told me about a wall-sized collage completely covered with Dean photos and clippings chronicling his and her life. When she wished, she would sit and speak with him, like in the morning with coffee, before going to work. She described how, when she would look at Jimmy she would have "this feeling," then she cited Neil Young's version of the song "Forever Young." "I can still be back as a young person [and] can think about pursuing my writing." Regardless of her age, she explained, she can look at him and reflect on his/her life, the things he/she did. From that hot day in Chicago on, her life has been intertwined with his. "Jimmy, you and I are forever young," she said. In her life from Chicago to Fairmount to New York to San Francisco and back, there is this "thread of Jimmy."

May's story underscores a not untypical journey of a lifelong devotee. But May is not an isolated example. Rather, she reflects or epitomizes most Deaners in her reaction to James Dean. Deaners often speak of seeing themselves, or "a part of" themselves, reflected on the screen. These first encounters are often described as "like being struck by lightning," as Kenneth Kendall, the late obsessed artist, has stated (Riese 1991, 284). Others have encountered Dean not in the movie theater, but in books. As noted above, David Loehr discovered Dean and himself in 1974 through reading David Dalton's *James Dean: The Mutant King* (1974). Today, Loehr is known as the "Dean of Deanabilia" because of his vast collection of Deanabilia, a collection that began only after reading Dalton's book. Others have told of having their first "reaction" to Dean from seeing a photo or poster of him. Still others claim to have been contacted by Dean from "beyond" or "feeling a psychic connection" to him or having felt his presence in some way.

At this juncture, let's take an intermission among the interviews for a change of pace to examine some of the writings of Di Elman.

ADORATION AND PILGRIMAGE

Girl on a Motorcycle

The journey of re-/discovery of Di Elman is retold in her book titled *James Dean...Just Once More* (1990). It is a collection of her poetic reactions to self/Dean and the associated sites. With the book open, the poems usually appear on the righthand page and a photo either of Dean or of Di, sometimes on her motorcycle, appears on the left page. Here are a few samples of her writings:

> [1][24] ... Who says you can't go back? Grab
> the music. Buddy Holly–and our soul.
> James Dean –
>
> ... Let's get going, Back in time–
> Before we're too late. And we miss
> the party–
>
> [2] ... James Dean? Who was I going to be?
> And, Where were you taking me? In the
> dust–on the screen. Up there–
>
> ... Tell me again. Please? Who I was
> going to be–I want to go there.
> Again.
>
> [3] ... Once. I tried to be perfect. And
> walk a line. A line inside of a line.
> Until the lines came apart.
> ... And I fell off. It hurt so bad.
> I couldn't stand it. So I found my
> leather jacket. And went back in
> time.
> ... To find James Dean.
>
> [4] ... I was just a child when you died.

> I never got to say thanks. I never got
> to touch you.
> … I was the ugly girl in thick glasses.
> Seated in the 12th row of the Arlington –
> Holding no one's hand.
> … When I grew up. I met you James
> Dean. I ran into your pain. Understood
> it. Walked with it.
> … and you took my hand.

The "mirror image" or *interchange* involves feeling what the other feels and believing the other feels the same. "He would understand what I feel" or another similar expression is typically heard or written. In this way, they are one and the same—blended so to speak—and the fusion is given expression. There is the mixing of "then" and "now" in many expressions. Then is now, and now is then.

The next two poems by Di Elman refer to Fairmount, Indiana, and Cholame, California, respectively, and are made part of the pilgrim's process of re-/discovery and the move through space and time.

> [5] … Fairmount. To be with you. I need
> you privately. Alone. Like you were.
> Dancing with yourself.
> … I need to touch where you are. Run
> your fields and tell you. I love you.
> I mourn you. I miss you.
> … James Dean.

> [6] … I need to say thanks. So, I take a
> tiny crystal from my pouch. And throw it
> where you were –
> … Along this lonely fence.
> … Thank you James Dean. For all you
> gave me. And us. And the world.

Another example, though not a poem, is much more to the point: "Every time I return to Fairmount it's like 'going home again,' and I feel a very definite connection with James Dean, a very personal, warm and yet sad feeling. I can't even begin to describe the connection" (*We Remember Dean International* 1994, 18).[25]

Vignettes

Little Prince

I hesitate to include Tom Burghuis among the Deaners. He is certainly a serious fan, but maybe not a Deaner by his own admission. I interviewed him on September 30, 1992, in Fairmount. He was in his late forties, from Michigan, and retired from General Motors. He indicated he wasn't a collector, though he said he did acquire a small Dean bust personally from Kenneth Kendall. He recalled having seen Dean's films when he was an adolescent, but Dean apparently had no impact on him at the time and he didn't become a fan.

Tom's route to becoming a fan and a regular at Fairmount's yearly Festival is a unique story. Sometime in the mid-1980s, a friend from Indiana loaned him a copy of *The Little Prince*. He read it and fascinated, reread it, finding it "very deep." His friend told him later the book was one of Dean's favorites and hearing Dean's name he remembered seeing the guy's movies back in the 1950s. Tom began reading more books about Dean and listened to his friend's stories about Fairmount. Tom's interest was pricked, and his friend suggested they make a trip to Fairmount. In March 1985, they spent two days there. Besides going to Dean's grave, they visited the Winslow farm and met the Winslow family.

Back home, Tom continued to read books about Dean and eventually discovered the *We Remember Dean International* fan club and became a member. He made a return trip in early September 1985, then returned later that month for the Festival and the memorial service. During these trips he eventually met Adeline Nall, Dean's high school drama teacher, and others associated with the Museum and some of the regular fans and Deaners.

He was fascinated by what he was learning and decided to do a video of Adeline. He hired a film crew and did the filming in the old Fairmount High School building. That allowed her to tell her stories about Dean in the setting where much of it happened. Tom continued to read other books on Dean as well as repeatedly rereading *The Little Prince*. Unlike most Deaners, Tom said he read Dalton's *The Mutant King* only once, preferring other biographies.

His focus on Dean remained on his acting, and he does not "identify with James Dean the way…[I] think that some people who come here do." Tom thinks Dean's "sensitive side" came from growing up in Fairmount and his "rebellious side was created."

With Adeline's encouragement, Tom got involved with the Museum's programs (the Festival and the memorial service). Under her guidance, he began serving as the emcee for the memorial service, a role he continued for thirty years. His expanded role established him as a regular among the fans and Deaners as well as many citizens in Fairmount.

West Coast Woman

"Judy," a medical transcriptionist, was born and raised in a small West Coast town. Her father was a Dean fan. At the time of my interview on September 30, 1991, she was twenty-four, a medical transcriptionist. This was her first visit to Fairmount and said she had wept when she arrived. She was "hooked" by James Dean about three years earlier after seeing *Eden* for the first time, and it remained her favorite Dean film. She started reading "all the books" she could find on him and collecting memorabilia and was planning to have a James Dean room in her apartment. Her favorite book was Dalton's *The Mutant King*. She had visited Cholame for a Dean memorial celebration on September 30, 1990, and planned to visit Griffith Planetarium.

Judy's attraction and identification with Dean derived from his sad childhood, his "brooding" sexuality, and his talent. "He has a way about him—it's hard to explain—he has a way about him that makes you want to get close to him. You feel sorry for him. You want to comfort him. You want to be a friend to him." I also asked Judy about any continuing inspiration, and she said, "I feel he gives people hope because he had a dream and he followed through with it." He inspired her to pursue acting.

A Loner

An example of the solitary Deaner is "Jeff," who spoke of being strongly discouraged in his early fascination with Dean: his father thought it was "silly," "childish," and "unmanly." His mother mediated the situation by recalling her early enchantment with Frank Sinatra, then cautioned him against "idol worship." Some of his mates thought he was strange, while others shared his early interest in Dean (though not to the same degree) and two of his best buddies were fans of Brando and Presley (creating a kind of symmetry). He had first become aware of Dean when he saw *Rebel Without a Cause* at age twelve. James Dean, he said, "just grabbed me...as if he had taken possession of me. After that, I began to notice him on lots of magazine covers and television reruns." There wasn't really any memorabilia then, so he sought out magazine articles on him. He also began wearing a red jacket, white T-shirt, jeans, and boots in *Rebel* style in junior high school.

Back then, Jeff wanted to rebel against authority of all types; now Dean is much more to him: Dean is the example who pointed the way whether Jeff knew it or not. "I wanted to be free, but I didn't understand then what that meant—Dean helped me get there." Jeff has remained a lifelong Deaner on his own terms, with some "ups and downs." The "downs" happened during college and early in his professional work although, he said, Dean would creep into his thoughts from time to time and usually at times of personal reflection.

East Coast Writer

I interviewed "Frank" on September 30, 1993; he was twenty-three and living in Fairmount with plans to move on soon. He was born and raised in a small East Coast town and has a degree from an East Coast college. He didn't have any especially difficult problems with his parents while growing up. He became a Dean fan at age fourteen after he and a chum saw a double feature of *Eden* and *Rebel*. His response: "We were just in awe–totally sucked in–totally–just part of this movie I couldn't believe.... I was exhausted." His reaction to Dean was "he was so right-on with everything we were living through right then." He thought Dean was the "real deal" and "just perfect." Wanting to know more, he bought a copy of John Howlett's biography *James Dean* (1975) followed by other Dean bios. Later, in speaking about those two films, he said: "I could put myself in there—I walked out of there feeling like either he was me or I was him." Frank said Dean was his role model and inspired him to take chances, become a writer, and led him to Fairmount. He was currently reading through David Loehr's Dean archives with plans to write a book.

I Had a Dream

On September 30, 1996, I interviewed "Jennifer," a married woman in her mid-fifties from a major East Coast city, where she worked in a hospital. Along with her husband, she was visiting Fairmount for the second time. A fan since age twelve when she first saw *Eden*, she explained she wasn't a rebel and didn't have family problems like some others but "something happened to me—it was a transformation." She claimed she locked herself in her room and cried for "months." Along with her husband, she also has visited Cholame and was working on plans to visit New York City so she could visit the places where Dean lived and maybe Los Angeles. She had read some of the Dean biographies, but not many, and recalled having read Dalton's. She's indicated not being into collecting memorabilia. She had made some friends from the visits to Fairmount and is corresponding with some. She explained that several years earlier she "woke up with tears streaming down my face, and I had been dreaming of Jimmy Dean." She said she still wonders what the dream meant.

Adoration and Pilgrimage

Obsessed...Now Mellowed

Twenty-five-year-old "Angela" had a deeply felt experience from watching *Rebel* in 1984 and when interviewed (September 30, 1991) was in Fairmount for the sixth time. She had also visited Cholame and Los Angeles. She met Kenneth Kendall while in LA, and he showed her some of the Dean sites there. She also wanted to visit the Dean sites in New York.

Angela is originally from the upper Midwest, had lived on the West Coast, and was then living in a southeastern state. After watching *Rebel* she asked her mother about Dean and learned he was dead. She began reading books about him and started collecting: "I got real bad, to the point where it was like an obsession, at one point, like nothing else existed in my life. But now it's mellowed out a lot.... It comes from the heart more than anything. It's not like I want a piece of everything he had; it's just I can relate to who I think he really was as a person as opposed to a character." In expressing what attracted her to him, she mentioned several characteristics such as his "looks," sense of humor, gentleness, sensitivity, and kindness to animals. From reading Dalton's *The Mutant King*, her favorite, she said, "It sounded like I was reading about me. That's how I really felt—like I was in tune with Jim, and I felt like, wow, I should have known him." About Dean's influence in the arts she said, he's "the greatest inspiration" in her life. She's been interested in the arts since grade school and draws, sculpts, and writes poetry.

Latin American Writer

I met and interviewed "Sofía" on July 4, 1998, during her third trip to Fairmount. Sofía, who came from a South American country, was forty-four and had been a Dean fan for many years. She first visited Fairmount in 1996 with her son, age about sixteen. On that trip, she had planned to travel to Italy, and her son suggested stopping in Indiana and they eventually made it to Marion. They continued on to Italy, where they spent six or seven months, then returned to

Fairmount and back to South America. In her home country, she taught philosophy in both middle and high school. Sofía explained her feelings for Dean as love and devotion. She became a fan when she was very young after watching *Rebel* on TV. Sofía said he wasn't "just a face or just an actor—something different—like a feeling." Subsequently, she explained, she was always looking for him in others, without finding that "something" that is like a star, comet, or angelic. She claimed he was an existentialist. A bit later she remarked she's always looking for "immortal people." At home Sofía would display photos of Dean, frequently changing them, and she would place fresh flowers in a vase near the photos. From Dean she seeks valor, which I took to mean heroism or perhaps gallantry. As the interview went on, she continued to attribute more qualities and characteristics to Dean, describing him as intelligent, a beautiful actor, overwhelming, dedicated, simple, unselfish, lonely, artistic, and innocent.

She began writing her book in Spanish while in Italy, noting she was the first woman to write about him. Her book, first, she said is from love, but the idea motivating her was the notion that Dean was/is a tragic hero. Realizing he was a hero, she began thinking about the heroes in Greek mythology, starting to compare him with Achilles. She planned to use quotations from Homer in her book along with "Jimmy's story" and lots of photos, some rare ones.

Discussion

"History" repeats again and again. The young woman who found herself through Dean in 1955 is re-/created, echoed, in similar fashion by young people in Australia, Germany, Japan, and elsewhere today and every year in between. This conjunctive being or phenomenon of self/Dean repeats and repeats. In this way, the ritual lives on and on timelessly, i.e., "everywhen." Dean on the screen, Dean on the wall, Dean and Fairmount, Dean in a book, and Dean within. Dean becomes the icon and the setting of the altar or shrine. The mirror may be revealed through any medium, visual or verbal, or by place. For many, the mirror is found in David Dalton's *James Dean: The Mutant King* (1974). Through the experience of reading Dalton's biography of Dean, some begin to see Dean and themselves in analogous terms. Others have the mirror revealed through other works, including photo collections of Dean or other biographies (or, more to the point, hagiographies). Another common path is through experiencing Dean in his films, especially *East of Eden* and *Rebel Without a Cause*. A path to the mirror may also be revealed with the aid of another person, such as an older sibling, friend, or parent.

"Oliver" said in a letter to David Dalton he wanted *"to be part of James Dean's life."* But he told me he didn't know what he meant at the time, "I had no idea."[26] Though not often expressed so directly, most Deaners have a desire to somehow intertwine their lives with his. How is this possible? Perhaps some believe they can fulfill or complete the unfinished trajectories of Dean's life. Certainly, in this way, time is bent or compressed, or perhaps, eliminated completely. How are separate "histories" joined except through such a process? This is not "objective" history, it is "private" history, or *even* the beginning of *a* history for some Deaners. Why do Deaners continue to re-/write Dean's history except as self-expression and as a way "to be part of James Dean's life?"

Many Deaners, if not most, write, paint, film, sculpt, build monuments, or seek some other creative avenue to express their feelings for and adoration of Dean. The subject of their work is Dean—either directly or indirectly—and this work serves as an exercise in self-expression, exploration, and renewal. (I don't mean to suggest that they only produce art of Dean, though for some that's apparently true, only that he is often the inspiration.) The "blending" of their lives with his occurs through these works and the transformation of self. In some cases, Dean is an "interpreter" or intermediary between a self and what is felt, expressed, or interpreted. In this way, Dean again fulfills the role of guide to continuing renewal. Each time this happens, the Dean/self virgule is also re-/created or renewed.

In the case of these artistic and creative expressions, what can't be seen or read is equally, if not more, important as what *is* seen or read. That is, these creations are the result of, or attempt at, collusion or symbiosis of the maker with Dean, or to oversimplify, the *interaction* of emotion, mind, and icon.

These interviews and interactions with Deaners reveal an existential dimension of renewal and transformation coupled with strong feelings and even desire. Dean's hometown of Fairmount, Indiana, is itself critical to the transformation for many. This setting provides for the movement through, in, and around space imbued with Dean and for the requisite peak experience. As ritual becomes history in Fairmount—and a multi-mirrored one—the break with normalcy again moves the pilgrim via nihilism to another state of being. The pilgrim again views the metaphorical looking glass and in seeing her other (in *a* form of James Dean, perhaps) steps through; the virgule of self/other dissolves at least for a time.

5

Exploring Semiotics and Meaning

How do we compare the behavior of anger, joy, hope, expectation, belief, love and understanding? Act like an angry person? That's easy. Like a joyful one—here it would depend on what the joy was about. The joy of seeing someone again, or the joy of listening to a piece of music…? Hope? That would be hard. Why? There are no gestures of hope. How does hoping that someone will return express itself?

—WITTGENSTEIN

A simple "dialogue" metaphor can be used to understand the interaction between devotee and *icon*. However, since consciousness and this metaphorical dialogue, which involves consciousness, between devotee and *object* of devotion cannot be viewed directly, the thorny issue arises of how best to "get at" either. That is the problem. What happens and what feelings occur between a devotee and the *object* of devotion that is registered with the devotee? That question led to an initial encounter with Charles Sanders Peirce's semiotic via Milton Singer (1980; 1984) and is found in a chapter written for Adams and Salamone (Hopgood 2000, 351, 354-358). This first exploration was anything but extensive or exhaustive yet appeared promising as an analytical tool. The purpose of bringing Peirce and his semiotic into play is to explain the type of interpretation employed here for the study of meaning vis-a-vis the Deaners. Beyond this piece I will not continue the use of the Peircean terms, although they may reappear in discussion or the conclusions.

Peirce's Semiotic

This problem could be examined using other cases, for example, what do the *icons* (renderings or visual conceptions) of the Virgin of Guadalupe communicate to people of somewhat different, but related cultures, such as a second-generation *Latina* of Mexican descent living in Dallas versus a Nahua woman in rural Puebla, Mexico? Such questions as this raise all sorts of problems related to consciousness and meaning. But, to simplify the problem let's say that in both cases the women produce poetry devoted to the *guadalupana*. Clearly, close study of the resulting poetry would provide a means of approaching the nature of what transpires between the devotee and *icon*. Interviewing the women and speaking with others will provide additional insights.

Or consider a Huichol shaman (*maraʾakame*) who following a vision proceeds to make a "yarn painting" of the experience, as is the custom (Furst 2003). In this case, the *object* would be the vision itself (which given present technology cannot be known directly) and the yarn painting is the *sign-icon*[27], and his interaction is with the *object* (vision) directly or at least shortly later and one could say with further interaction with the *sign-icon* during the process of creation. A person doing an oil painting directly does not paint exactly what is viewed, but some representation of it, even a type of preconception of it, and so on, and during the process the painter may change this or that in minor or major ways. But what if the artist is only responding to a pre-existing image, not to any representation of that image? The original *object* is not present or available. And to complicate the matter even more, the artist is attempting to grasp, to re-create a feeling and an image experienced some time before and to put that into physical form. In a case explored elsewhere (see chapter 6), this was the circumstance with the late artist Kenneth Kendall. He met Dean only once, and although he had access to a life mask and numerous photographs of him, Kendall claimed for years that he was never able to "capture" the image he sought, which existed in his "mind's eye" and was derived from that only face-to-face meeting.

Basically, by employing such Peircean concepts as "*quale-consciousness*" along with other elements of his theory of signs, this issue can be illuminated. Peirce's "*quale-consciousness*" refers to "a consciousness of the quality of feelings" (Singer 1984, 158). However, this notion cannot be understood without reference to Peirce's theory of signs, nor can an exploration get very far without this.[28] Peirce's theory of signs, however, is much more complex than the usage here indicates.

From the beginning I held to the notion that the key to understanding what was happening with fans, and Deaners especially, was the interaction between each of them and the persona of James Dean along with certain special places associated with him. What was this adoration about? That nagging question was basically just how to get at this process of interaction. The notion of a dyadic relation was explored initially, but this approach ignored a key component and oversimplified the process. Digging deeper into Peirce seemed to only result in more permutations of his semiotic *ad infinitum* and at times an endless exercise of logic. I soon learned this was a frequent issue noted or experienced by others (e.g., Fisch 1978; Maquet 1982, 2-3). At one level, for example, an image of James Dean can be viewed as an *icon* and is iconic because it resembles the person James Dean. The image can also be considered an *index* because he marks certain characteristics, e.g., a rebel, movie star, and so on. Likewise, his image may be regarded as a *symbol*, having become a *sign* representing, say, method actors (*cf.* Scott 2009, 135).

However, Peirce's triadic semiotic in the basic form of *object–sign–interpretant* is introduced here to provide a model of the process involved in the interaction of the viewer/participant with the images and places associated with the object of devotion (Fig. 5-1).[29] It must be kept in mind that before an *interpretant* is produced, there must be an *interpreter* (Innis 2004,198), though for economy the interpreter is not shown in the figure. To paraphrase Singer, this triad allows for dialogue between the *sign-object* and interpreter of the *sign* resulting in an inner dialogue as well as outer dialogues with others (1984, 158). The fact that the *object* of devotion considered here (James Dean) is no longer living would seem to simplify matters. This is not the case. Dean (the "*object*," in Peirce) is fixed in a very real sense and cannot age or change, yet interpretations ("*interpretants*," in Peirce's terms) have continued to appear. This is because devotees (as viewers or interpreters) continue to interact with the images of him (the "*sign-object*," in Peirce).[30] Of course, the *sign-object* does not have to be an image of him but a place or thing associated with him that may stimulate an *interpretant*. For a Deaner they all have significance. Another issue, of course, is what the viewer brings to the encounter in the form of beliefs, ideas, past history, bias, and so on. Even though the *sign* is derived from the *object,* the *sign* has a life of its own. The interpreter or viewer-devotee (or self) is "within" this triad in creating or using an *interpretant*. It is necessary for the viewer/interpreter, or self, to be understood as an intrinsic part of the process, otherwise other problems will arise.

```
SIGN-OBJECT→ →→→INTERPRETANT →→→→SIGN
                    ↕              ↘    ↕
          ADDITIONAL INTERPRETANTS      OTHER SIGNS
```

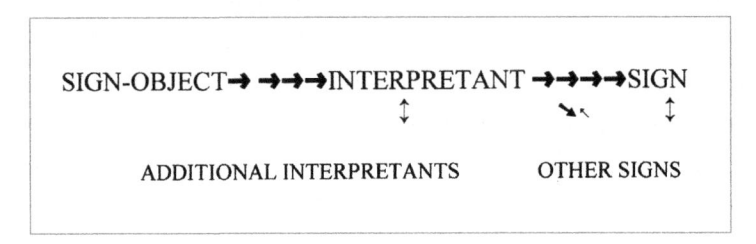

Figure 5-1. Peirce's Semiotic.

It is the *interpretant* of this interaction that is of most interest and will reveal something about consciousness vis-a-vis the self. It should also be noted that the *interpretant* may not only lead to other *signs* but may loop back to affect the original *sign* or *interpretant*.

More needs to be explained about these terms and how they work, as well as several additional terms from Peirce. Certainly, an important point to keep in mind is the ambiguity or lack of determinacy in this method, i.e., each viewer/interpreter of a *sign-object* is "free" to respond in a predictable but nondeterministic manner. In fact, each viewing of the *sign-object* by the interpreter may generate different *interpretants*. Regarding these *interpretants*, Peirce indicates three types: *emotional, energetic,* and *logical* (1998, 409; *cf.* Colapietro 1989, 107ff). It is also probably important to underscore the obvious: that the *interpretant* effect or affect may not only lead to other *signs* but may loop back on the original *interpretant*.

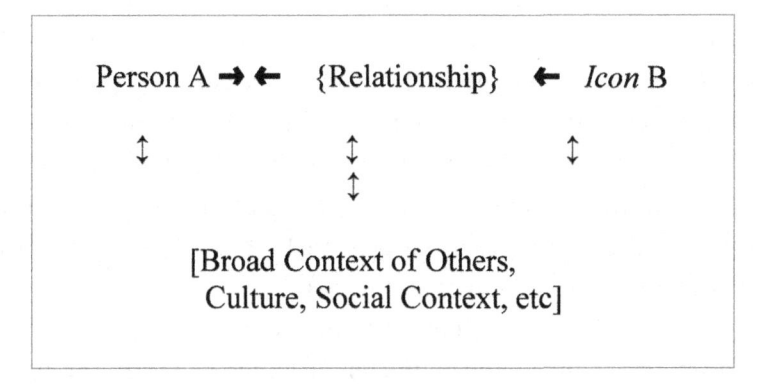

```
Person A → ←   {Relationship}   ←   Icon B

    ↕              ↕                   ↕
                   ↕

         [Broad Context of Others,
         Culture, Social Context, etc]
```

Figure 5.2. Triadic Model.

Still another way to view these relations is as follows. Dyadic relations are always *triadic* due to the *content* of the *relationship* between the two parties or things. That is, how is it possible in any dyadic relation not to refer to the relationship or specifically what results from the relationship? I have purposefully not included a third, fourth, or more persons in the model. They are subsumed in "Broad Context" in figure 5.2.

This model can be used to analyze the "relationship" between a person A and an *icon* B. In this case there is considerable "baggage" attached to both A and B. A, being a person, carries with her a whole complex of meanings, behaviors, history, and so on. And B, being itself an *icon* [complex symbol] carries a host of other symbols, meanings, and so on, which exist in the non-living world but are carried and perpetuated by persons such as A. This is useful in "modeling" what transpires and is not necessarily what actually happens. The actual nature of the interaction (thoughts, emotions, actions) is much more complex than this simple model. Likewise, it is not necessary to create models as involved as those employed by Warner (1959, 449ff), given that the aims here are less complex and the focus is on the individual interaction with an *icon* (*sign-object*). Consequently, this model does not readily deal with communication from other persons, although in reality such communication has occurred and continues to occur. Warner recognizes the "internal conversation" issue, but models it differently (1959, 468). Nor is there speculation about how much "reasoning" participates in this exercise. What is of interest is the "relationship" and what results from this sort of interaction. The "relationship" in this case is entirely in the head of person A, but something is missing if the point is left there. What is missing is the loop, the "back-and-forth" over time between person A and icon B.

An example of how Peirce's semiotic works is as follows. A hypothetical Deaner views a poster of James Dean in one of the famous "rebel" poses used to promote *Rebel Without a Cause*. She is the interpreter and the *interpretant* in this case is created via her viewing of the poster (the *sign-object*), creating another *sign*, a mental image or thought. As such this initial *interpretant* may create a series of associations or responses. There will certainly be an *emotional interpretant*, that is, a feeling or series of feelings associated with James Dean, the film itself, and other feelings associated with viewing the film. Say, she shares her reaction with a close friend who has already seen the film and has formed an opinion (*sign*) on her own. Both are interested in learning more and begin sharing their reactions.

Another example of this semiotic came from a telephone conversation I had with "Jeff." Though he was not a serious collector yet, I knew he did have some items from the 1950s. I asked if he had any of the special issue magazines that were devoted entirely to Dean. He said he did and added he had recently retrieved one from his collection. He said that as he began glancing through it, memories of those days when he was a teen began coming back to him. Without repeating any of his details, it was apparent this *interpretant* had led him on a journey into his past.

An *energetic interpretant* may also result. For example, whenever she sees this particular poster, she may want to watch the film again or not. If a *logical interpretant* results, the Deaner may decide she needs to make plans for a trip to Fairmount or make a phone call to a fellow Deaner who is a dear friend. In another actual case, a longtime Dean fan in her forties views the same "rebel" pose, and her initial *interpretant* is a rejection of the image, thinking he wasn't a rebel at all—another *sign*, is followed by yet another. This time it is an *emotional interpretant* of Dean as a sensitive man with good looks, followed by yet another *sign* of when she learned he was killed in the car accident.

The Porsche

There are many examples of this process in action, though not written using Peirce's semiotic. James Morgan, a former magazine editor, provides an excellent example in *The Distance to the Moon* (1999), his book about his road trip across the US in a Porsche Boxster. After noting that in developing his adolescent persona he combined some Elvis with "a dash of *Blackboard Jungle,* and a whole lot of brooding James Dean," he details his reaction to a certain photograph that he had taped to his bedroom wall as an eleven-year-old. The photograph was of Dean's wrecked Porsche, and "[it] was the first thing I saw in the morning and the last thing I saw at night" (1999, 4). Morgan continues to describe the impact the photograph had on him, after describing the wreckage itself:

"To an eleven-year-old romantic, Dean's aura somehow metamorphosed the twisted steel [sic!] so that it was no longer wreckage—it was sculpture. Signifying exactly what, I've not sorted out" (1999, 4). Since then, he writes, he "lusted" for a Porsche.

Eventually Morgan's road trip and pilgrimage takes him to Cholame and the scene of Dean's death. From there he visits Jack's Ranch Café and takes note of the Dean memorial monument. He takes stock of his trip and reflects once again on that photograph that seems to have motivated his journey. He attempts to find meaning in this and finds it "marked by desire, glamor, speed, selfishness, excess—and inevitability" (1999, 279). Referring again to the wreckage as abstract sculpture open to many interpretations, he writes that it could be seen as "a depiction of freedom, which always comes with trade-offs… [or maybe] it was a brilliant comment on the clashing forces of restlessness and consequences." This is followed by Morgan imagining Dean's wrecked Porsche ending up at the Museum of Modern Art with a brass label "American Century" (1999, 279).

Certainly, in this case Dean's wrecked Porsche has become an *object-sign* with a significant number of *signs* and *interpretants*, not only with Dean but a series of non-material *interpretants* attached to both Dean and Porsche.[31] The various steps of arriving at *interpretants* are clear in Morgan's narrative even though he does not resort to semiotics or to its logic. It is also clear that since his first interaction with the photograph he brings much more to his series of *interpretants*. A different person with a different history would no doubt have different reactions (*interpretants*) to the same photograph. This makes clear that one's *interpretants* change over time, and the whole complex of meanings, behaviors, history, ideas, and so on carried by the person affect those *interpretants*. The complexity of this process simply indicates the limits of the model. What transpires as "modeled" is only an approximation of what happens. The actual nature of the interaction is much more complex than the model can manage. Fortunately, the aims here are less complex and the focus must be limited to the "surface" of the interaction.

Peirce recognized the importance of the "internal conversation" as well and points to added complexity of the issue.

> It follows from our own existence...that everything which is present to us is a phenomenal manifestation of ourselves. This does not prevent its being a phenomenon of something without us, just as a rainbow is at once a manifestation both of the sun and of the rain. When we think, then, we ourselves, as we are at that moment, appear as a sign (1992, 38).

This position rejects epiphenomenalism, as needed. This means, as Hoopes notes: "Thinking *is* behavior" (1991, 9) and not just phenomena *somehow* related to behavior or irrelevant to behavior (*cf.* Searle 1993, 8ff). For current purposes, this leads to the suggestion that some introspective dimension of consciousness is in interaction with the *object-sign* as a reflective "amplifier" that results in an extension or alteration of consciousness. It is the creation of significance, the attachment and amplification of meaning in this process that is of major importance.

The Professor

Another excellent example to demonstrate this system is "the professor," "Albert." He is not a Deaner but rather one who brings the insight of someone who closely approached that status earlier in life, along with details of the impact Dean did have on him. It would be economical to simply list the personally appealing characteristics of James Dean mentioned by the professor, but that would ignore the dialectics at work and the value of semiotics. It is the interaction of the *interpretant* (the professor) with the *object-sign* or *icon* (Dean) plus a host of other thought streams creating a triadic interaction. That is, between the *interpretant* and *icon* there are more streams of thought at work than a straightforward, single line reaction to the *icon*.

At the time of his interview in 1990, Albert was a philosophy professor in his mid-forties, and the interview was conducted in a small conference room at the Ohio Valley university where he worked. Albert explained that he was an adolescent when he first encountered Dean in magazines. But interestingly he linked his initial interest in Dean with his experience of living in the desert West, where he spent several summers. But in response to my first question about Dean's impact on him, he immediately began a lengthy testament. Let him explain:

> There was a sense of extreme isolation and loneliness…and being in the desert there was a lot of heat, of course…Part of the experience involved a sense of isolation together with a sense of silence that I later discovered in Camus's work in terms of an emphasis on those things. That is, a sense of nature that is "valid" that can't be expressed or understood through business or science…[i.e.,] appreciation for silence, appreciation for loneliness, lending itself perhaps even to alienation.…Here in the desert you felt a sense of isolation… you didn't feel a part of anything…[and] the sun seemed to exacerbate that and make one turn inward…[and] tends to focus your attention on yourself as the individual. And your mind tends to wander as opposed to being logical or connected.

Not long after those experiences, he saw his first Dean film, *Rebel Without a Cause*. He continues:

> I guess it was the element of individuality in his movies that made a connection with me, and Dean was obviously a charismatic actor—part of his charisma attached to the notion that one could identify with his individuality, *per se*.… [In] contrast to the others around him that were conspiring to make him straight, not to be a rebel…, I keenly felt that

because of the isolation and sense of individuality that I got from the desert as opposed to what I felt back East. Especially in the straight establishment society that I was raised in—where that kind of thing—the individuality and sense of aloneness, possibly even alienation—was disparaged.

Speaking of Dean's scene in *Rebel* where he is confronted by the caring counselor/police officer and in a rage tries to hit him and then pounds on his desk, coupled with the cowardliness of his father, represented to Albert "rebellion against the hypocrisy around him."

Referring again to the desert and how it affected him, he said, "I would later discover the same kind of feeling of some degree in Camus because in Camus…there's a stress on silence and peace in the desert, there's also a sense of alienation…. The desert gives one courage to stand alone, which I highly valued." After citing Natalie Wood's character speaking of the importance of sincerity, Albert cited sincerity as a characteristic of Dean's: "That's exactly what James Dean was—sincere….He said what he meant, and he meant what he said."

Albert next turned to Dean's manner of speaking in a staccato style, referring to an isolation of words or distance between words. From there Albert linked this speaking style to referencing Martin Heidegger's speaking style as an "existential way of speaking." After interjecting a comparison to Robert F. Kennedy's staccato style as reflecting his sincerity and emotions, he notes that "Dean anticipated that kind of thing…[and he] reflected some kind of existential aspect…." Saying that about Dean does not imply Dean was familiar with Heidegger or other existential philosophers, Albert notes, stating: "There's something more fundamentally existential about his very being than can be articulated through formal modes of thought." Referring to that "something about him," Albert notes:

He stood apart and alone—you could see it in his eyes. You could see it in the way he combed his hair and the way he dressed, his smile, the way he spoke. It comes through in the parts that he played. Somehow or other he transcends organized religion or morality or those kinds of things. In the same way that I think Camus did.

Digging deeper, I asked Albert to return to that initial impact, how he felt when seeing Dean on the screen. I was unprepared for what followed:

> I felt like he underscored a part of reality, individual reality, an external reality that I knew was there.... he made explicit that broader understanding of reality or degree of reality....I'm talking—about the reality of individuality—the questionableness of society—the "validity" of isolation and aloneness of the distinctively unique individual. He underscored the reality of that to me—I already knew it, but he expressed it in his acting—more than just said it—expressed it. He made the heat sufferable. I can remember sitting on the curb and reading stuff about James Dean...with my foot on a cigarette butt in a street by a shopping center in the middle of summer...when it was 85 degrees, and I should have been insufferably hot, in pain, but sitting there and seeing Dean in the desert with his feet up on an old car in front of the house in *Giant*—somehow, he made it sufferable. Somehow, he made it my heat.... he drew attention to the fact that it was my experience—it wasn't something packaged and presented that I should just suffer but that it was something for me to experience and if I was going to suffer, it was going to be my suffering.

So, the experience of the heat, of being uncomfortable in one of life's situations was not just something to be avoided, but

> Dean helped underscore that—helped one think in a new way about the things one was experiencing even if they

were bad. And he helped one to laugh at that in a typically spontaneous way that Dean laughed or get mad in the way that he typically and spontaneously got mad. And spontaneity and staccato and monosyllables and the way that he was emphasized the fact that those kinds of things could not be grasped by the scruff of the neck in terms of systems of thought.

I next pushed for how Dean affected him behaviorally.

> For one thing it made me respect true "individuals" that I met....I would tend to lean towards friends who were not orientated toward groups or group behavior or peer groups or in-groups in high school. I tended to respect and, therefore, be attracted more to individuals...[who] were merely alienated in some pejorative way—they were often exceptional individuals.

Referring to one of his friends whom he regarded as an exceptional person, Albert said:

> He was my friend in high school, and he had those characteristics of saying what he meant, meaning what he said. He seemed purveyed with a sense sometimes of loneliness and isolation and yet had a tremendous sense of humor to overcome that. And yet his humor was somehow in a way anti-establishment to some degree. So, I think that Dean affected my behavior at least in terms of that—being attracted to those kinds of individuals and respecting them. Probably in some indirect way maybe giving me increasingly courage to do that—he affected me to some degree in that way....I probably would have been that way anyway though; when I look back at it, I was—that's the way I've been pretty much.

A few moments later, after I had said that such a thing is difficult to measure, he replied, "Probably I wouldn't have been attracted to [Dean] if I hadn't been that way in the first place." Referring to conformity and anti-conformity that Dean came to represent, Albert said, "Maybe he represents for us that figure that didn't compromise, and maybe that's why we still like him. And maybe that figure is still with us to some degree—symbolizes that." And later, this: "Dean comprised a kind of antidote to the overworked society notion of man."

Still, reflecting on the passage of years, Albert said: "I've periodically gone back to James Dean....But then I would always return to him—he never left my inner self, my inner consciousness. He was there; he made a mark."

I asked him, well into the interview, to sum up what Dean means to him. His reply was:

> What he means to me is most relevant to an artful way of looking at reality. He reflects that side of reality as opposed to a logocentric or rational side of reality. He represents the other—not necessarily irrational but perhaps one more orientated toward art and literature—that's just as valid, indeed, necessary for appreciating life; without it we become boring—we forget the importance of our emotions and feelings—that Dean evidences so much in his pictures.

My questions and at times our discussion covered more ground including the Beats, rock and roll, sexuality, Dean's role in *Giant*, and the milieu of the 1950s. Interspersed there were additional or emphasized characterizations of Dean as the "outsider" and "loner" in *Giant*, emphasis on individuality, authenticity, integrity, charisma, anti-establishmentarianism, and vulnerability.

Turning to question of semiotics and meaning in our dialog, Albert immediately linked the desert, heat, isolation, and loneliness to his reaction/connection to Dean followed by a valid "sense of nature" and an enhanced inner focus of the self/individuality. All of these are *signs* in the Peircean system and linked to *sign-object* (Dean). These are some of the first steps of establishing meaning for the *interpretant*. In the early part of our dialogue, Albert refers to the philosopher Camus's work as reinforcing the sense of isolation, silence, and loneliness. All of these "pieces" become part of a bundle linked, at least for a time, to the *sign-object*.

I wondered if in another setting a student's question about Robert Kennedy or Camus would stimulate a *sign* from our professor of Dean or the desert. I should have asked him.

Art, Semiotics, and the Sacred

How is the sacred handled, if at all, with Peirce's semiotic? Peirce appears to have been silent regarding the sacred, as if it were "out-of-bounds." Whatever the case, it is of interest to explore the processing of the sacred. A likely avenue is via one of the three *interpretants* and highly likely the *emotional*, yet it could well be all three to some degree.

The basic question is this: what are the processes by which ordinary, profane, and secular things and places, natural or human-made, are transformed (and mediated) into sacred ones, and beyond that, sacred "art." Artists accept the idea that ordinary things may become art, of course, but then, what makes a creative act or product sacred? In terms of "art," a parallel question arises: what transforms a secular thing into art and then into sacred art? It is the first question that is of most concern, but the other cannot be entirely ignored. Such issues are related to some especially puzzling aspects of Deaner behavior—especially the unusual amount of creative work they do in tribute and adoration of Dean. This point needs an emphasis: Deaners do a truly astonishing amount of artwork, write poetry and prose, and engage in other creative or "arty" activities to express their feelings for Dean. The nature of these creations ranges from professionally executed oil paintings and sculpture to pencil sketches and from flower arrangements to tattoos. A related issue involves the transformation of ordinary and mass-produced memorabilia (commodities) into sacred objects. This may be unique to twentieth- and twenty-first-century capitalist societies, but there are analogous products from much earlier times (Hahn 1990). And the role of transformed "memorabilia" in the context of Deaner behavior and ritual is key to understanding the nature of this process. Then there is the impact Dean had on many artists (chapter 6).

Analysis

Another way to demonstrate this process is to examine works devoted or dedicated to Dean. The analysis then turns to answering the question: What do these works tell us about the metaphorical dialogue with self and James Dean? A poem that exemplifies the interaction of the *interpretant, sign-object,* results in this:

> James Dean
> You are everything
> The one who sustains me
> The one who sets me free.
> You are my idol, my savior,
> My hero, my redeemer.
> You're the legend that
> will never fade.
> You've been immortal since that
> September day.
> There was only one like you before
> Nor has there been since.
> There will never be a
> James Dean again.
> You're the one that gives me
> life,
> The air that I breathe.
> You, James Dean, are everything.

(from *We Remember Dean International* Newsletter, August/September 1996, 7)

Another one, by a Deaner who also regularly contributes drawings of Dean, goes in part as follows:

> He held life's answers down deep inside;
> His secret we couldn't discover, no matter how hard we tried.
> If only he hadn't left us so soon,
> We might have uncovered the man in the moon.
> But alas he has flown; the secret with him did die,
> And we're left with the mystery of How? What? And Why?
> What James Dean means depends on with whom you speak:
> Saint or Sinner? Talented or Genius-streaked?
> No matter.
> The irrefutable truth will always fly high:
> The Legend of James Dean Will Never Die . . .
> (from the *We Remember Dean International* Newsletter, August/September 1996, 1)

A few Deaners have self-published collections of their poems. *The Red Ribbon: James Dean in Poetry* by Yvonne Lubov Rusiniak (1996) contains in its twenty-one pages a series of fifteen poems devoted to her feelings, reactions, and effects of James Dean. One sample from a poem titled "Anniversary" (co-written with James Robiscoe) relates a visit to Fairmount and places associated with Dean, including the Winslow home:

> Steady as a hand in a pocket,
> I alone slip in
> to touch the things he used.
> Alone in his room, I run my hand
> across the drums, the books, the bed.
> Years press into a twist of the wrist.

An even more intimate expression comes from her poem "On the Marquee:"

> Every time there is some sort of crisis
> in my life and I feel that I am about
> to faint, my Jimmy comes to hold me
> for awhile, giving me his shy smile
> that seems a haunting mixture of joy
> and pain.

A strong expression of worship is found in her "Communion:"

> In the worship of James Dean
> when I was a teen, I followed
> the path of his promise religiously,
> thinking I would like to act.
> And later,   ………
> I wanted to kiss the gold chalice
> of Hollywood, at the altar of all he was,
> and wipe my lips afterwards
> with a red cloth as it
> is done in church, the material
> of his red jacket.

A more elaborate approach is taken by James Courtney in his *James Dean: Back Creek Boy* (1990) with illustrations by Mark Heckman and a focus on Dean's three film roles. The final chapter is given over to "James Dean: Actor," which is a chronicle of Dean's life from age nine to his final day. Courtney reveals little of his own feelings toward Dean, though it is clear he is a serious fan if not a Deaner.

Douglas Allen was inspired to write and paint about his feeling toward James Dean with a series of poems and paintings that provides further insight into what inspires his fans and Deaners. A sample (2010, 10):

> An end of life we see him yet
> > Life beyond living vow we not forget
> The beginning and the end, or is it the other way round
> > Visions of James Dean beget us anew
> A stream of emotion unbound

This poem is accompanied by a painting adapted from a photograph by Roy Schatt showing Dean in a circular window, hand to mouth with cigarette (1982, 82).

These are just a few of hundreds and hundreds of poems that relate devotees' thoughts and feelings about Dean. Just a few of the motifs, or *interpretants*, that emerge from the poems include love and desire, friendship, loss and sorrow, lifestyle, particular mannerisms, talent, beauty, gaining strength, savior or redeemer, worship, immortality, and saving one's life ("he saved my life"). Some also deal with the interaction of the writer and the image as in this segment from a longer poem:

> "No matter what troubles confront me anew,
> Jim's always there to see me through."
> (from the *We Remember Dean International* Newsletter,
> December 1994 / January 1995, 12)

A Preliminary Conclusion

One obvious result of the triadic interaction at a general level is the effort at expression of affect in relation to the *sign-object*, i.e., James Dean. This contributes to or sets the devotee off on a quest for "self-understanding," "self-exploration," or development of abilities and talents via interaction with the *sign-object*. However, this process also includes other observations. In some cases, the quest leads to significant changes in the direction of the devotee's life, what Peirce calls "habit-change." The affect or effect (*interpretant*) may be at the level of "tone" or "attitude" and may lead to modified or new behaviors. And, certainly, over time it may become all-embracing, leading to some transformations in a person's life. Some Deaners would say "major transformations" and this claim is striking. Also, the number of people who have claimed that profound changes have taken place in themselves since discovering or finding Dean is striking. Perhaps it is, after all, only another manifestation of a particularly American version of the hero myth or perhaps just a narcissistic exercise. Even so, that can be said to be true only regarding certain kinds of questions and at a certain abstract level of analysis. To understand the relationship of consciousness and this interaction with a *sign-object* is a different order of question since it attempts to probe the inner life.

What is useful here is the use of the *sign-object* to get into touch with another aspect of the self, explore a different level or dimension of consciousness, or to try to "expand" oneself in some way as a creative process of self-exploration and self-definition through deep involvement. This introspective/extrospective dimension of consciousness in interaction with the *sign-object* as a reflective "amplifier" result in modifications of consciousness. Finally, the deep attachment to the *icon* and the resulting amplification or creation of meaning is itself significant.

6

Artists, Their Art, and the Sacred

Whatever is holy to people inspires artistic conception.
—SUSANNE K. LANGER

While it is true that since prehistory and throughout history, the joining of images with the sacred is well established, actual cases are not necessarily clear. What turns mundane, profane, and secular things and places, natural or human made, into transformed (and mediated) sacred ones? What is usually considered "art" in a broad sense is an obvious area to explore that question. But then, what makes a creative act or product sacred art? Of course, for something to be sacred it doesn't have to be art. Consider a strand of hair from a dead child kept safe and carefully stored by her mother. The hair is "sacred" to the mother, but not art. While the creative aspect of art is the focus here, at times things will get "blurry" between these categories.

Put another way, what transforms a secular thing into art and then into sacred art or just a sacred object? This issue is related to some especially puzzling aspects of Deaner behavior, especially the unusual amount of creative work they do in tribute and adoration of Dean. To repeat a point made earlier in this book: Deaners do a truly astonishing amount of artwork, write poetry and prose, and engage in other creative or "arty" activities to express their feelings for Dean. The nature of these creations ranges from professional works in oil and other media to amateur works and from simple poems to visual creations. As noted previously, the transformation of common and mass-produced memorabilia may be unique to twentieth and twenty-first-century capitalist societies. In that case the role of art and transformed memorabilia in the context of Deaner behavior and ritual is key to understanding the nature of this process.

The Creative Dimension

Deaners turn out a large assortment of what may be broadly labeled "creative products" and "creative activities." Among these products are a good deal of poetry, prose, sculptures, paintings, and drawings. In the previous chapter, poems written by Deaners were discussed in the context the interaction of self and *sign*. Here the discussion moves on to other creative forms of expression by other artists. Most are directed, primarily, toward James Dean, and they reveal much of the artists' thoughts and feelings toward him.

Visitors to the Fairmount Historical Museum will see many paintings of Dean created and donated by Dean fans. Several scrapbooks kept by the museum contain numerous poems dedicated to Dean. Formerly the James Dean Gallery maintained a room known as the "Kenneth Kendall Room" that contained a large assortment of Kendall's paintings, sculptures, and other artwork devoted to Dean. Additionally, a book of paintings of Dean created by Dante (1984), prints of Dean by Andy Warhol (e.g., Feldman and Schellmann 1989, 112), a collection of paintings, drawings, and illustrations of Dean published in book form (Dawber 1988), and even a pornographic graphic novel (Manara 1992). Additionally, an amazing variety of posters by an assortment of artists also demonstrates an interest in Dean. Perhaps the best known are from the series called "Boulevard of Broken Dreams" by Gottfried Helnwein. There are also several biographical films and plays about Dean, including some by well-known directors and producers.

We Remember Dean International (*WRDI*) fan club's newsletters were an excellent source for finding Deaner and fan creations. Each newsletter contained an assortment of news items and information of all kinds for fans. The newsletters also included occasional drawings by fans and frequent personal accounts, which I refer to as "testimonials." Of particular interest were the poems that appeared in nearly every issue. Among the "rank and file" Deaners there is a wide range of such expressions, exclusive of the newsletter. In addition to poems, paintings, drawings, and sculptures, some have written plays about Dean or his influence, filmed their own videos dedicated to Dean, published books of prose about or inspired by Dean, downloaded creations to YouTube, posted their collections on *Pinterest,* or taken up a creative activity such as floral design. One especially inspired and gifted Deaner at one time contributed an occasional leaflet he called "Collectors Illustrated Poetry," which he wrote and illustrated. This Deaner left his home in Arkansas for Hollywood trying to get into acting. Then there is the case of the man who, beginning many years ago with his devotion to Dean, eventually built the James Dean Gallery in Fairmount.

Following up on this dimension of the Deaners, I posed interview questions exploring many activities not usually regarded as creative (in the "arts" sort of way), such as public speaking. What emerged in these interviews was a consistent story that goes something like this: "Before I became interested in James Dean, I was afraid to attempt writing [or acting, or drawing, etc.]." "I was shy, I was afraid to speak up, I didn't try to write [or act, or draw, or sculpt, etc.]." "I was afraid to express myself." And so on.... So, what does this have to do with James Dean and his image? In every case, when asked about that connection, it was James Dean who was and is the inspiration. It is his origin (modest), his background (rural America), his looks, his perseverance, his struggle for success, his challenging work, drive, and enthusiasm, his talent and creativity, his daring, his quest for fulfillment, and so on that have served as catalyst and continuing inspiration. What is cited may be any number of Dean's interests in painting, drawing, sculpting, music, photography, dance, cinematography, bullfighting, writing, directing, and, of course, acting.

The Deaner whom I call "May" told me of her continuing dialogue with "Jimmy." Since 1955, when she first "saw herself" on the screen in the form of James Dean, she has relied on him for psychological support, especially in times of difficulty in her inner life. May told of a large portable mural of Dean photos she took with her everywhere she lived, from Chicago to New York to Los Angeles and back to Chicago. She placed this mural on the wall in her kitchen near the breakfast table, and each morning over coffee she could "speak" with Jimmy. (May is among those interviewed and is covered in chapter 4.)

Music and Musicians

In addition to these types of creative activities, there is Dean's influence on American popular music, which is surprising given he was not engaged in the music field. What is curious is the effort to tie rock and roll music to Dean's influence. To drive home this point, a pulp magazine appeared titled: *James Dean: A Tribute to Rock's Greatest Influence* (May 1977). Most of the magazine is devoted to retelling Dean's story with plenty of photographs but Christopher May tries to connect rock and roll and Dean. He proclaims Dean the messiah of rock and roll, proclaiming its coming long before anyone else had any inkling that the winds of change were blowing (May 1977, 6). Such a claim may satisfy many fans, but it is unlikely to be upheld by historical evidence of the genesis of rock and roll. In any case, May's approach is largely one of chronicling the numerous singers and songwriters who were influenced by Dean, in lifestyle or outlook, as well as paying homage to him in their songs. Among those he lists are Lou Reed, Loudon Wainwright, David Essex, Roger Daltry, Peter Frampton, Garland Jeffries, and The Eagles. May notes that Don McLean's "American Pie" refers to Bob Dylan as the Jester singing to the King (Elvis) and Queen (Joan

Baez) "in a coat he borrowed from James Dean" (1977, 7). Elvis is often cited as one who was obsessed with Dean and attempted to emulate him in his early films. But Dylan is a case worthy of some examination of Dean's alleged connection of rock and roll.

Bob Dylan sang "May you stay forever young," and knowing that Dylan was a Dean fan many Deaners believe he was singing about James Dean (but the song was about one of Dylan's sons). Like many young people across the country in the mid-1950s, young Bob Dylan had pictures of James Dean covering his bedroom walls and experienced conflict with his father over his adoration of Dean (Shelton 1986, 23-24). Dean was more than just a movie star to young Bob. He wanted to look like Dean, and he copied his style as best he could, including the perceived attitude and the red jacket from *Rebel*. Trying to measure Dean's inspiration to someone as prolific and creative as Bob Dylan is a difficult task. But most Dylan biographers manage to mention Dean's impact and influence. Clinton Heylin, for example, writes:

> In September 1955, [Dylan's] second idol, James Dean, was killed....If Hank Williams gave the young Zimmerman [a.k.a. Dylan] a sound, Dean gave him an image. A composite of the characters Dean played in *Rebel Without a Cause* and *East of Eden* became the first adopted image of Robert Zimmerman. The teen angst of Dean seemed to mirror directly the sense of isolation of Robert Zimmerman... (1991, 24).

And he quotes Dylan as saying in 1987 that he liked James Dean for the "same reason you liked anybody, I guess. You see somethin' of yourself in them" (1991, 24). Dylan is also reported to have said of Dean, "He let his heart do the talking" (Cott 1984, 20). Bob Spitz, in writing about Dean's performance on the screen and its impact on the young Bobby, notes that he was "inspired by the whole package—the defiant posturing, the attitude, the mumbling, and especially The

Look" (1989, 25). In the booklet included with Dylan's *Biograph* release of 1985, the notes for the song "Every Grain of Sand" include a Dylan quotation: "People like to talk about the new image of America but to me it's still the old one—Marlon Brando, James Dean, Marilyn Monroe, it's not computers, cocaine, and David Letterman, we gotta get off that—Hedy Lamarr, Dorothy Dandridge, that's my idea of America...." Many observers noted resemblances between Dylan's style and persona and Dean: Bob Spitz states that Dylan "was the epitome of cool. James Dean with a guitar" (1989, 270).

If Dylan ever made reference in his music to Dean's influence, it may be from 1965's "Like a Rolling Stone:"

> You used to ride on the chrome horse with your diplomat
> Who carried on his shoulder a Siamese cat
> Ain't it hard when you discover that
> He really wasn't where it's at
> After he took from you everything he could steal.

The "chrome horse" is probably a reference to the motorcycle he rode in his hometown of Hibbing, Minnesota, (or to Dean's motorcycle), "with your diplomat" maybe Dean, "and carried on his shoulder a Siamese cat" could be referring to a series of photographs taken of Dean by Sanford Roth (e.g., Roth and Roth 1983, 38-39). In any case, Dylan did make a pilgrimage in 1988 to Fairmount, where he walked the streets and visited the farm, the Historical Museum, and Dean's grave.

Among other musical artists who exhibit influence from, if not some degree of obsession with, James Dean is the English singer Steven Morrissey (with or without The Smiths). One obvious indication of Morrissey's fixation on Dean is the music video "Suedehead," which he filmed in Fairmount. In the video Morrissey is seen visiting the various locations in and around Fairmount where Dean was photographed by Dennis Stock (1978)—it's like following a pilgrim visiting sacred sites. Morrissey is shown striking the same poses as Dean did in the same locations. Other pointers include publicity photos of Morrissey in poses clearly copied from those of Dean and album covers with photos from Dean's films (*cf.* Slee 1994). To further cement his dedication to Dean, he published a thin book in 1983, *James Dean Is Not Dead*. With a large selection of Dean photographs, the text is a retelling of Dean's life with an emphasis on personal struggle, rebellion, sexuality, self-doubt, non-conformity, and alienation. According to internet chatter, on April 8, 2008, Morrissey purchased a pocket watch Dean wore during the filming of *East of Eden*. His winning bid was reported to be $53,000 at the Heritage Auction Galleries, Dallas, Texas. Dean's influence on Morrissey, like Dylan, is in lifestyle and outlook, if not worldview. Any influence on his art, in contrast, is not apparent.

To those already mentioned can be added (in no certain order) the Beach Boys, Robbie Robertson, Jim Morrison, Paula Abdul, Elton John, Mick Jagger, Madonna, John Miles, Tom Petty, Billy Joel, London Wainwright III, David Essex, John Cougar Mellencamp, Bruce Springsteen, and Lou Reed. They have either written a song about Dean, included references to him in their songs, or exhibited some measure of his influence in lifestyle. From this list, Jim Morrison deserves special mention.

Morrison is believed to have been influenced by Dean, is often compared to him, and has a postmortem following of fans and devotees. David Dalton, the author of *James Dean: The Mutant King* (1974), also wrote a biography of Jim Morrison. Dalton notes Dean's influence on the young Morrison and finds several similarities between the two. Dalton, in examining the formative years of James D. Morrison (b.1943) notes that "Everything was changing, and it all reached a critical mass by 1955. Jim was twelve" (1991,16). What was so significant about 1955? It was *Rebel Without a Cause* along with Morrison's discovery of Elvis, rock and roll, Jack Kerouac, and Jackson Pollock (1991,40). While Morrison was not raised in the Midwest, he was a "Middle American messiah" and was "by nature more like James Dean" (1991, 32). Morrison "emulated" many art and literary figures, including James Dean, "all of whom had the distinction of dying young, and in hindsight their sudden, violent, untimely deaths seem the only possible conclusion for their lives" (1991, 82). Despite the strong language, charting actual lines of influence remains very elusive. Perhaps it is, after all, only by an extension of Dean's perceived lifestyle that allows such a linkage.

An examination of some of the songs written about Dean provides a few clues to the persona these performers presented. There are these from Taylor Swift's "Style Lyrics" repeated three times:

> You got that James Dean daydream look in your eye
> And I got that red lip classic thing you like
> And when we go crashing down, we come back every time.
> 'Cause we never go out of style.

Loudon Wainwright III refers to Dean in two of his compositions, "School Days" and "The Acid Song." In the latter he sings of taking LSD and the psychological effects and sings "I was sure I was James Dean." Then there was David Essex's "Rock On," which was performed by a long list of rockers. It begins:

> Hey kid, rock and roll
> Rock on, ooh, my soul
> Hey kid, boogey too, did ya
> . . . .
> Still looking for that blue jean baby queen
> Prettiest girl I ever seen
> See her shake on the movie screen, Jimmy Dean
> (James Dean)
> . . . .
> Jimmy Dean
> Rock on
> Rock on
> Rock on

The Beach Boys sang "Little Deuce Coupe" (1963) originally written by Bobby Troup about "a young man is gone." The band changed some of the lyrics to make it a tribute to James Dean with these lines "Now a young man is gone, but his legend lives on...." And "For this daring young star met his death while in his car...." Continuing with, "And they say that he'll be known forever more…as the Rebel Without a Cause."

The Eagles song "James Dean" is all about the actor and was written by Jackson Browne, Glenn Frey, John "J.D." Souther, and Don Henley. With lyrics like "James Dean, you said it all so clean," "You were just too cool for school," "The only thing that got you off was breakin' all the rules," "Along came a Spyder picked up a rider, / And took him down the road to eternity // James Dean, James Dean, you bought it, sight unseen," and finally "You were too fast to live, too young to die, bye-bye."

Then there's Don McLean's classic "American Pie," a song about his early days with a long tribute to many early rock and roll stars, with his lyric reference to "the jester" (Elvis Presley) "In a coat he borrowed from James Dean."

Many others make some sort of reference to Dean. There's "American Roulette" by Robbie Robertson, which references Dean without naming him:

> He was born in the belly of the country,
> Over east of Eden, yeah,
> Confused by the big city blues,
> He didn't know whose life he's leading, no,
> Put yourself behind the wheel
> And see if you can get that feel, oh,
> Move faster by night, yeah,
> Move faster by night, uhm,
> The windows were all shattered
> And the body was all battered:
> American roulette,

Stake your life upon it,
American roulette

To mention a few more who make reference to Dean are Mick Jagger in "Primitive Cool," Billy Joel in "We Didn't Start the Fire," Madonna's "Vogue," John Cougar Mellencamp in "Jack and Diane," Bruce Springsteen's song "Cadillac Ranch," Lou Reed's "Walk on the Wild Side" with an androgynous reference, Joan Jett's "Ridin' With James Dean," Hilary Duff's "Mr. James Dean," Bette Midler's "Come Back Jimmy Dean," Def Leppard singing David Essex's "Rock On," and Elton John in the love song "Amy." There are many more, of course.

Plastic Arts

Even excluding fans and Deaners, the sheer variety of artists producing sculpture, ceramics, drawings, paintings, collages, public art, and other forms of art is impressive. Given the time frame—the era of pop art—that is perhaps not surprising. Andy Warhol did him a couple of times, along with Ray Johnson, among others. There's automobile art by professional artists, usually focused on the 550 Spyder, in paintings and sculptures. For example, in 1994 Stanley Wanless of Astoria, Oregon, produced a limited edition of fifty-five bronzes and a limited edition of fifteen sterling silver sculptures of James Dean in his 550 Spyder. The bronze was selling for $16,500 and the silver version for $26,500. Wanless is one among many who have done Dean in his 550 Spyder. The sculptures are only one example of the automobile art produced and still being produced. Dean and his Porsche usually as paintings, lithographs, or prints are often seen for sale at car shows and on eBay. Sometimes pictured along with other "icons" of the 1950s and '60s including Brando, Monroe, and others.

This genre blends into collectibles, such as cookie jars, ceramic plaques and statues, cups, and other items, often produced by professional artists and amateurs, some of whom may be fans or

Deaners. Vladimir Gorsky, a professional, has produced a series of pop-culture portraits but is unlikely a serious fan. A brief mention of public art should be noted as well. Too many to cover in detail, these typically appear in locations associated with Dean. Consequently, Hollywood has several, including a large mural at Hollywood Boulevard and Wilcox Avenue, where he is one among a multitude of famous Hollywood stars. Public murals of Dean as the only, or main focus are also seen elsewhere in Los Angeles.

Professional Artist: Kenneth Kendall

A consideration of Deaner art must include the work of the late Kenneth Kendall (1921-2006). A professional artist who had met Dean only once, Kendall became obsessed with doing representations of him and capturing him in a certain way; "just right." In Dean he found his muse. Although he has done probably hundreds of images of Dean, he wasn't his only subject. Before Dean there was Robert Mitchum, Steve Reeves, Marlon Brando, and later Jan-Michael Vincent, Leonardo DiCaprio, an occasional fan, and many others. Raised in Los Angeles, he also acted in bit parts in films, such as *Julius Caesar* and *Babes on Broadway,* and served as a stand-in for Yves Montand in *Let's Make Love*. It was a bust of Marlon Brando that caught Dean's eye and created his desire to have Kendall "do" him. It is often claimed that "doing art" itself is a ritual act—an expression of sacred feelings—even perhaps a form of prayer. This is certainly the case among many artists in the history of Western and non-Western cultures. Kendall, it appears, came closest to this expression in his endless efforts to reproduce what he recalled seeing and feeling in his only face-to-face meeting with James Dean.

Kendall sculpted the original bust of Dean that was given to Fairmount High School in 1956, and a replica was later placed in Fairmount's Park Cemetery in 1957. Nine months later, it was stolen—rumored to have been stolen by unhappy veterans—and has never been recovered. A new bust was erected at Griffith Observatory and in Fairmount for the James Dean Memorial Park. The latter was dedicated on September 30, 1995. From my interview with Kendall that day, being there when he visited Fairmount on various occasions and spoke publicly and privately, published accounts covering him, and his correspondence with David Loehr, I arrived at some insight into his motivation and that moment of epiphany when he was inspired to "do Dean." Apparently, at a certain moment during his visit with Dean he experienced something extraordinarily beautiful that continued to haunt him for fifty years. Understanding of Kendall's obsession will be helpful with the larger questions here.

The Meeting

Kendall's only meeting with James Dean was in January 1955 at his studio. Dean's interest in Kendall was due to a bust Dean had seen of Marlon Brando sculpted by Kendall. Via a go-between who called by phone, Dean was described as an actor and a friend of Brando's who wanted to meet with him. Kendall agreed, although he had no idea who the actor-friend was. During the visit Dean was interested is speaking about Brando and seeing Kendall's portfolio of Brando. Eventually, Dean worked up the courage to ask if he would be interested in sculpting him. Kendall was a bit taken aback by this request; still he agreed, but no definite plans were made. Here is Kendall's description of the meeting, in his own unique style, as he recalled it in 1982:

> The Dean who came through my door that night was wearing the brand spanking new leather jacket with the fur collar and enamel…buttons in the lapel—white turtle neck pullover, grey whipcords, and black Wellington boots—he needed a shave—looked a little "lippy" and mouth very pink—he expressed himself about the Brando head and I told him about Brando's "no interest" [in the bust]….I hadn't done any "homework" on Dean and didn't know that the big moment in my life was happening although

> I had a terrible case of "stage fright"....one could feel his intensity...something drawing the energy out of the air to itself....He got on the subject of accidental death of famous people and he admired a painting of 3 skulls I had painted.... Dean seemed quite impressed with [Steve] Reeves and liked my almost finished head of Reeves....They were there long enough for him to smoke 6 cigarettes (I later gave the 6 butts to someone who prepared an elaborate horoscope of Dean. I recall Sept. 30 was listed as a "good day" for him!!!) (Letter to David Loehr, May 24, 1982).

Yet, Kendall writes that Dean

> left on an upbeat—"to be continued." In the doorway he put out his hand—lowering his head and looking me right in the eyes and as we shook hands he broke into that dimpled laughing smile—I have looked in vain for that particular smile in all the photos—but it's not there—I think that it was an act or "art." He knew just what he was doing.

A bit later in the letter Kendall continues:

> [Dean] was well aware that he could melt steel with that smile—absolutely beautiful—I'd say he's as close to an enchanted Prince as we will ever see and he is the Lord Byron of our time—it is nice to see that Dean was as important as I felt that he was—that it was not "the end." (Letter to David Loehr, May 24, 1982).

In a somewhat different version of their parting and one of his more extended recollections, Kendall wrote:

> He looked up into my eyes and smiled and in that instant transformed himself into some radiant angel—apparently

he threw the entire personality at me and saved that final smile as the final touch—nothing was ever the same again—two weeks later I was to see him on the screen [in *East of Eden*] and realized his genius—from our original encounter to the big screen he was wielding thunderbolts—I thought to myself Jesus Christ!—I know this guy—he knows me! He wants something from me. But now I was in awe of him. (Letter to David Loehr, June 3, 1985).

In 1995 on the occasion of the dedication of his bust of James Dean in Fairmount, Kendall worded his encounter with Dean in 1955 somewhat differently:

He stepped outside the door, turned around, and in a half bow extended his hand and looked into my eyes—his mouth half open in a smile—and suddenly his was the most beautiful face I had ever seen (Kendall 2004, 9).

Yet another somewhat more elaborate variation on this event with Dean is found in Martin Dawber's *Wish You Were Here, Jimmy Dean*, as told once again by Kendall:

He stepped outside the door, put out his hand, positioning himself into an almost-bow, and looked up into my eyes opening his mouth into a smile he threw the whole personality at me. He had turned himself into a most beautiful thing God ever created. It was like being struck by lightning. That kid knew what he was doing (1988, 54)!

When he learned of Dean's death "that bright spirit was gone but I was in a position to give him his wish—he had ordered his own memorial" (letter to David Loehr, June 3, 1985). Kendall began immediately working on the Dean bust, which eventually was erected in Park Cemetery.

This was only the beginning for Kendall, who for the next fifty years would produce works of Dean in various media. He drew, painted, and sculpted in his quest to recapture that instant when he saw Dean as a "radiant angel." As if this was not tribute enough, Kendall welcomed untold numbers of pilgrims to his studio, where he retold the story of their meeting and his continuing quest. A chair that Dean had sat in during his visit with Kendall was a favorite item among his visitors. He also held an annual birthday party at his home in Dean's honor and spoke publicly and in numerous interviews about him.

I first met Kenneth on one of my many trips to Fairmount on September 29, 1995. He was dressed in his trademark black outfit including black hat. This was at the Gallery following the "big weekend," and with the annual memorial at the Back Creek Friends Meeting, there were many fans and Deaners gathered there, sitting on the front porch and wandering among the exhibits. He was always one of the favorites among fans and Deaners, and he was being interviewed, filmed, photographed, questioned, approached by autograph seekers, and generally being pursued by fans and Deaners in the Gallery. He often provided autographed copies of his paintings on large postcards to be distributed to subscribers of the club fanzine. Eventually I found an opening and arranged for an interview that took place the next day.

The dedication of the new James Dean Memorial Park with his newly cast bust of Dean had finished earlier but was still on Kenneth's mind when we finally sat down for the interview in the Gallery office. A train whistle sounded during his speech about Dean for the bust dedication, and he was saying to me that "Dean registered like a train whistle or a foghorn in the harbor—that it was something moving—something very nostalgic, melancholy about those sounds—to hear a train whistle in the distance—it's moving, it's going away. And the same with the boat thing—so then Jimmy fixed me with the train whistle."

During the interview he spoke at great length about his background in art and working in Hollywood, including with many well-known actors he had known over the years. He spoke at length about Brando. From there he moved on to his meeting with Dean. He remarked that his first impression "wasn't that much," and he didn't see a fabulous smile (like Brando's) "at first in James Dean." After Dean asked about doing his bust, Kendall let him know he couldn't do it for free. "I was thinking like $400 or something," he said. Later in their conversation, Kenneth told Dean to make sure he had the studio do a life mask of him and make them give him a copy. He spoke at length about his efforts to donate his copy of Dean's life mask to the Smithsonian and about life masks more generally.

Kenneth tended to wander or free associate in his responses to a degree that I didn't anticipate. Many subjects were touched on, including several unexpected topics. In other words, no matter my questions, he had other things he wanted to bring up. He was very free in expressing his opinions about actors, Hollywood types, and others connected with Dean (e.g., Sanford Roth, Mr. Onishi, and Ann Warr, among others).

One unexpected bit of information from Kenneth was a description of how Dean worked to change some aspects of his appearance. He styled his hair to be higher so he would appear taller, which had the added benefit of making the back of his head appear less "flat." He added that Dean combed his hair with his hand to achieve the effect he wanted. Now, who knew that?

I asked Kenneth his opinion of Dean's acting: "Here's the thing with Jimmy. Jimmy had acting coming out of his fingertips—he was a natural—of course, he studied, but it was natural—it was there—he could project." Later we talked of Dean's efforts in sculpting and other arts. Kenneth thought Dean wanted to be able to sculpt, play the piano, etc. without much study, "because that was what he could do with acting."

About his own career, Kenneth gave me considerable detail and coverage of his life, which he capped with this: "I'm kind of amused at—that all of this has happened—my mini-celebrity here in signing autographs and being the big artist—that's all Jimmy's gift." A moment later he added: "It wouldn't have happened otherwise, and I don't know if he hadn't pumped into my life—what I would be doing because everyone I was working on, has, you know…turned into nothing."

Kendall was a regular in Fairmount over the next several years and always a center of attention by the fans and Deaners. Although I saw him off and on, my next chance for interaction came when the "world premiere" of *James Dean: Race With Destiny* (subtitled later changed to *Live Fast, Die Young*) on September 29, 1997. The film, with Casper Van Dien as Dean, was being premiered at the Eagles Theatre in Wabash, about 35 miles from Fairmount. It was significant to the Deaners that the showing was on the twenty-ninth, the day before the annual memorial service at Back Creek Meeting. That year's memorial service was doubly important because it would also include a memorial for Dean's high school drama teacher Adeline Nall.

When I entered the Gallery, there were several regulars in addition to David Loehr and Lenny Prussack, Kenneth Kendall, Maxine Rowland, Kathie Wilson, and Phil Zeigler. Phil had recently retired and moved to Fairmount and had settled into the small house near the Winslow farm where Winton Dean had lived in recent years.

We had a quick dinner upstairs, supplied by David and Lenny, before leaving for Wabash. Lenny rode with me, but neither of us knew the route from Fairmount and we briefly lost our way, arriving at the theater after everyone else. David and several others were still outside the entrance. David looked worried and I explained about getting lost. Inside there were many familiar faces. The cost for me was three dollars as I lacked a pass.

I sat next to Kenneth, who made very knowledgeable, detailed observations about the artistic aspects of the theater's decor. The building was an example of the art deco style so popular with theaters during the 1920s and '30s. His comments on the film were more limited than I had hoped or expected. He found the film "professional," and he wondered why it took so long to be released. I found the film disappointing.

Other comments later offered by the Deaners were guarded, with "pretty good" and "not bad" being common remarks. One fellow offered a "not as bad as expected" comment. Phil said he liked the film and was pleased to see Dean tell his father that he loved him. Lenny noted that it was "low budget", and that Van Dien didn't look much like Jimmy. Someone said it was a "TV movie." Some liked the music, others didn't.

Kendall's Art

Kendall only had photographs to work from after Dean's death along with a copy of the life mask he borrowed from Winton Dean. In the 1995 interview, he admitted he was "just a little painted out on him." He cited a need for additional photos, which might reenergize his interest, adding, "If one could take *East of Eden* and run it through a Moviola—just click, click, click—there's a thousand new faces in that." Despite those feelings, he cited one of his works that perhaps had achieved "that particular smile" that he sought to capture from his only meeting with Dean. He was thinking and looking at one picture he did from *Giant*, and it finally hit him "that's him, that's Jim…it worked perfectly for me." He had, perhaps, captured his "enchanted Prince" his "radiant angel" (Fig. 6.1).

Given that his body of work depicting James Dean is extensive and wide-ranging, a brief note of the individual works is informative. Kendall's work is within the representational/pictorial tradition. Some of the paintings are pastiche and clearly influenced by such well-known artists as Édouard Manet and Vincent Van Gogh. The Manet is a rendition of Dean as "The Dead Toreador" (Figure 6.2). A majority of others can be linked to specific photographs or movie stills. Among those are "Dean as Malcolm," "Hamlet," "The Torn Poster," and "New York." A bit more imaginative are "Jacob Wrestles With an Angel" featuring Dean and Brando and one titled "Byron" with Dean and Lord Byron face to face.

ADORATION AND PILGRIMAGE

Figure 6.1. Kenneth Kendall's painting "Giant" (original in color). (Copyright Kenneth Kendall Estate)

Figure 6.2. "El Torero Muerto" by Kenneth Kendall (original in color). (Copyright Kenneth Kendall Estate)

Photography and Photographers

While there were others, three photographers in particular stand out for their photos of Dean: Roy Schatt, Dennis Stock, and Sanford Roth. Schatt knew Dean in his New York days, where they became friends, and Schatt began teaching him photography. Like many other photos of Dean, some of Schatt's have taken on a life of their own, such as his "Torn Sweater" series and others such as "The Photographer." Most of his photos were taken in 1954. His photos would often appear in books, magazines, and even in stage productions without giving him credit. The Beats adopted as their own one or more of the "Torn Sweater" photos, including similar ones by Phil Stein (e.g., 1993). Schatt didn't publish his book *James Dean: A Portrait* until 1982. Sanford Roth (Roth and Roth 1983) was the final photographer to shoot Dean and was traveling along behind the Porsche Spyder the day of Dean's fatal accident. Among his photos to achieve a label were some he shot during Dean's final scene in *Giant*, which are known as "The Last Supper."

It is Dennis Stock who gets the award for most-cited Dean photographer. Of the three, only Stock visited Fairmount. Stock, a Magnum photographer, published at least three versions of his book of Dean photographs (1978, 1987, 2005), and he seems inseparable from that association. He was introduced to Dean by Nick Ray, and after attending a sneak preview of *Eden* in Santa Monica, Stock began to develop an idea for a photo essay on Dean. The next day they met for breakfast, and he presented the idea to Dean, who agreed. The next step was convincing *Life* magazine editors to do a photo essay piece on the rising young actor. He felt the best approach for understanding Dean's genesis was with a trip to Fairmount and subsequently to New York. They could explore his roots in Fairmount, then follow his development by shooting in New York before returning to California, where Dean was to work on *Rebel*. Stock's photos of Dean were to appear years later in his *James Dean Revisited* (1978), although individual photos were seen in other media prior to that date. While considered a photojournalist, he regarded himself as a photo essayist. The kind of attention brought to Dean by his photos cannot be measured. Many of Stock's photos of Dean and others have become classics of Americana.

It was Dennis Stock who captured what many consider the most famous photograph of James Dean (Miller 1997, 125), yet it goes without a fixed label. That stark black-and-white photo captures Dean in a long coat, cigarette dangling from his mouth, walking in the rain in Times Square and looking downcast, dejected, alienated, haunting, or "beat." The photo could be a take on any young male artist struggling to "make it." But it communicates beyond the mere fact of just a man walking in the rain in Times Square. According to Wayne Rowe, Stock's photo is a "visual haiku" (2010, 9). Rowe's analysis explores the role that the Zen concept of *satori* (or enlightenment) can play in photography and along with two concepts, *studium* and *punctum*, from Roland Barthes in reference to the Times Square photo (2010, 11-14). Briefly, he states:

> [It has] an existential mood and a mysterious romantic poetry. It represents a perfect interaction between the photographer, the subject, the setting, and the moment. It is, in fact, a silver halide haiku. It records satori experienced by the photographer and his subject, and it provokes satori in the viewer as well (2010, 12).

These qualities are not limited to the Times Square photo. In my interview with Stock, he mentioned how Dean collaborated with him in "staging" many of the photos (September 29, 1991). In one example, he referred to a photo he called "You Can't Go Home Again" captured in front of the farmhouse and its driveway with the barns in the background. Dean is looking to the left and away as if looking to a future elsewhere (see Stock 1978, 62-63).

I often asked an interviewee about their favorite photos of Dean. One of those I asked was "Jane," a young Midwestern, college-educated woman of twenty-eight. She had several favorite photos, including one taken of Dean while at the farm posing with a large sow. She described the photo as "sarcastic" because it shows the "playful side of him…because he was multifaceted, he's not a static character." Stock referred to the same photo as "Tintype with Sow." (I think a better name would be "American Gothic, II" in reference to the Grant Wood painting "American Gothic" from 1930.)

In November 2014, Life Books published *James Dean: A Rebel's Life in Pictures* with a foreword by Martin Landau, who knew Dean in their early days in New York (Baker 2014). It was perhaps published in anticipation of the sixtieth anniversary of Dean's death. It highlighted photos taken by Dennis Stock, Roy Schatt, Phil Stern, and Sanford Roth. And a new film "biopic" titled *Life* was released focusing on the period when Dennis Stock was photographing James Dean for *Life* magazine (Corbijn 2015). Stock was also honored with a documentary film, *Beyond Iconic*, shortly before his death in 2010 (Sawka 2011).

Two stills from *Giant* shot on location near Marfa, Texas, have gained "iconic" status as well. One called "The Outsider" or "The Loner" shows Dean as Jett Rink sitting in the back seat of a limousine convertible with legs stretched out onto the front seats, gloves in hand, Stetson hat on head, with the Reata mansion in the background. A second, known as "The Crucifixion," has Dean standing above a kneeling Elizabeth Taylor to the side of the limousine. Dean is standing in a Christ-on-the-cross-like pose, looking down at Taylor, with his arms stretched out and supported across his back by a shotgun. Neither of those two shots appears in the film, and the stills are not credited to a specific Warner Bros. photographer.

Perhaps the best-known photos of Dean among the "general public" are those from *Rebel Without a Cause*, and they have taken on a label simply of "Rebel." All have him in the red jacket, T-shirt, jeans, boots, and originally with cigarette in hand. Some appeared on the posters, lobby cards, promos, and movie flyers for the film and have been adapted for reproduction as life-size cardboard cutout stand-ups or small stand-ups, and endless reproduction in books and magazines, T-shirts, and numerous other forms for memorabilia. The "Rebel" poses are favorites for artists including a few famous ones like Andy Warhol. Nearly all those photos were publicity photos by uncredited Warner Bros. photographers and did not appear in the film.

Florist and Amateur Chef

Greg Swenson, a prize-winning florist formerly working in St. Louis, is well known in Fairmount and among Deaners for his special floral arrangements honoring James Dean. My first interview with Greg was during the Festival weekend 1992. Greg studied painting and illustration at the American Academy of Art in Chicago after graduating high school in Paxton, Illinois. After an unfulfilling position in textbook publishing, he switched to floristry or floral design. His awareness of Dean began when he was ten or eleven years old, but it wasn't until his first year in college in Chicago that his interest was aroused after seeing *Rebel* and *Eden*. With his interest piqued, he read Dalton's *The Mutant King* and was "hooked." During his summer vacation in 1987, he made his first visit to Fairmount.

Given that James Dean is the inspiration for many of his floral designs, I asked him whether any particular photos served as his sources. His favorite photographs of Dean are the "Torn Sweater" series, but as reference sources Greg usually prefers the later photos taken around the time that Dean was filming *Giant* because he was "more mature looking." He liked the "Torn Sweater" photos because they are "dramatic and show him kind of how I think of him."

I learned that in addition to his floral design work, Greg paints and prefers portraits. I asked him about Dean's appeal and inspiration to him, and Greg responded: "I use him in my personal life [and] daily life as sort of an inspirational sort...his attitudes about experiencing life and trying all sorts of things and eventually you hit on something which goes beyond and works and everybody loves it." He continued, referring both to the "depth of his acting" and "the Method" [of acting], and said that even though he had no desire to be an actor, he thought "maybe this way of thinking was to be transformed into other art forms, like painting...to give things a little more expression and feeling...." He referred to his former job doing illustrations for textbooks as too restrictive and deadline driven, which led to his desire to go in a "different direction." Dean was an inspiration in that change, and he now loves his work as a florist.

I returned to questions of inspiration and exploring something different. Greg said he doesn't think of himself as an adventurous person, but sometimes he gets an urge to go off and do things others might not do. For example, he mentioned in 1983 that he went to "Central America and picked coffee in the mountains for a couple of months." His experience there got him painting again and opened his eyes to the difficult lives of the workers and natives.

My second interview with Greg was during the Festival weekend of 1993. I returned to the issue of Dean's inspiration and influence on his work as a florist, and specifically "the Method." He explained that he uses the Method in his own way, bringing some interpretative results with more feeling, and said "Jimmy plays a big part of it too." Before getting ready to design a new project for a show, Greg said he "always does this 'Jimmy thing'" for the preparation with some "rituals." He might wear a Dean T-shirt, for example, or some clothing combination of jacket and tie. It's whatever works and feels right at the time. But, interestingly, on his way to do the show, he spotted some graffiti on a bridge near Mount Vernon, Illinois, that read "James Dean." After seeing that, he felt it was going to be the best show ever.

I asked what the secret to doing that was. He replied, "It's something that you have to practice and work out, and things didn't come easy for Jimmy either. He worked at it all the time." In explaining how he won a recent contest with a creative idea, he said, "It's a Jimmy thing." Since then, he has kept using his ritual—sort of like, he explained, athletes who always do or wear the same thing before a game. Also, when he travels, he always takes along his copy of *The Little Prince*, Dean's favorite book.

After learning that Greg was the author of *Recipes for Rebels: In the Kitchen with James Dean* (2015) and recently moved to Fairmount from Greece where he had been living for a time with his partner, I gave him a call (September 17, 2021) as I was curious about his progression to recipe book writer. In the phone call, I learned he had been diagnosed with prostate cancer seven years earlier. While undergoing treatments including chemotherapy, he focused more on his cooking hobby and began collecting new recipes along with, no doubt, some experimenting. Collecting recipes was not new for him—it dated back many years to when he found a recipe attributed to Natalie Wood. For some years he had expected to see a "James Dean cookbook" appear, but it never happened, giving him the opportunity.

Fetishism

Examining art and memorabilia from the point of view of their possessors leads to issues of collecting and fetishism. Collecting in many cases takes on elements of fetishism and is perhaps most apparent when the objects once belonged to or were touched by Dean. Such things are not only unique and rare, but *special* in nonutilitarian terms—a shirt is not just a shirt to be worn, but a shirt worn by James Dean, and it may be touched and perhaps even briefly tried on, but it is absolutely not to be worn. It is sacred. There may be only *one* such object, and to possess it reaches well beyond any usual understanding of collecting. A chair Dean sat in, even if only briefly, is perhaps imbued. This sort of identification of object with person is also apparent with other items that may be uncommon, though originally mass produced. Take, for example, the red jacket worn by Dean in *Rebel*. Undoubtedly thousands of the jackets were produced in the mid-1950s and available for purchase throughout the country. Yet only one was worn by the star of *Rebel*.

In standard anthropological terminology, a fetish is an object held in awe because of its ritual or supernatural potency and/or its connection to a spirit or supernatural agent and may confer a benefit to its owner. In Catholicism, there are sacred relics that carry supernatural power. And, of course, in the psychoanalytic tradition and in the popular imagination, a fetish is an object that stimulates a sexual response, even when the fetish is not sexual. Both dimensions may also be present in many cases.

What is special in this case is problematic. Perhaps it is a certain photograph, magazine, or other such item. Many Deaners have stated they *always* carry a photo of Dean on their person. Or higher up the fetishism scale, a comb, slacks, shirt, pack of cigarettes, or anything for that matter that belonged to Dean. Somewhere in between could be an original painting of Dean by Kenneth Kendall, an original photo by Dennis Stock, an original print of Dean by Andy Warhol, or a work by other artists. There is the issue of what is rare and unique, but also what is authentic and/or original, such as a movie poster from the first release of a film versus a poster from a rerelease of the same film. The meaning attached by the viewer is what is critical, and on the upper end of the scale the item may approach that of traditional religious "icons."

Tattooed

Then there is a kind of ultimate expression of devotion by having one's body parts tattooed, perhaps expressing a form of "sacrifice?" Review of Dean club newsletters from 1988-2007 revealed fifty-two people who wrote of or pictured their tattoos of Dean. The count of fifty-two constituted nearly 14 percent of the counted acts of devotion. One issue of *The Deanzine* of 2007 (Vol. 77, Issue 25, 14-19) pictures forty-four Deaners with tattoos on various body parts. I was fortunate that among those I interviewed was a man, whom I call "Matt," with a large tattoo of Dean in rebel pose on his back covering the length of his spine. Matt was in Fairmount with his wife on their honeymoon and first trip to Dean's hometown.

Matt was 25 years old, from the East Coast, and in the car business. He's not a big collector of Dean items, though he has a few books, posters, and tapes. He said he "always has Jimmy's picture with him all the time" (a likely fetish).

He met David Loehr in 1988 at a car show where David had an exhibit. They had a conversation, he showed David his tattoo, and David invited him to attend his Dean "walking tour" in New York City, an invitation he followed through on. He got his tattoo in 1987 but explained that he'd been a Dean fan since he was about fifteen years old. His sister worked in a poster factory and brought home a large poster that she placed on her closet door. It was of Dean from *Giant* in a scene after striking oil. Asking her who the young man covered in oil was, his sister replied, "That's James Dean. He's cool." She gave him the poster to put on a wall in his room. Later, he explained, when he got his driver's license, he put Dean postcards on his visors and began watching his movies and "that was it." "I relate to him in *Rebel Without a Cause*. He struck a familiar note with me."

He mentioned Dean being the "epitome of the '50s" and he expressed wishing he had been there and grown up during that period. Explaining more of Dean's appeal, he said:

> I think a little bit of James Dean belongs to everyone. It can never disappoint—no matter what anyone could say about him—he belongs to everybody. There's something everybody can relate to—to a certain thing—whether it's a look or something you've seen on the screen or something you read about—maybe being rebellious as you're growing up through your teens. There's something there.

He explained why *Rebel* was his favorite film:

> Growing up, I was in a family business. And it was rough, working with my father and my brothers, and in certain

scenes in the movie and certain things that happened, I related to in the movie with him not getting along with his parents. And, just trying to separate from my parents, it really was hard…and seeing the movie [and] how he was separating from his parents. That inspired me a lot. And, when I started reading about him, how he got started with his career and just set his goals to do and that was his number one priority. I went into business very young. I was eighteen when I got my own business together, and I always thought of him—how he did it. And he always was in me as a positive attitude. Always have a positive attitude: if you want something, you'll get it. He was always in the back of my mind. He did it, and I'm going to do it. He was always there in my thoughts as I was doing things.

About other sources he mentioned Dennis Hopper and the way Hopper described Dean's influence on the youth "movements" of the 1950s and '60s, giving credit to Dean for giving them a voice while citing both *Eden* and *Rebel*. I asked next about any favorite photographs, and he said his favorites were those taken by Dennis Stock in New York City, because Dean was "more like a Beatnik" in those. He continued, "That's Jimmy, that's not…someone he's portraying on the screen, that's the real him right there."

Next, I asked Matt if there were other ways Dean was an inspiration. Referring again to Dean's family conflict in *Rebel*, he repeated the story of growing up and working for his father and the disagreements they had about ideas he had or something he wanted to do. "It was always quite a mess, you know?" The only hint he gave as to why he had gotten his tattoo was: "You gotta sacrifice to be cool."

Discussion

Art is often referred to as a "slippery fish," and perhaps that is a useful metaphor. Rather than belabor the issue, a shift to Armstrong's notion of aesthetics is helpful: *"the theory or study of form incarnating feeling*" (1975, 11). The phrase "incarnating feeling" allows for the idea of an object embodying or incorporating affect. The concern remains with the interaction of the viewer/possessor as well as creator of a piece of "sacredness;" and, by extension a sort of "participation" with the sacred thing.

As a practical matter, the term "art" is used in a broad sense to include painting, drawing, and sculpting, of course, but also poetry and verse, various types of prose, theater, dance, body decoration, and dress. Still another category of things that is involved when investigating the sacred are natural objects and things, like water, soil, or stone. And finally, there are human things originally made for a utilitarian purpose. None of these things may ordinarily be thought of as art, but they may become memorabilia and are candidates for transformation into sacred things. If these categories seem blurred in the context of the sacred, that is how it should be.

So, whether the drawings, paintings, poems, and other creations are art should be moot. Likewise, most of the work is done by amateurs and should not be approached in terms of professional standards. What matters is that the creations are personal expressions of a creative and emotive feeling focused on James Dean.

But what about the more specific issue of art and religion? As often happens when exploring a new area of inquiry, there are the dangers of stumbling and of error with the existing body of literature. Eliade (1986) has written on the subject generally, but philosopher Susanne Langer (1953) has provided several useful insights. In writing about how art affects the quality of life, Langer suggests that: "In this way it [art] is akin to religion, which…in its pristine, vigorous, spontaneous phase, defines and develops human feelings" (1953, 402), and what "art expresses is *not* actual feeling, but ideas of feeling" (1953, 59). These creations are expressions of feelings about James Dean, or to follow Langer, they are attempts at expressing ideas of feeling. She also remarks that: "When the arts become 'liberated'…from religion, they simply have exhausted the religious consciousness, and draw upon other sources" (1953,

402). This needs some modification, however. The suggestion that arises from this study is that whatever ignites the sacred impulse may find expression in any number of activities, including the arts.

A Pause

On the issue of the transformative process of secular to sacred, a notion of means or "energy" is needed. In this connection, thinking of beliefs, ideas, and thought generally as behavior and, therefore, real, and potentially having effect, as well as affect, partly solves the problem. Another helpful concept is "witnessing" in a sense like the religious one but taking a physical form. Or, put another way, an object, and an associated act (e.g., placing flowers before it) *may* become a type of witnessing. Regarding the present problem, it provides a general premise for framing the change or transformation of apparently secular and mundane things into sacred ones. What it does not tell us is anything about why a particular thing is transformed or what the rules involved in any particular case are. These points will be revisited later.

Now, exploration of some additional examples of objects is in order. It's clear that Kenneth Kendall has a special place in the minds of Deaners because of his connection to Dean (brief though it was) and his decades of work to capture that special look he once witnessed. That effort makes his works closer to Dean and more significant. But, beyond his products what else can be of similar significance?

For Deaners, dozens of other kinds of items may come to make up a sacred or quasi-sacred space devoted to Dean, and many have just such an area—a special room or place within a room—where these important items are kept and displayed. Items considered the more important and/or sacred are those having special meaning to the individual, of course, and often these are the older, scarce, or rare items made during the 1950s. Also, items that are of an individual, original, or handmade nature take on added significance. Often original or reproductions of paintings or drawings of Dean are in this category of special significance. Items that are of the utmost importance are those that *link* the individual to Dean in some unique way or to the experience or sense of *being* with Dean on a certain occasion. And certainly, the term "fetish" is appropriate for some of these items and how they are handled by the devoted.

Another category of secular object that may be transformed into the sacred includes such obvious things as anything worn by Dean like articles of clothing or costume, personal items such as a comb, a wristwatch, and so on. There are also examples of artwork by Dean that are high on the list of sacred things. In addition, other natural and secular things that become sacred when obtained by a Deaner include: (1) marble chips from his gravestone, (2) water taken from a natural spring near the Winslow farm and where, it is said, he often stopped to get a drink, (3) soil from the farm, (4) soil from the Cholame crash site, and (5) fragments of structures associated with Dean (such as movie set items, the stage on which he performed in high school, etc.). A candidate for sacred object can be something as simple as a pebble picked up at one of the sacred locations in and around Fairmount.

It is somewhat like the collection of objects for a medicine bag among Navajo medicine men in that some of the items appear common and of no value. But, of course, the value is to the medicine man and the particular and special associations of the objects. Again, in some cases, these items are best termed fetishes, depending on how they are handled and honored by the possessor. Sacred places are also covered elsewhere (see chapter 7), but one especially interesting site is located on the farm where Dean spent much of his youth. It is a concrete slab where as a child Dean made impressions of his hands in the still-wet cement. This was a profane act and a common one. In this case the traces of that act are transformed into a sacred spot and object.

Further Discussion and a Conclusion

If these various things are viewed as forms of "witnessing" (or even theophany) as in the case of medieval *loca sancta* souvenirs (cf.

Hahn 1990), then a link is made in the transformative process. On the one hand, these things "bear witness" to a significant affective experience, and, on the other, they may "contain" or "possess" a special quality that is sacred from their association with Dean. There is a wide continuum of things that range from mere souvenirs and memorabilia to special productions that *may* become sacred in the correct circumstances. Except for things that were in direct contact with Dean, it is difficult to predict what will become sacred. I think items regarded as "art," as in popular art, folk art, but also fine art and not mass produced, are especially susceptible to the transformation, although at present it is difficult to be confident of this point. It seems that the transformation of mass-produced memorabilia into sacred things requires time to produce scarcity and/or depends on the quality of art.

The transformation of mundane or profane items into sacred ones, including those classed as art, occurs when those items come to represent *affect made concrete*. That is, they represent a special reality, and usually deeply felt, and expressive of the individual who processes them. At one level, these articles of memorabilia are only representations of a person, place, or event. At another level, they take on an additional affective and meaningful nature. The point is that such items may take on significance (meaning) via their interaction with a thinking and feeling person and simply because of that person's affective relation with Dean.

The transformation of ordinary and profane things into sacred things is common in the history of religions and human relations. I have not found much in the literature that details the specific process(es) of transformation. Still, items that are believed to be intimately associated with the divine, items from associated sacred places, and so on are customarily regarded as special and sacred. But even so, there is often a requisite personal connection required. Likewise, professional art produced or commissioned to depict or represent the divine may also become sacred.

This is also the case with the Deaners. What may be different here is the transformation of selected mass-produced items and memorabilia into sacred things. While this may say something about post-modern, post-industrial society, it also basically mirrors the usual case of transformation. What is important is that these things can be viewed as a form of witnessing that provides a connecting link to experiencing the sacred "icon." These items bear witness to a significant affective experience and possess a special sacred quality due to the linkage to or association with Dean.

7

Deaner Pilgrimage and the Role of Fairmount

*Fairmount, Indiana, is a peaceful, wholesome
little farm town near Marion.*

—WILLIAM BAST

The Deaner devotional activities play out every September in Fairmount with traditional public and spiritual/religious activities, along with many private acts. Fairmount is the most important of the several places Deaners visit. But, before we visit Fairmount, a summary of the other pilgrimage sites is in order. Many Deaners are committed to visiting all these places, ranging from New York City to Marfa, Texas, Los Angeles, and Cholame. A true diehard with camera in hand will even travel to Mendocino, California, where much of *East of Eden* was filmed, or the numerous places in the Los Angeles area associated with Dean's life and the filming of *Rebel Without a Cause*.

The February birthday party on a Sunday features a showing of one of Dean's films, followed by refreshments and birthday cake, and is sponsored by the Museum. When this event was first started the Museum also opened on the day of the party when it would have normally been closed until summer. Over time it has evolved to a "birthday weekend" with a dinner and dance on Saturday evening sponsored by the Gallery. Some years, a rockabilly band fest precedes a dinner and dance, all also sponsored by the Gallery. In 2008, the program expanded to include a Friday "get-together" dinner, Saturday morning breakfast, and Saturday evening all-you-can-eat buffet dinner. These events precede the Museum's showing of one of Dean's films and the cake and punch celebration.

The birthday celebration never brings in as many people as the September events, with perhaps twenty-five to thirty or so attending. Indiana weather in February can be problematic and directly affects attendance. Also, additional events have been added at other times in the year, including the James Dean Spring Fans Get-Together in May and the Annual James Dean Fans Weekend and Film Festival in July (since 1998). Each of these events includes scheduled activities such as banquets and films. Both were begun by David Loehr and sponsored by the Gallery. The weekly "Deaner Breakfast Club," also begun by Loehr, is another added get-together. It is held at one of the local diners, the Gallery, or perhaps someone's home. Local fans and Deaners and any out-of-town visitors are invited. A "James Dean Spring Car Show" in June also added to the list of events available to fans and interested persons. Except for those who live in Fairmount or very near, it's unusual to see the same people at all Fairmount events. In any case, many longtime friends find these events an excellent venue for visits and catching up.

The other pilgrimage sites are associated with places where Dean lived or worked on his films. At one time an annual "James Dean Walk" in New York City was conducted by David Loehr. The tour included Dean's habitats and hangouts from the years when he lived and worked there. Although there are numerous sites in Los Angeles, the most important is Griffith Park and Observatory, where two major scenes in *Rebel* were filmed. A special monument with a bust of Dean was erected there in 1988 by Dean's most dedicated artist, the late Kenneth Kendall. The June 24, 1996, US Postal Service's release of its James Dean stamp presented another special occasion for fans to gather in Los Angeles and elsewhere. Other important film locations include Mendocino and Salinas, California, where parts of *Eden* were filmed, and Marfa, Texas, where much of *Giant* was shot. Both locations are on a "must-do" list of many Deaners.[32]

Cholame, California, where Dean's fatal accident occurred, is another important pilgrimage location, although some Deaners prefer not to attend. In 1977, Japanese businessman Seita Ohnishi erected a monument to Dean at Cholame at a cost of $50,000. Organized "car runs" (another form of pilgrimage for some) are periodically conducted in Dean's honor between Los Angeles and Cholame, retracing his route on the day of his death. This somewhat desolate location is clearly out of the way for most fans. With only one business, the Jack Ranch Café, and no population, Cholame is indeed a lonely place. The monument is showing many signs of abuse and neglect. It has been picked over by visitors, perhaps wanting mementos. On September 30, 2005, the fiftieth anniversary of Dean's death, the site of the crash was designated the "James Dean Memorial Junction," as an official California state memorial. Located at the junction of California 41 and 46, near where the accident occurred, this memorial consists of a sign only. Nearby are mementos left by fans and another memorial of sorts erected by an unknown person or persons. Some fans collect soil from the site. For those who can't visit all sites themselves, there are books covering many of the locations, photos and videos are available from fans, and online at YouTube and other sites.

But why go to Fairmount? Specifically, what are the meanings sought, experienced, created, or renewed by a pilgrimage to Fairmount for Deaners or fans? Since 1975, thousands of people visit this small Indiana town each September for what began as "Museum Days," a festival manifestly in honor of several "famous sons." These are persons, all men, who were born or raised in Fairmount and went on to gain some degree of fame. But there is little doubt who among them is the focus, and at one time the name was changed to "Remembering James Dean Festival." Some refer to the event as "Jimmy Dean Days," "the Big Weekend," or simply "the Festival." Any of these will do as they are interchangeable among fans. In distant second place are cartoon cat *Garfield* and his creator Jim Davis.

A first-time visitor, during the September events or anytime, can pick up a homemade map of the James Dean sites around Fairview at the Museum or the Gallery. It includes the locations of the Winslow farm where he lived, the Back Creek Friends Meeting church that he attended, and the Indian Motorcycle shop building (no longer in operation), one of his favorite hangouts as a youth. A visit to the farm is especially significant if one is lucky enough to be invited. Unlike Graceland, there are no tours of the farm. For many years, Dean's Fairmount High School was one of the sites, but over time it continued to crumble with various sections collapsing. Off-and-on efforts to raise money to restore the school began in 1989 and raised several thousand dollars, but the building was finally demolished in 2016. For true fans and Deaners, souvenir bricks from the school with a certificate of authenticity are available for purchase at the Gallery. Likewise, initial efforts to save the school stage on which Dean had performed failed. Later, partial success was achieved when it was dismantled and rebuilt in a pavilion in Fairmount's Playacres Park. It is now used for local events including plays.

Added to the sites for fans and the curious is the James Dean Memorial Park on Main Street, which boasts a large bust of Dean by the late Kenneth Kendall (Fig.7.1). Of course, his grave in the local cemetery is mandatory for the casual visitor as well as for fans and Deaners. At any time of the year, a visitor will observe many mementos left at the grave by previous visitors.

Figure 7.1. James Dean Memorial Park, Fairmount, Indiana. (Photo by author).

Visitors may pass by most of these places without giving any note, but to Deaners they are very special, if not sacred. Not mentioned on any tour map, but known to most Deaners, are several other special spots at the farm: his bedroom in the farmhouse (maintained as he left it), his foot- and handprints in concrete at the barn, and a spring between the farmhouse and the Back Creek Friends Meeting church where he is said to have drunk water (Deaners like to take samples for keeping). If these places are not enough, as they aren't for many, there are the streets of downtown Fairmount immortalized by Dennis Stock, which look much the same as they did in 1955 (1978, 1987, 2005). It is a must for any devoted fan or Deaner to walk and photograph (and be photographed at) those locations. In recent years murals depicting Dean have appeared on some of the walls on a side street near the Museum.

Beyond Fairmount, there is his mother's grave in Marion, where a plaque explains who she was. A plaque in a sidewalk marked the house where Dean was born in Marion until it was replaced in 2015 with a parklike memorial designed by David Loehr. Following the 1996 release of the Dean postage stamp, Grant County, home to Fairmount and Marion, upped its commercialization of James Dean with large roadside billboards pronouncing that Grant County is where "cool was born." The county also increased its coverage of Dean in its tourist brochures and online. Currently (2021) they highlight Dean under "Experiences" and list all the associated public sites and events during the year along with a map of "James Dean Trail Landmarks."

But it is in Fairmount, of course, that James Dean, the icon, the image, becomes "real." Like pilgrims in Jerusalem who follow the steps believed taken by Jesus of Nazareth, Dean's progeny can follow his steps. Fairmount attracts thousands of visitors yearly, with the greatest numbers appearing on certain special days; days that are sacred to Deaners—and the most important being the day of his death, the weekend festival, and the anniversary of his birthday. On any day, however, visitors and pilgrims will be found visiting Dean's grave, the Museum and Gallery, and other special places. Many Deaners prefer less chaotic times for their visits if possible, and it was on such a day that I informally interviewed "Jeff," one of the first Deaners I met.

But according to fans and Deaners alike, no other place is as central to the Deaner experience as Fairmount, where the young Jimmy Dean was nurtured and his budding genius began, and where they feel closest to him and perhaps can experience that very special feeling of connection.

Returning to the "Big Weekend," this is no Midwestern Mardi Gras or Caribbean festival, of course, nor does it have the elaborateness of Graceland. That would betray Fairmount's Quaker roots, not to mention its rural, farmer conservatism and its "original" 1950s look. The festival is well managed and structured. Even the leather-clad motorcyclists demonstrate exceptional self-control.

Fairmount's Museum Days, the Mecca of Deaner Pilgrimage

The festival itself is currently (2021) called the "James Dean Festival" though previously known variously as "Fairmount Museum Days," "Museum Days," "Fairmount Museum Days/Remembering James Dean" or "James Dean Festival and Run" and held in this small Indiana town of around 3,000. Many just call it "Jimmy Dean Days." Regardless of any name change, everyone knows what it's all about. The festival is sponsored by the Fairmount Historical Museum. Since the beginning in 1975, it has always taken place the last full weekend in September, and manifestly to celebrate the "famous sons" of Fairmount—living and dead.[33] However, above all else it is James Dean who is honored, and many visitors think the events are entirely in celebration of Dean. The festival's late September schedule is no coincidence—rather, it's because Dean died on September 30, 1955. Long a separate activity, fans, friends, and family also hold a memorial service for Dean and always on the thirtieth. When the thirtieth follows that longest weekend in September, even larger crowds can be expected.

Fans and devotees of the late actor began making annual pilgrimages to Fairmount that very first memorial service in 1955, and many came in following years (although the first service was on October 3). The genesis of the Museum Days festival twenty years later is in those pilgrimages and with those first pilgrims.

Throughout the weekend, the steady stream of cars and motorcycles traveling to Dean's grave is interrupted only by the night and resumes each morning. Some of the devoted have been known to spend the night near his grave, though it's prohibited and they're subject to removal by police. Some simply drive slowly past the grave, while others park and walk to the gravesite where they spend time in reflection and prayer. Many leave "gifts" and mementos such as photos of Dean, love letters or prayers, toy cars, rocks, a pack of cigarettes (sometimes Chesterfields, his favorite), kisses on the stone, paperback books, and flowers (Fig.7.2).

ADORATION AND PILGRIMAGE

Figure 7.2. Flowers and "gifts" left at Dean's grave during a Festival weekend. (Photograph by author).

The scheduled activities for Museum Days start on Friday and continue through Sunday afternoon. Main Street is closed off to allow for the carnival rides and concessions. There are a number of activities held each year (with variations, of course): the "James Dean Run" (begun in 1980 as a pre-1970 car and custom show in Playacres Park with a series of events), crowning of a "James Dean Festival" queen and king, the Annual James Dean Memorial 10K Run, a children's pet parade, a kiddie tractor pull, perhaps a stage play or production about Dean, showing of one or more of Dean's films, James Dean Rock Lasso Contest, the Grand Parade, a "Garfield" cat photo contest, best of the '50s dance and/or costume contest, the James Dean Look-a-like Contest (adult and child versions), James Dean Bicycle Tour, assorted entertainment (like high school bands, rock and rockabilly bands, barbershop quartet, dances, and other live entertainment), a fashion show, and a golf tournament.

During the festival, the James Dean Gallery and the Fairmount Historical Museum are open all day and into the night to accommodate visitors. Attendance in Fairmount during Museum Days is often estimated as high as 20,000-30,000, which includes the James Dean Run car show at Playacres Park. In nearby Gas City, the annual "Rebel Run" is held on the same weekend. The Gas City car show resulted from a split in 1989 from Fairmount's car show and is not part of a larger festival nor officially focused on James Dean. A lawsuit prevented them from using the James Dean name. In recent years the Festival has expanded in various ways. For example, in 2019 (no Festival in 2020) it began on Thursday with a "Pre-James Dean Run" and car show on Main Street along with a "kickoff party." The "James Dean Run" car show has its own schedule in Playacres Park, and bands perform on the old high school stage rebuilt in the park's pavilion. Though a separate coeval event, there are numerous signs that James Dean is a focus with a replica Porsche 550 Spyder, 1950 Mercs, and cars from the Winslow family collection, as well as other indications.

For Deaners and many fans, the climax of the festival is the James Dean Look-Alike contest held Saturday night. Contestants come from all over the United States, as well as from several foreign countries. It began as a strictly young adult affair, but eventually expanded to include a James Dean as a child segment. And a few brave fellows have appeared as the elderly Jett Rink from *Giant*. Some of the young look-alikes are professionals or wannabe actors. There is an "East Coast James Dean," among many others. The Hollywood actor and director Damien Chapa competed for the honor in several contests, including Fairmount's, and is said to have won.

During the festival Dean's image is seen everywhere yet is not literally *everywhere*. His image in various renditions is sold at the Gallery, the Museum, in stalls, on the street, at the car show, and so on. Some people wear him on their jackets, ties, and T-shirts, while others are dressed like him. Now and then you can glimpse a Dean tattoo on an arm or peeking from under a T-shirt. Dean seems to be everywhere. Yet, curiously, he is largely absent from the Grand Parade. No floats feature him, and no look-alikes are featured in the parade. Formal acknowledgment of him in the parades I attended was strangely absent—though he has been observed in the parade peering out from a side window of a '49 Merc like the one he drove in *Rebel Without a Cause*. (Of course, that was a photo attached to the window of one of the Dean Run cars.) His image is also evident at the car show in the form of stand-ups, T-shirts, jackets, and posters.

As noted above, a trip to the Grant Memorial Park in Marion is also a likely destination where Dean's mother, Mildred, is buried. In 2010, I and "May" attended what some would call a "seance." This event was conducted by Marlene Isaacs of Indianapolis. She bills herself as an "intuitive counselor," a "spiritual teacher," "healer of people, places and animals," "intuitive historian," and "paranormal investigator." When we arrived, the session was in process with eight people participating. Isaacs was sitting on the ground near Mildred Dean's gravestone. She was speaking in a halting, searching manner about things that Mildred wanted cleared up, but it was quite vague with many references to Mildred's feelings and emotions. Ms. Isaacs said Mildred "is hiding something," and may have had a lover and Jimmy wasn't her child. Near the end of her intuitive exploration, she remarked that we would have dreams that night as well as questions that might be answered tomorrow. She also mentioned receiving messages from Jimmy while on the way to the cemetery. Unfortunately, she failed to explain just what those messages were. Those gathered reacted mostly with disbelief, though perhaps some were undecided, and at least one participant took the session seriously.

The Memorial Service

Although the memorial service is often days after the Festival, it is appropriate to include it here as some Deaners attend both, while others only come for the memorial service due to the absence of large crowds and greater intimacy. The service mirrors a Christian funeral in many respects, while the image of Jesus with his flock looking down on the service is an ever-present reminder to the audience that they are in a church. If there is a contradiction implied here, it somehow never surfaces. This is followed by a procession to the gravesite, where the service continues. For many years the procession would follow "Nicky Bazooka" on his motorcycle in place of a hearse. In reproducing a funeral service, it reinforces the process of sanctification, and the familiar routines make it all seem comfortable.

The memorial service is held in the Back Creek Friends Meeting, which is both the church Dean attended and the family church of the Winslows'. It was founded in 1829, with the small meetinghouse constructed in 1899. An annex was added in 1997, which provided space and facilities for the church to begin offering brunch for the fans before the annual memorial service. The chapel is small with a normal seating capacity of perhaps 100 to 110, reflecting the small congregation it serves. When Dean's memorial is held, seating can be expanded to 130 or so with extra chairs, but as many as 200 can crowd into the chapel by standing in the back. When an overflow occurs with people standing outside, a public address system is employed.

For many years the emcee and most-honored guest at the service was Adeline Nall, Dean's high school speech and drama teacher. She was often called upon for interviews for films, television, and magazines, becoming a regular spokesperson for the Dean story and legend. She was perhaps the most sought after by fans and Deaners who wanted to know what he was like and what she taught him. As emcee she directed the service, and her stories of Jimmy were the highlight. With her advancing age, she turned over the emcee role to Tom Burghuis, a longtime fan from Michigan, but continued to attend and often spoke to the gathering. She died in 1996.

Attendees include a mix of ages and genders. There are regulars who rarely miss a memorial service, and members of the Winslow family, including Mark, his wife, and usually his late sister (seating is reserved for the family), local friends, first-timers, and Dean look-alikes. Usually a reporter and/or film crew is present, and some years there have been several. On the stage, Burghuis is joined by other regulars, such as the late Phil Zeigler for many years, and one or more of Dean's former high school classmates (though they are becoming fewer). Special guests are a standard feature of the service and may also be seated on the stage or in the audience. Those who have come to speak have included (in no special order) Dean's former New York and California friends and co-stars Arlene Sachs (a.k.a., Arlene Lorca), Liz Sheridan, Christine White, Frank Mazzola, Bob Hinkle, Lew Bracker, and the artist Kenneth Kendall. Over the years, efforts to enlist the likes of Elizabeth Taylor or Dennis Hopper for appearances were unsuccessful. Martin Sheen appeared in 1980. Other special guests have come from foreign countries, including Japan, Australia, Germany, England, and Canada, among others. Sometimes, Dean's high school classmates have also shared their recollections of "growing up" with Jimmy. For many years, a frequent classmate to appear was Bob Pulley, who often recounted his last visit with Dean in February 1955 or told a story from their youth and the good times they had on the farm, their mischievous deeds, or Dean's love of speed.

The memorial service follows a typical church service pattern in many ways. There is organ music and singing (e.g., "Amazing Grace"). Burghuis opens the service with a greeting and a reading from one of the Dean biographies, such as Dalton's *The Mutant King*, from Dean's favorite, *The Little Prince*, or from another piece about Dean. He often mentions his debt to Adeline Nall. Prior to his death, Phil Zeigler would follow with announcements, perhaps read a letter from an absent fan, and then recite one of his own poems honoring Dean. Usually there is a guest speaker from among those who knew Dean at some point in his life. (Fig. 7.3).

Figure 7.3. "Nicky Bazooka" addresses the audience during the annual memorial service at the Back Creek Friends Meeting; the late Phil Zeigler, left, and Tom Burghuis, right. (Photograph by author).

After the presentations, for many years "Nicky Bazooka" would appear from the back of the chapel dressed in a black leather motorcycle jacket, boots, special scarf, and cap. After saying a few words, he would then invite everyone to meet him outside, where his motorcycle awaited with a carefully arranged bouquet of flowers. From there he would lead the procession to Park Cemetery and Dean's gravesite. Once there, he would always place a set of flowers on the grave and present his scarf to one of the other attendees. (Until Adeline Nall's death in 1996, he always presented the scarf to her; after Nall's death, he would present it to another longtime Deaner.) Once he had completed his tasks, Bazooka would fire up his cycle and speed out of the cemetery. He led the procession from 1980—the year Martin Sheen appeared as a special Festival guest—until 2013. Bazooka was a mystery man whose true name was unknown, though speculation about his identity abounded. His death in 2014 left a large gap in the ceremony (Fig. 7.4).

Figure 7.4. "Nicky Bazooka" places special flowers at Dean's grave following the church memorial service. (Photograph by author).

Returning our attention to the church ceremony, a sampling of my (somewhat edited) field notes on the 2005 service outlines some of the events:

> I don't know how many people were there—it was packed with some overflow outside. I sat next to a reporter from the *Chronicle-Tribune* in Marion, and she asked me a few questions. (I'll have to see if she quotes me in tomorrow's paper.) Many familiar faces were there and many unfamiliar ones. There were several Japanese there. One fellow was all over the place taking photos. Tom Burghuis mentioned folks from France, Germany, Belgium, among other places.
>
> On the stage, in addition to Tom Burghuis, was Phil Zeigler, Bob Pulley, Jim Grindle, actor Christine White, and Lew Bracker (the car guy). This was the first time for him [Bracker] to visit Fairmount, and he didn't say much except they were "best friends" for two years but referred to himself and Dean being friends for "52 years" several times. All of it was pretty much the usual routine. White went on and on for what seemed like an hour about when she knew Jimmy—much of it hard to believe, but she began by referring to the hurricanes that have hit the Gulf Coast region as basically a "wake-up call from God" or a "message from God," some such thing. (I recall in 2001 at the memorial service she tried to make Dean out as some sort of patriot—this was just after 9/11 of course.) There was a long bit about the sweater she said she gave Dean, which was the same one known from the "Torn Sweater" series. Everyone else kept it short. Bob Pulley told the story again of the last time he saw Jim and they went out "partying" and a fellow asked for his autograph and then tore it up [because Dean had avoided the draft]. Jim Grindle, another classmate who

has spoken there before, also told of some of their times together in Fairmount, covering some familiar ground. After Bracker spoke, Tom called on a young man in the audience who then went up on the stage. He looked familiar, but I didn't get his name. He said he was from Marion. When he was about 10 years old, he saw *Rebel* for the first time and was hooked. He was a bit emotional about his attachment to Dean. He talked about being inspired to do what he wanted to do. In his case it is acting. (I later learned that he works at Disney World in Florida as one of the dressed cartoon characters.) Somewhere in here Zeigler read a letter from [actor] Perry Lopez, who knew Dean briefly in '54-'55. In the letter Lopez spoke highly of his friendship with Dean and, among other things, remarked about their playing chess together. Zeigler also read one of his own poems. Tom closed the service by reading Xen Harvey's eulogy from Oct. 8, 1955—the whole thing [and something he has done on previous occasions]. Then Nicky Bazooka arrived to say a few words and went outside to lead everyone to the cemetery. But this year…everyone stood and sang "Auld Lang Syne," then filed out. Outside I took a few photos of Nicky and the gathering crowd.

Since Nicky Bazooka's death, the procession to Dean's grave is led by others. Amid the visiting, filming, and photo-taking outside, the gathered fans began the walk toward the cemetery about a mile away. They moved slowly, having to give way to traffic coming from both directions to the cemetery entrance and then on to the grave. When all have gathered about the grave, following tradition someone will say a few words or recite a poem. Also following tradition, someone will place a bouquet of flowers on the gravestone (Fig. 7.5).

Figure 7.5. Naomi Yamada, a pilgrim from Japan, places her origami cranes on Dean's gravestone in 2005. (Photograph by author).

For several years, Naomi Yamada, a young woman from Japan, has prepared a special crane origami arrangement to place on Dean's grave. This is not unusual as many others bring special "gifts:" special flower arrangements are frequent, such as those by Greg Swenson, a professional florist formerly from St. Louis who has made special flower arrangements with a Dean theme for the grave. Others have left items believed to be favorites of Dean's, or a tract of prose or poetry. Some years a bagpiper was hired to play "Amazing Grace" during the event.

For many years Arnold Siminoff, a regular at the memorial service and other September events, would read one or two of his poems. He was famous among the Deaners. Siminoff would travel to Marion each year for the Festival and then walk the ten miles from Marion to Fairmount. He always wore a Dean-style red jacket and western-style straw hat. Born in Missouri, he lived in New Jersey and worked at Caesar's Palace for many years. His plan to retire and live in Fairmount never materialized before his death in 2001.

A candlelight vigil to the cemetery was added to the memorial events by the Gallery in 2005 and seemed an appropriate addition for the fiftieth anniversary of Dean's death. People gathered at the Fairmount Friends Church downtown, where Dean's funeral had been held, and Mark Kinnaman and Lenny Prussack handed out candles. This procession of seventy-five or more had a police escort, which was a good thing given the approaching darkness. At the gravesite fifteen more people had arrived by car, and their cars were scattered in the cemetery. It was completely dark by the time the procession began arriving.

What followed was an informal ritual as people gathered in a circle around the grave with their candles. The darkness made it difficult to see what everyone was doing, but the event was solemn for the most part. As we stood around the grave, every now and then someone would say something out loud for everyone to hear: "Dean will live forever," "Dean is king," "He is the true son of God," "He is eternal," and so on. There was some singing of religious hymns, including "Amazing Grace." Someone referred to *The Little Prince*. David Loehr said whoever was the youngest person there should make sure the commemoration continues for another fifty years. A Japanese fellow was taking photos. Lenny and several others were sitting and squatting by the tombstone. Lenny seemed especially focused on the grave and appeared to be in deep thought. Someone did a countdown to 7:45 pm (5:45 p.m. California time, the approximate time Dean died in 1955), and then someone read Psalm 23, said to be Dean's favorite.

Semiotics of Pilgrimage

In exploring meanings (semiotics) associated with Deaner pilgrimage to Fairmount and their devotion to James Dean, Milton Singer's *Man's Glassy Essence* (1984; *cf.* Singer 1980) and Victor Turner's *The Ritual Process* (1969) are both helpful with many aspects of this effort. In addition to exploring pilgrimage and its role, the interactions and relations of the devotee and follower *and* the object of devotion need to be explored. What *passes* or *transpires* between the two, specifically, what meanings are "received" or "created" by the devotee are of special interest (also see chapter 5). The central question is what are the shared and individual meanings of the pilgrimage for the Deaners? For present purposes, some degree of analytical separation of reactions to the *place* (Fairmount) from the *icon/object* (Dean) of the pilgrimage is maintained.

Pilgrimage can be viewed conveniently as an emotional or intellectual movement, or *transformation*, from one state or condition to another, an application clearly related to Turner's use of *liminality* (1969, 94ff; Turner and Turner 1978, 1-38).[34] Deaners are transformed from the everyday world of the ordinary (or profane) to the extraordinary (or sacred or special). This transformation is given sharp relief on many occasions when observing pilgrims visiting Dean's grave. While some pray silently, others may express their feelings out loud. The emotional impact felt is part of a transformation with such experiences "packaged" together. Sometimes, asking a serious fan about her feelings the reply will elicit something like "If you have to ask, you'll never understand," close to a famous Louis Armstrong response to questions about jazz.

Emotion, as in many religious and secular contexts, is an important ingredient in establishing and maintaining a personal connection with an event, place, and person. Why visit a loved one's grave in one's hometown unless remembering and reestablishing that connection is intended? So it is in this case. Who doesn't feel for the little boy of nine who lost his mother to cancer and then was sent (some say "abandoned") by his father to live with relatives thousands of miles away? Who doesn't feel for the handsome young many of twenty-four with a bright career of fame and stardom ahead dying tragically in an automobile accident? There is strong emotional content attached to Dean from the three major film roles played, as well as to the roles he was scheduled to play and his so many plans. Likewise, strong emotion is associated with the annual rituals in his honor. For some there are the emotions from when Dean helped them sort through a crisis or problem. Others may simply feel a great loss.

There are six types of transformations connected with Deaner pilgrimage employed elsewhere (Hopgood 2000, 352-356): physical, temporal, existential, tactile, completion, and *communitas* (communal understanding). None of these are necessarily exclusive or discreet acts or affects.

One of the obvious examples of physical transformation are the Dean "look-alikes" who participate in the look-alike contest. While usually male, white, and young, recent years have seen both child and elder (ala Jett Rink in *Giant*) look-alikes. There are "play-acting" activities associated with the activities in Fairmount, including dressing up in the styles of the 1950s and engaging in '50s dancing. Some appear for the events of the weekend in red jackets, white T-shirts, and boots like Dean in *Rebel*. The dress may only provide the "trappings" for a more significant emotional process. A temporal transformation back to a generalized or "mythical" past may also be part of the experience. Perhaps the illusion of "the good old days" is useful in setting oneself *apart* from the current or ordinary into another frame by seeking transformation through the sights, sounds, and feelings of this place and that "other time." Most Deaners are not the least nostalgic, but the experience of being in Fairmount is helpful in getting close to Dean. Deaners are on an existential quest for insights into the self: seeking answers to who they are, the meaning of one's life, what it all means, or direction about where or what to do next. What is it about this place that produced a James Dean, and can I find it too? Attempting to get in touch with Dean and his roots—to get *closer* to Dean by exploring those places where he was—is a major reason for visiting Fairmount. You may be able to actually touch things and places that he touched and experienced. While tactile transformation may not be magic, it may fill the soul.

There are also many who knew and remember him, though fewer in number today. Speaking with Dean's high school buddies, his teachers, members of the Winslow and Dean families, and others who knew him is an important step in their efforts. Is there something about Fairmount and its people that produced someone like James Dean? Perhaps the answer may be in the qualities they find in Dean's teachers, family, and classmates. In stark contrast, some find in Fairmount the antithesis of what Dean means to them and say, "Dean had to get away from here to survive and flourish."

There is, after all, something very solid about this place. Dennis Stock's photos show Dean walking the streets of Fairmount, speaking with people along downtown sidewalks, and posing with farm animals on the family farm. He is seen in real places, and many of those very places are still there in contrast to a world that is often virtual, artificial, and always changing. In Fairmount things seem more fixed, all together, and unchanging. He was *real*, and he was *here*!

Journey completion applies when the Deaner, as part of her quest, believes this—trip, journey, or trajectory—is a necessary part in her life and destiny. It may be the completion of a pilgrimage or a step in a pilgrimage. Some may want to visit all the pilgrimage places. Others who were touched by Dean years and years ago (in some cases as early as 1955 or even before his death) may be seeking to "get back" to that time.

Some semblance of community exists during the memorial day's events; though real or imagined, it may be perhaps fleeting. But feelings of community also reinforce other forms of transformation. Visits to Fairmount and meeting like-minded people often create connections and the feeling of community. Being with others of like mind and sympathies is important for many and an important reason or consideration in making the trip. It is an occasion to share one's latest creation (poem, photo, art, etc.) or latest "find" of Dean memorabilia. Or just a time to renew old friendships and maybe make new ones. Sharing experiences, hopes, and problems is of continuing significance for many Deaners. Many Deaners have made numerous friends on their trips to Fairmount and maintain those friendships by keeping in contact and visiting in Fairmount. Some of these friendships have existed for many years and are often strengthened by taking trips together to other sites associated with Dean and visiting each other at their homes. These characteristics are aspects of what Bellah et al. have called a "lifestyle enclave" (1985, 71 *ff*), *and* what Turner terms "*communitas*" (1969, 96 *ff*).

When I interviewed twenty-four-year-old "Fred," the subject of Fairmount was paramount in much he said. He told how he started visiting Fairmount when he was sixteen and had tried to visit every year since. He's a second-generation Deaner and collects Dean memorabilia. About his trips to Fairmount and getting with fellow fans and Deaners, he said

> I still come down here because of Dean.... it's [also] because of the friends you meet.... I mean, there's like—it's amazing—like the other night I think there was eight or nine of us out—there were like four different states represented and a couple of different countries. It's amazing what you can learn.

He had previously referred to becoming good friends with David and Lenny, and later in the interview he referred to the lack of "hustle and bustle" there and said "like Kenneth Kendall put it a couple of years ago.... it's still America there. That's how I feel. I feel—you know, there's twenty people back there eating pizza and a guy from Uruguay...it's great!" Finally, late in the interview Fred expressed a desire to move to Fairmount and mentioned he had quit his job at one point and was going to move there, but things kept happening to keep him at home.

Certainly, another dimension of community involves those Deaners who decide to move to Fairmount, either permanently or only for a while. Phil Zeigler provided his personal views and experiences in our 1996 interview at his house after he had moved to Fairmount. He liked the people and the area beginning with his first visit in 1977, and those feelings only strengthened over the years. It was clear from my interview with him that he was very comfortable with his new life in the community. Many others I spoke with expressed similar feelings about the area, while others pointed to the negatives they had experienced.

Another example is provided by a young man from a European country who came to Fairmount because of his interest in James Dean. He stayed on and began working in the Gallery. Eventually he established a successful business near Fairmount, married, had two children, and became involved in the local community.

Mark Kinnaman, a well-known and very active Deaner, has lived in Fairmount since 2001. He grew up about fifteen miles from Fairmount, where he was born in September 1956—"I just missed Jimmy by a year...," he said—and he's "considered a local." He grew up knowing about Dean through his father, who was a fan and photographer, but Mark didn't start getting into him until seeing *Eden* at age thirteen and becoming "mesmerized." Later he saw *Rebel* and *Giant*, which continued to strengthen his fascination with Dean, but he continued to believe Dean's performance in *Eden* was his best and best represents the "real" James Dean. Mark joined the US Army after graduating from high school at age eighteen, reached the rank of sergeant and served until after the first Gulf War's Desert Storm.

After leaving the Army, Mark worked for a time in Fort Wayne as a quality-control inspector and later at Daddy-O's in Marion. He began returning to Fairmount in the late 1980s and eventually met David Loehr and Lenny Prussack at the Gallery and got to know others in the town. He became a regular at all the Dean events and began getting involved in the local activities and especially those associated with honoring Dean. At one time, he began selling Dean memorabilia during the September festival and by mail. One of the activities he started was a "James Dean Walking Tour" of Fairmount and environs, and later he started the previously mentioned candlelight walk from Fairmount to Dean's grave on evenings following the memorial service. His attachment to Dean is also evidenced by a head shot of him tattooed on his upper left arm. His commitment hasn't ended there as he became the vice president of the "James Dean Remembered" fan club publisher of the *Deanzine*. Many other Deaners have moved to Fairmount or nearby for varying periods of time. A woman from Spain lived there for a while. A woman from Uruguay, a middle and high school teacher, moved to the area with her son from 1996 to 2003. Her son eventually married a local girl, while his mother moved on to L.A. One Australian bought a house in Fairmount, which he rents to visitors when he is not in town. David Loehr acts as his agent for the house.

Perhaps an integral dimension to the quest is seeking self-identity, individuality, *and* community within the dominant homogeneous but increasingly fragmented culture of the United States. Of course, I doubt any Deaner would speak of their reasons or experiences in those terms. Still, most Deaners are white, with little special or strong ethnic identity beyond "American," and perhaps are seeking a form of community analogous to an ethnic group.[35]

Discussion

Perhaps the parading of Dean's image, or even giving him an obviously predominant place in the Grand Parade is too "Catholic" for the Protestant sensibilities of the larger community. It is significant to note that the memorial service for Dean is *always* held on the September 30, regardless of what day of the week that happens to be, and that the Museum Days festival is always the last full weekend in September. This means that the most "sacred" activity undertaken, the memorial service, is usually separated from the "secular" Museum Days activities by as much as a week, although some years the memorial service occurs at the end of Museum Days. So far, commercialization has not altered the practice of holding the memorial service on the anniversary date of Dean's death.

The festival consists of many separate "performances" played out conterminously. There is overlap, of course, but the agendas of the casual visitor will be quite different from the long-term Deaner or any serious Dean fan. There are many levels and dimensions to the various activities. For example, there is an interesting combination of activities commemorating Dean with activities celebrating America. The festival is held on a *weekend* in traditional Protestant American fashion, in deference to the work ethic and in the autumn (like a harvest festival).[36] The Grand Parade looks like a thousand other parades throughout the US with beauty queens, high school bands, clowns, hand-shaking politicians, Shriners, military color guards, trucks, farm tractors, floats of many kinds, Scouts, plenty of American flags, and the ultimate American symbol—the automobile in its multifarious forms. What might distinguish Fairmount's parade is the appearance of someone dressed like Garfield the cat, the possible appearance of a replica Porsche Spyder, or the car he drove to his high school prom.

The broader social and economic issues involved are yet to be systematically studied. Nevertheless, there are some obvious and interesting issues, such as the local and regional economic effects. Not only Fairmount, but the nearby towns of Marion, Gas City, Anderson, and others benefit greatly from Fairmount's Museum Days. Fairmount, for example, has no hotels or motels, although a few "bed and breakfast" type arrangements are available. These in no way meet the demand. The nearest motels are in Gas City and Marion, each about ten miles away, and reservations during Museum Days usually must be made a year in advance. The car shows in Fairmount and nearby Gas City during Museum Days are, in themselves, a major draw for thousands of people. In addition to local people and organizations that open concessions on South Main Street, many use this opportunity to sell various items from their houses and front yards.

Some streets look like one continuous yard sale with everything from knickknacks, antiques, and old furniture to toys and household goods. A few also turn their yards into temporary parking lots. Some locals simply disappear during the festival or stay at home to avoid the traffic and general "hustle-bustle."

Another indication of the impact is indicated by the retail sales by the James Dean Gallery (Hausknecht and Casper 1991, 610-612). In 1989, its second year of operation, retail sales were reported at $13,500, plus admission charges of $2 per person with approximately 6,000 *recorded* admissions.[37] Similar data are not available for the Fairmount Historical Museum, and, in any case, admission is free with a request for a donation at the entrance. The Fairmount Historical Museum reported 8,329 visitors during 1994 and 5,157 during 2006—however, during Museum Days, when long lines of people stretch around the block, no effort is made to maintain good records. Local newspapers typically report many thousands of visitors on Museum Days. Generally, attendance has been lower since 2005 and especially during the COVID-19 pandemic.

One clear reason for the continuing success of the festival is that Fairmount still looks like a small, typical Midwestern town of the not-so-distant past. In fact, Fairmount still looks much like it did when photographed by Dennis Stock during his visit there with Dean in 1955 (Stock 1978).[38] I find this enduring, unchanging quality of Fairmount to be of utmost importance to many Deaners and fans: Fairmount *itself* is symbolic of another time and creates or re-creates an important setting for those seeking James Dean (*cf.* Hopgood 2005b). Fairmount presents a time out of place and a place out of time, but that is its appeal and very fitting for a person who is perhaps timeless and forever young.

For the Deaners, visiting Fairmount is more than a mere trip to Dean's hometown, it is a pilgrimage on at least two interlinked levels: (1) it is a quest for self, self-discovery, and meaning in one's own existence, future, and struggle through James Dean, and (2) it is a tracing backward, a struggle with the present and at best a foggy future. In either, it is a search for meaning, perhaps lost or past meanings, or unknown meaning, in or through this place and the critical link, James Dean. The Deaners, then, are the siblings, the sons, and the daughters of James Dean, and his true descendants.

Perhaps a better understanding can be achieved by moving beyond the rather mechanical notions of sacred time and space through which Deaners move (*cf.* Eade and Sallnow 1991). Obviously, notions of time (or history), space, and being in some form are critical in this context. The sense of timelessness or suspension of normal time by the pilgrim may be as important as a more conscious effort to connect with Dean. Though timelessness may be sought, it cannot be maintained and must be given up, unless sanity is to be put at risk. This thought recalls a few lines from Lou Reed's song "Walk on the Wild Side": "Jackie she's just speeding away/thought she was James Dean for a day/then you know she had to crash…." Is this a sort of Deaner version of "dreamtime" or "everywhen?"

8

Deaners as a Movement: A "Cult" or What?

Burning in effigy. Kissing the picture of a loved one. This is obviously not based on a belief that it will have a definite effect on the object which the picture represents. It aims at some satisfaction and it achieves it. Or rather, it does not aim at anything; we act in this way and then feel satisfied.

—WITTGENSTEIN

The questions associated with applying the label "cult" or any label for that matter to this phenomenon are not easily solved nor are the issues easily sorted. Can or should the Deaners be referred to as a "movement," and if so, of what sort of movement? I have referred to the Deaners as an "iconic movement" elsewhere (e.g., Hopgood 2000, 346-347), but with misgivings together with the label "quasi-religious" movement. Or is this some sort of "cult?" In the *classic* sense, yes, it is. But this is not the sort of thing the man or woman in the street means by "cult." It is only in that sense or as in general usage of the term that it is rejected here. While it is perhaps neither "cult" nor "movement," those terms can be quite useful for understanding this phenomenon.

What exactly are we dealing with regarding the Deaners as an organization? Can any of this be even called an organization? Is it more than a fleeting thing of momentary substance? A loose amalgamation of like-minded folks? Perhaps it is only imagined. Perhaps any group where many or most of the members are focused on the self cannot, in any "real" sense, function as an organization.

Who are the Deaners and serious fans? I cannot supply complete demographics; however, a thumbnail sketch is helpful. Most come from the United States, but many come from other countries, including Canada, Mexico, most European countries, South Africa, Japan, Australia, Malaysia, and the Philippines. Deaners are all ages and genders. The youngest Deaner I have formally interviewed was nine and the oldest in his sixties. There are many teenagers and young adults who regularly participate in Dean-related activities in Fairmount and elsewhere. Another large bloc are adults in their thirties and forties, and beyond. Economic and occupational statuses cannot be specified in detail. My impressions are of a wide range of income groups and occupations being represented, although many would fall into the middle-income and white-collar occupations, along with lower-income and working class.

In terms of American ethnicity, most Deaners are Anglo-American, with an occasional person of Italian descent or Jewish identity. I have only seen a few African American and Latino participants in Fairmount. Most Deaners are from the Midwest, East, and far West. Southerners and Southwesterners are fewer in number. A count of 368 subscribers to *We Remember Dean International* from 1990 found California number one, followed by Illinois, New York, Indiana, Ohio, Pennsylvania, Michigan, New Jersey, Massachusetts, and Texas. All other states had eight or fewer members. Among other countries Canada, Japan, and Germany were highest, followed by Australia, United Kingdom, and France. Other countries had three or fewer members.

A more recent listing in 2005 from the Gallery for its newsletter has a similar distribution with Indiana at the top, followed by California, New York, Illinois, Ohio, Michigan, Pennsylvania, and Maryland. Other states had nine or fewer subscribers. Among other countries, the United Kingdom ranked first, followed by France,

Australia, and Canada. Other nations had one or two subscribers. Once a year the Museum sends a letter to its members outlining the past year's events and future plans. Included each year is a count of foreign visitors to the Museum. Dates of these visits are not given, though many occur during the annual festival. Covering the years 1989 through 2012, the total number of foreign visitors recorded was 7,401. For 1989 through 2009 overall, the Museum tallied 147,316 visitors from all countries (no total figures were given for 2010-2012). Given that the Museum was not open all year during those years that is an impressive figure.

Given this range I can only approximate numbers of stalwart fans at approximately 2,000 to 3,000 worldwide, while the number of Deaners would only be a wild guess. Certainly many, but not all, were members of the *We Remember Dean International* club and its successor the *James Dean Remembered Fan Club* begun in 2000 and now simply called *James Dean Remembered*.

What Is This?

Some of my research with the Deaners has focused on comparisons with religious movements, including folk saints, and exploration of the semiotics of Deaner pilgrimage (e.g., Hopgood 2000, 2005b). For lack of a name, it is a "phenomenon" dedicated to and continues to receive inspiration from the words and acts of a charismatic person, through the person's example, actions, creations, desires, and aspirations. While it does not qualify as a typical social or religious movement, it shares some characteristics with Robert Bellah's "lifestyle enclave" (Bellah, et al. 1985, 71-75) as well as having ingredients of Bellah's "expressive individualism" (1985, 32-35). There are also obvious similarities to the notion of a person as "sacred *symbol*" representing a kind of "collective charisma" ala Durkheim (1915; and via Lindholm 1990, 27-34).

This phenomenon shares some similarities with charismatic religious movements generally, although in this case it is *ostensibly* a secular cluster of social processes devoted to a charismatic person. Such an assemblage of processes may be an organized expression of popular or folk culture, as is the case with the Deaners. In certain other cases, however, it could be argued that it is a charismatic movement of a *formatively religious* variety. I no longer hold that view.

However, the "concreteness" of this Durkheimian-derived approach does not exhaust the issues involved, and the exploration of associated semiotics are helpful in distilling the brew of movement significance to its participants. For example, on the issue of the *transformative process:* How do ordinary things become "sacred" things? In this connection, if beliefs, ideas, and thought generally are regarded as *behavior* and, therefore, *real* and potentially having *effect*, and *affect*, then the problem is partly solved. This provides a general premise for framing or allowing for the change or transformation of apparently secular and mundane things into sacred ones.

For those who continue to refer to this as a "cult," in the derogatory sense, it is informative to quote Roof. In referring to "Sheilaism" ("my own religion") as a type of religious individualism from Robert Bellah's *Habits of the Heart* he writes:

> [The] Sheila-like expressive now generates, paradoxically, both highly individualistic spiritual quests out of church, synagogue, and temple *and*…with religious communities, mostly notably within Pentecostalism, Evangelicalism, and the Charismatic movements (1999, 149).

In the present case, it is suggestive that persons who turn to James Dean may be in an exploratory phase of their lives—seekers in the "Who am I?" stage. This certainly appears to be the case with many of the younger persons, and one can only wonder where the quest may take them. James Dean may just be a stopping-off point. With many of the older Deaners, he has remained a guide and ideal throughout their lives, regardless of what other directions their lives have taken.

Not a Cult?

The problem with the term "cult," like the term "icon," is its usage is all over the spectrum of meanings. In popular usage it is often used as a derogatory expression of disdain, contempt, or intense dislike toward a group, or as a label for "weird" activities and groups practicing mysticism, the occult, psychic phenomena, or "new religions." On the occasion of the Hale-Bopp comet in 1997, thirty-nine followers of the Heaven's Gate cult committed suicide believing their souls would be taken away by a spaceship. A more recent example is when some news program consultants referred to the followers of a certain recent president as a "cult." Certainly, to say Dean fans collectively are a "cult" in this popular sense is simply not correct.

Turning to legitimate usages of the term is helpful in exploring what is actually at play among fans and Deaners. Beginning with a classic definition of cult, it is typically grounded in an established religion and refers to: "The ritual observances involved in the worship of, or communication with, particular supernatural persons or objects or their symbolic representations" (Winick 1958, 143). From prehistory to contemporary times, there have been an amazing array of cults, such as cults for specific saints in the Catholic Church as well as other established world religions (Buddhism, Islam, Hinduism, etc.). Among non-Western societies, the array is seemingly endless. Ancestor cults are common in many African societies, as are guardian spirit cults among many traditional Native American and First Nations societies. Initiation cults are widespread in Western and non-Western religions and societies. For example, the so-called "Ghost Dance religion" among some North American tribes was a cult that believed a dance, if performed correctly, would bring back the buffalo and the ancestors, and cause the white people to disappear.

Colin Campbell, referring to the work of Howard Becker from the 1930s, explains how the term is applicable to "small and transient groups…stressing the private, personal character of the adherents' beliefs and the amorphous nature of the organization" (1998, 122). This is still being applied only in the context of religion and refers to "a group whose beliefs and practices were merely deviant from the perspective of" an established religion or orthodoxy. Also as conceived, these loosely organized groups are short-lived, and members would then move on to another pursuit (1998, 122). Does this solve the problem of where to place Deaners? Not exactly.

There are aspects of Deaner behavior and activities that are cultic. The most obvious example is the September 30 memorial service held each year in the small Back Creek Friends Meeting and the ensuing procession to Dean's gravesite and the acts carried out there—along with, starting in 2005, the candlelight walk to the grave, where participants can express their feelings out loud or privately. It's important to remember that rituals accomplish many things, including sociality, guidance, consolation, and celebration. The personal dialectic is renewed, but the group is ephemeral.

Other events, perhaps less ritualistic, include the annual February 8 get-together to honor Dean's birthday. One of Dean's films is shown followed by birthday cake and visiting. For some, a visit to Dean's grave followed by a prayer, leaving a memento, or just sitting silently for a time is required when visiting the area. Driving by or even stopping at the Winslow farm may be included, as well as visiting the few remaining locations that are remembered from Dean's days in Fairmount. Then there's the new Dean memorial on Main Street, where private meditation can take place. Those events and activities all happen in Fairmount, of course, but similar ones are held by other individuals elsewhere, such as organized car drives to Cholame or birthday get-togethers at one's home. The late Kenneth Kendall always held a birthday party to honor Dean for fans at his home in Los Angeles. There are unknown numbers of other private rituals: placing flowers or burning candles before his image in one's own "James Dean room," or praying for his help and guidance, drawing, painting, or sculpting his image, writing a poem devoted to him, and more. Or, simply meditating with one's thoughts of him.

What Deaners Are Not

The Deaners lack the usual characteristics and refinements of an established movement. For example, Deaners as Deaners do not await the "end of days" or the coming of the millennium (e.g., a golden age)—they lack an eschatology, in other words. If some adhere to such beliefs, it is not due to their attachment to Dean. Theirs is entirely a personalistic/individualistic "theology." A Deaner may be quite comfortable with her Christian or Jewish beliefs with no apparent conflict with her devotion to James Dean. Nor is this a mystery cult. There are no secret ceremonies, no secret initiations, secret books, and so on. Social movements have specific, concrete goals beyond the adoration of a founder or charismatic leader, while this type of emergent "movement" is clearly focused on the adoration and perpetuation of the persona of a single person but lacks a program or plan beyond the continued honoring and adoration of James Dean. They have not generated a continuation of Dean's charisma in another person (Weber 1968,48ff).

This "movement" as a movement can best be described as "ambivalent," "loose," or liminal. There is no leader. It requires very little of its "members," who may come and go with little or no notice of any organizational requirement. It lacks an ongoing crusade, the notion of proselytizing is rare, though not unknown. A potential contradiction here is the strong emphasis on individualism versus the hypothetical demands of an actual movement, should Deaners ever move in that direction. This is not a necessary condition for this phenomenon to survive, but it will never achieve the close-knittedness or intra-group solidarity associated with actual movements.

Sosis's (2004) "costly signaling theory of ritual" is of use here. Basically, this theory states that the more that is required of members (believers, followers, etc.), the stronger the group (movement, sect, etc.) will be. The greater the individual and personal sacrifice, the stronger the group will be. So, if it costs little or nothing (no sacrifice) to become a follower, there will be little in the way of commitment. What are the types or kinds of costs involved? This appears to apply well to conventional social movements and religious organizations but does not work well in the case of the Deaners. With a few exceptions, there are few costs in being a Deaner. There is, after all, no place to sign up. There are no demonstrations, rallies, political causes, etc. attached to being a Deaner. Still, there may be costs. There is the potential of ridicule or harassment by friends, family, and associates. Several Deaners have told me that they don't discuss Dean with coworkers or friends because of doubts that they will understand. Fathers are often mentioned as unapproving or worse. A few tell of losing a boyfriend or girlfriend because of his/her devotion to Dean. One woman told me she never mentions Dean to her husband because he gets upset. And one young woman told me that her last boyfriend was jealous of Dean and they no longer date. On two occasions when participating in the procession from the Back Creek Friends church to Dean's grave, I heard passersby shout "weirdos," "get a life!" and "go home!"—as well as other less charitable expressions. There may be costs to bear but certainly nothing like some possible examples.

Ideology

After Dean's death, there were substantial outpourings of anguish, disbelief, mystery, and speculation combined with anticipation of future revelations that produced what newspaper and movie magazine writers, among others, eventually came to label a "cult." This notion was born in the public imagination, assisted by the print media of the day. The intricacies of the development of Dean's public image will not be comprehensively explored here (*cf.* Tysl 1965), nevertheless certain aspects of that image and persona are clearly important to the analysis of his significance to the Deaners in particular and to fans in general. In part, the continued good reviews of Dean's work in the two unreleased films during 1955 and 1956 continued to add to his growing fame and image, and since *Giant* was not widely released until November 1956, anticipation heightened, and interest increased for his third and final performance on film. Though mostly a phenomenon that appealed to the young of America, all ages were attracted, as well as other nationalities (*cf.* Truffaut 1978, 296-299).

Speculation about the details of Dean's personal life have been a favorite topic of the media, fans, and the Deaners since his untimely death. It remains so today. Given the ambiguity of much of the information, the details of his private life remain a rich field for speculation and personal projection. For Deaners, the life and roles of James Dean are blended into a mythic unity. Dean is loved and admired as much for his future promise as for his accomplishments. The known facts of his life are enhanced and blended with the less established material of his private life. Deaners find in him hope for the discovery and development of their abilities.

The belief system of the Deaners *qua* Deaners, their "ideology" or "theology," is not formally codified, nor is there an "official" body of persons charged with the task of judging issues that may arise concerning Dean's life and activities. As an emergent manifestation it is nonetheless one grounded in a broader American belief system, worldview, or "civil religion." A theology, in its usual Western Judeo-Christian expression, is text-based. That is, there are sacred texts from which mortals attempt to speak rationally of the divine. Following Mark Taylor's liberal conception of theology and texts (2000, 33-45), I employ a liberal understanding of "texts." Deaner texts consist of images of Dean (in movies, television performances, photos, drawings, paintings, and sculptures), locations, artifacts, and memorabilia associated with Dean, biographies and hagiographies (including film, video, and staged versions), other published media, and Dean quotes, writings, and artworks. Deaner epistemology, if you will, is to study Dean's person and special *persona* as revealed through these texts. And, as with the reading of sacred texts in other contexts, there are contradictions in interpretation.

The emergent Deaner ideology is in flux around a core of common understandings and generally accepted truths regarding Dean, his life, accomplishments, and potential. James Dean, person and icon, is associated or identified with a series of values and ideals characteristically, though not uniquely, American: creativity in the arts, courage and daring, eternal youth and beauty, hope, rebellion against authority, individualism and "lone wolfism," self-seeking introspection, struggle—the struggle to achieve, the struggle for tolerance, and the struggle of the "common person." From the combination of Dean's lauded talents and creativity, along with such qualities as the "boy next door," "like you and me," and "from a small town," a powerful all-American image and ideal emerges. But, of course, in there somewhere is the "real" James Dean. Maybe that's him in *East of Eden,* maybe it's him in *Rebel Without a Cause*, or maybe he's to be found in Fairmount.

The view of Dean as potential, often phrased in terms of "if only he had lived, he would have accomplished so much," is common among Deaners. They refer to his wide range of interests, not only in acting, but in directing, writing, painting, sculpting, dance, music, auto racing, bullfighting, and so on. This view is a strong source of personal inspiration for Deaners to achieve in their own ways, as he would have done. Dean is the guide in a Deaner's search for his/her own special talents and gifts.

Dean's appeal in terms of "nostalgia" for the "good old days of the 1950s" can be demonstrated, as well. However, for most Deaners, this nostalgia is not a central element in their devotion of Dean, and for some Deaners, it plays a small or no role at all. The 1950s may have an appeal apart from the actual 1950s, that is, an intrinsic appeal. But, when this appeal is expressed today by a teenager who only just "discovered" James Dean, clearly it cannot be nostalgia. The inter-/cross-generational aspect of Dean's appeal continues to sustain the fan and Deaner phenomenon, as demonstrated by the continuing flow of young people from England, Australia, Western Europe, and Japan to Fairmount in search of Dean.

Conclusions

Deaners are perhaps simply too inner-directed or introspective to require or desire anything like an established organization. A Deaner's commitment is personal and individualistic (even narcissistic), it is not group-oriented, per se. Is that the crux of the matter? One does not become a Deaner to better the world or the lot of a particular segment of society. There are no long-range group goals, just individual ones. Even such efforts as preserving the old Fairmount High School—largely because of Dean's attendance there—lacked the strength and commitment for success. But, in fairness, it must be noted that eventually the stage on which the school plays were performed was saved and rebuilt in Playacres Park.

I no longer prefer labeling this phenomenon an "iconic movement" although this particular icon has acquired followers and worshipers from around the world amid a milieu of expectations and questing for personal fulfillment. At best it remains an incipient movement but does have cultic aspects given the annual and private rituals. In several ways, the adoration of and devotion to philosopher Friedrich Nietzsche in the United States during the late nineteenth and early twentieth centuries are remarkably similar to that toward James Dean, though the subject matter is obviously very different.

Examining letters from his American admirers, Jennifer Ratner-Rosenhagen explores the philosopher's cultlike following in her *American Nietzsche* (2012, 193-217). The letters, sent to Nietzsche's sister Elisabeth Föster-Nietzsche, document the range of sentiments expressed by his fans. It is tempting to make a point-by-point comparison here, but I must leave that task to others. For now, I will only detail a few points of similarity. They wrote about how reading Nietzsche "transformed their views of themselves and their world...how Nietzsche helped them critique the religion of their youth" (2012, 197). Some writers "conveyed their devotion to Nietzsche in expressly religious terms, referring to the way '*He*' saved them from despair and how they found new meaning in

'*His*' prophetic utterances." A large number "expressed their pious regard for him, not simply because he taught them new truths but because he helped give them the courage to speak theirs" (2012, 196-197). Ratner-Rosenhagen further describes Nietzsche's reception in America as creating a "growth industry" and an "intellectual romance," and how he emerges as a "celebrity in American culture" (while noting the similarities to contemporary American "culture of celebrity") (2012, 197). She refers to Nietzsche in the American context as "the personalist, secular savior, and the cultural critic," and from reading him his followers wanted to "'intimate' with him" and possess something of him or that belonged to him (2012, 216). These readers' Nietzsche "was never a being but a becoming; he was a product of collaborative meaning-making between text and reader, text and context" (2012, 204) and was "remade…in their own image" (2012, 216). Some apparently had shrines to Nietzsche in their homes. Many of his followers in America made the transatlantic pilgrimage to Weimar to talk with his sister and visit his personal library and archives (2012, 209).

Deaners share their feelings about Dean, and in that way lay the foundation for a sociality that may last for many years and could, but has not, provide the basis for the formation of a more conventional movement. There is no lack of social networks (and more will be said of this elsewhere). The networks and connectedness are strengthened by Deaner engagement in rituals devoted to Dean—and there are both public and private rituals. In the public rituals, there is something of a common *praxis* that has contributed to its continuity, and for Deaners these have their own beauty: chapel memorial service, procession to the grave, graveside service, and so on. Deaners do not go there only to "go through the motions." They are sincere. Once again: the personal dialectic is renewed and sustained each time.

It's as if the ritual groupings cannot be transcended, only regression is possible to the very individualism that brought them to the ritual. After the service at Dean's grave, David Loehr always walks back to town while others drive. Asked why, he said he prefers to be alone with his thoughts at that time. Group consciousness is dissipated, and so it is with many public rituals, but in this case, there is no larger structure or organization to which to return. Personal ties and networks remain, and there is strength there, but such dyadic relationships would not sustain any larger undertaking. Thus, this is a quasi-group, a quasi-movement, and perhaps at some level an "imagined community."

9

A Conclusion and Final Thoughts

Do not, my soul, long for an immortal life,
but make the most of what you can realistically achieve.
—PINDAR, PYTHIAN III

From the traces of Dean's life, I have *not* attempted to disentangle past and present perceptions of the various known and possible events and influences during his early, formative years and later struggles and accomplishments from a historical reality. Such an effort would require placing him in the context of the 1930s through the early 1950s first in rural Indiana, Southern California, followed by rural Indiana again and so on. Deaners, fans, and others (including writers) can pick and choose which influences and events, known or supposed, had formative importance on the young Dean and his later struggles and rise to stardom. What I have offered is a brief coverage of some aspects of his early life with some background on Fairmount and environs. I have not delved into historical sources in the exhaustive fashion required for an insightful exploration into "what it was like" to be the young and maturing James Dean. Most of the events and influences I have included are those referred to by most Deaners and hagiographers. Nor have I sought to demystify, but to clarify, who Deaners are and what they believe and what some beliefs address.

Given that today there is literally something "out there" for everyone in the electronically globalized hyperspace world, it's not surprising that James Dean continues to occupy a niche. Certainly nothing as large and spacious as Elvis Presley, Michael Jackson, or the current heartthrob, and many others, but a niche, nonetheless. It is also certain that the ready availability of media on the web and the ease of communication among interested persons allows those of like minds to exchange information and has facilitated the continuation the various forms of adoration of contemporary "icons."

This technological underpinning is, of course, only a partial explanation. Because there are uncounted choices for those looking for a group to follow (of various types), an "icon," role model, a leader, a god, or whatever, the major question becomes why that particular one? And, here, the question is why James Dean? Without resorting to an underpinning of evolutionary theory, the question is why has the adoration of James Dean survived for over sixty-five years? What is it about James Dean—his symbol, sign, icon, and history—that continues to appeal to and draw people to him? What attracts, and for some, sustains a lifelong involvement with this young man? What do they "get" from him? Why do so many make pilgrimages to Fairmount and seek out other places where he lived, worked, and died? Those are the questions that have driven this project.

Perhaps there is something, after all, to the position Louis Armstrong stated in his earlier quote regarding Jazz: "If you have to ask, you will never know." It is the notion that some things are beyond explanation or analysis and belong, perhaps, in a deep realm of emotion. Many fans and Deaners believe their feelings about James Dean are beyond academic explanation or easily categorized and dismissed. Verbal analysis just won't do. Maybe too close an analysis will somehow destroy, belittle, or reduce the thing adored. "You can't talk about this—you just feel it." Everyone is looking for answers—a new way through whatever mess—Deaners are no different in finding or giving meaning to one's life, beyond existence, toward something significant, lasting, meaningful. What is worth saving, knowing, understanding, keeping, treasuring, passing on? For them, Dean is a way, perhaps, through to another place, another state of being, or a new level of creativity or expression.

Perhaps the key is fame and wealth? That is a possible link to the narcissism many have noted in American culture. There is the narcissism angle/side to this adoration. Many have written on the link between narcissism and American celebrity culture and especially among the young (e.g., Sternheimer 2011). Perhaps just touching the source of the adored will be the key or a step toward a vaguely defined goal. To judge a Deaner or Deaners in general as narcissistic remains at best only a piece of this phenomenon; there is much more. Perhaps when taken as a whole, this phenomenon is just an example of seeking a contemporary version of myths, heroes, and gods as well as the magical and enchantment.

The Self and What Is Sought

Some Deaners are seeking a mutuality of being—a sort of kinship-like state—and belong to that greater whole: a journey of being via the community. For others it is a family of common participants, and it is a mix of Dean and Fairmount—keeping in mind that these relations often extend to people in Fairmount—that brought them together, and this shared participation maintains a continuity. It's as if Dean were an ancestral father. Leading to a renewal with each visit; maintaining a continuity through time. So it is not only participation in the events but the private reunions that solidify these relations. There is a range of who and what James Dean is among fans and Deaners. For many, there is an undercurrent of desire and love mixed with other feelings. Here are few aspects:

- Dean is very a *personal* "icon" and hero figure. There is a personal resistance—even hostility—when one's personal vision of Dean is challenged. This was most apparent when Alexander's book was published with its unsubstantiated claims about his sex life and an infamous photograph of a nude young man in a tree purported to be Dean.

- For many this is all the "religion" they require. At once, self-made, sacred, and secular. I continue to marvel at the amount of adoration he receives, not only by the older Deaners but by the youth who seek him out. It may be argued that all this is located somewhere between the sacred and the profane—the liminal—but it is nonetheless real for those engaged with Dean.

- This "finding" of oneself—self-expression and individualism coupled with a search for meaning—found here through Dean is, of course, a modernist value, yet one that has roots in Protestantism and other religions.

- Dean has been remade to transcend his actual life and his film roles—like many celebrities, heroes, and all saints. His fans and Deaners have "forced" him into these images, symbols, ideals, and molds. He is often a mix of legends (and role models) in identity and personality.

- The issue of Dean's physical attraction cannot be dismissed or overlooked. His image approaches a state of iconophilia for some. The various images or guises of Dean are important in understanding his appeal and attraction: the rebel, the misunderstood, the outsider, the artist, the struggle, a quest for experience, the weight of a certain sadness, the abandoned, the lost soul, the farm boy, the beautiful, and the complex. Many from this list are applied to Dean by the devoted.

- Dean serves as an inspiration to create something in his honor in the form of films, plays, drawings, paintings, sculptures, poetry, and prose. Others' inspiration is to strive toward acting, auto racing, or simply to achieve something of significance.

- There is something "concrete" about this James Dean in Fairmount—no digital creation here—he was here, he walked these streets, drove on those roads, worked at that farm, performed on that stage, and visited those places. He struggled to begin first in Hollywood, then in New York, and you can see that from photographs and even TV films. From these beginnings inspirational stories are woven, creating a canvas on which to create one's ideal.

Dean in life was a work in progress, in a process of becoming, a process with an uncertain goal. That process is one characteristic that has made him so influential and sought: seeking self-realization via a path treaded by James Dean. There is something very appealing about an unfulfilled promise of a young life or an unfinished work, especially a life's work, a short-lived, bright star. As for many political figures and movie, rock, and sports stars, the reinventing of James Dean is standard fare. Given his age at death, his brief career in television, stage, and film, and the absence of accounts of much of his brief life, reinvention has considerable latitude. There is the iconography, mythology, and events real, invented, or imagined contending with or molded into a personal ideal. Dean was, in fact, a work in process while alive, and this process has only continued since his death. Portions of his life have been exaggerated—if not distorted—while others have been played down or ignored. Much of this is underpinned by people's love of a good story and more specifically the comfort of the familiar story of early difficulties (in childhood and youth) followed by struggle and eventual triumph.

Following the fiftieth anniversary of Dean's death, his popularity again declined. Yet, as is the case in contemporary American popular culture, what and who is "in" changes rapidly. Film director, screenwriter, and producer Martin Scorsese pegged this characteristic well when he wrote: "Now, the cycles of popularity are down to a matter of hours, minutes, seconds, and the work that's been created out of seriousness and real passion is lumped together with the work that hasn't" (2013, 27). He was writing about the history of film in the United States and how certain films and genres are in and out of fashion, and not only is this the case with film genres and styles, but with actors, writers, and singers, among others. Many facets of American culture could be added to his list as it continues as a country of "fads."

Community

Despite the emphasis I've placed on the individual quest, it is clear from this study that additional important factors clearly point to the importance of community. Perhaps they didn't seek community or a movement, but what there is of it is a mainstay of this phenomenon, and in this case it derives from the importance of place. Fairmount and Dean's connection to Fairmount along with the common bond felt among his followers form the basis of a community. Long-term friends maintain contact throughout the year and meet up when returning to Fairmount. This was obvious during my first time attending the Festival weekend and memorial service in Fairmount. Though first-timers, my spouse and I were invited to join a group for lunch at the Crossroads restaurant near Fairmount. It was attended by many old hands, and the camaraderie among them was clear at the dining table. Present were David Loehr, Lenny Prussack, Bob Rees and his wife, and Tom Burghuis and many others I didn't know at that time. They all knew each other. At the center of the activity was Dean's high school drama teacher, the late Adeline Nall. In this connection, it is imperative to indicate this continues a process of hospitality began in the early days after Dean's death by many in Fairmount and in particular the Winslow family.

What fans and Deaners find in Fairmount may be a mystery to outsiders, but you must visit those places, they say, to find out for yourself. Some among the most devoted move to Fairmount permanently or for various periods of time, die there, and are buried there or have their ashes deposited near Dean's grave. The degree of devotion among Deaners does vary, but certainly at one end of this continuum one finds total immersion or, or for some, "obsession." The degree does vary over time as well and is noted by many Deaners in their own life stories. Dean's films, works, and life stories from childhood to death provide Deaners a basis for solidarity and sense of community—sense that comes from the rituals held in Fairmount and elsewhere.

While this phenomenon is acephalous and lacks any centralized organization, there are individuals who are highly regarded for either a connection to James Dean in life or for a high degree of devotion to him. Others have held those roles in the past, but currently they are held by Marcus Winslow Jr. and David Loehr respectively. Others among the Deaners and serious fans hold important participatory roles in local activities or the club. What there is of an *esprit de corps* is lax with connectedness more common among pairs or small groups. In this context, the Gallery serves as a base of sociality for fans and Deaners.

Fairmount

The Festival events in Fairmount are an occasion for the collective expression of local, state, and national sentiments with the parade, car show, and local pride in famous (and not-so-famous) men. Small town rituals—festivals, memorials, car shows, dances—express collective meaning via local history and emotional attachments to place. A Deaner may experience a flood of emotions along with a vague familiarity with the sights and sounds of this small Midwestern town. This familiarity may come from a generalized past or from the Fairmount of Dennis Stock's photographs. There's a sort of simplicity about it: the lack of complexity of everyday life with remembrance of past times. Fairmount seems authentic and solidly *real* but not unmodern, just a step "out of time."

The small town has played a very important role in maintaining Dean's history, legacy, and continuing adoration. In Fairmount we find a mix of the modern, the present, and the past with competing and contesting views of each among those engaged with the place.

Clearly for some it is a step into a past that appears to exist still, a past they want to fully engage and savor. Others, regardless of their feelings for Dean, view Fairmount with greater distance and perhaps as simply "old-fashioned." For the long-term non-Deaner residents of Fairmount, the present may simply be living their lives, making a living, and perhaps engaging in their own dialectical struggles with the past and present. For a Deaner, this dialectic between the past and present is too simplistic and is not, of course, just the past and present for the participant. It is also what the Deaner brings to the mix that results in a personal, though shared, synthesis.

Charisma

There is something of the universal in Dean's appeal—he is not just or only the American rebel, individualist, or what have you—he has something of that universal quality that appeals beyond the bounds of one nation or culture. Some call it charisma—his uniqueness and individuality—Deaners use phrases such as "there is no other" and "there will never be another James Dean." For Deaners, all "look-alikes" and imitators fall short. They only get close. Actors who have portrayed Dean are debated as to who best captured him in film, but none comes close to the original.

His charisma took several directions or forms. In the late 1950s he was viewed by many from the home, church, and political arenas as a "threat" to society and religion. Dean was seen as an archetype of young rebels who sought to undermine established authority from family to perhaps all levels of society. Those young rebels were not only seen on movie and TV screens in fictional roles but performing to large crowds of young people a new form of music—rock 'n' roll—and eventually in the streets protesting for civil rights or to end the war in Vietnam.

Dean's "threat" was and is via a style of expression in his life and film roles of nonconformity, individuality, seeking personal fulfillment in art, and pushing boundaries in work and play. His struggle in life and in film against problems of authority (from family to social class) was itself a form of self-expression. For a Deaner, it is the blending of Dean's life and film roles into one whole set that results in a matrix that serves as a guide in her own life's struggle. Yet, it can be added that Deaners are not rebels in the strict sense. Rather they are perhaps rebelling against the dehumanized struggle for a meaningful and sustainable life in the contemporary world.

This James Dean is what we made and continue to make of him. He will always be multifaceted, multi-imaged, projected, refracted, and remade. In this way he is an existential creation and no longer the author of his own being. For some he encourages rebellion, others conformity, while others find a creative direction of inspiration, and others find comfort in who they are. From their gazes and contemplation, they find direction and hope, too.

In the end I return to this: at its foundation this is a quest for that individualism long an integral part of American Protestantism and American culture generally and in that sense remains quite conservative. While not the sort of conservatism that necessarily seeks a return to an imagined past, it may remain a strictly personal idea. Never mind the contradiction by some in seeking their individualism by duplicating another persona. Some find their way out of this dilemma and instead seek those qualities that contribute to creativity, self-expression, and independence on whatever "works" for them. Here it is appropriate to recall Lindholm's statement: "Charisma is, above all, a *relationship*, a mutual mingling of the inner selves of leader and follower" (1990, 7). And in this case, it is often the supposed, perceived, or imagined inner self of James Dean.

The case for Dean post-2005 hasn't been optimistic. His popularity has declined at least as judged by the lack of media attention and the impact on Fairmount of poor national economics and a deadly pandemic's effects on travel. Still, the nagging question remains as to why this phenomenon has continued for over sixty-seven years. The fact that Dean's status as a popular icon has declined, and may decline further, is of little consequence to a Deaner or the serious fan. Deaners will continue their devotion. Less attention from the media may even contribute to an increased sense of "specialness" or exclusivity. That is not unknown from the past record of Dean's general popularity. Considering the availability of Facebook, YouTube, and other internet and web-based options, fans and Deaners can, and do, maintain their own networks of like-minded folks.

Standing adjacent to a loose community paradigm is that continuing quest of individuality. Even when temporarily breaking from the bonds of American individualism, the tension remains and pulls toward the allure of "the individual." And, as has been shown, many come to Fairmount seeking that "self" felt to be missing or incomplete and first awakened by James Dean. Some seek a sort of salvation, liberation, and deliverance along with justification: "This is how I am, and it's OK." While seeking a guide or role model, they also seek a redeemer. Dean, of course, is not just a role model; there's too much adoration to leave it there. For some he has become a savior, a saint: a secularized, nonconformist saint. Still, those who have dug deeper have found much more than the "rebel" persona. Perhaps rebelling can be much more than taking a pose and can go in other directions and take other forms. For them, Dean is an intermediary in seeking something deeper in oneself leading perhaps to an inner place of desire, motivation, and direction while Dean remains in a state of perpetual becoming. This question remains: Will pilgrims and travelers continue seeking a new beginning, the sources of the creative impulse, of daring, of hope, transcendence, and a new or complete self through James Dean? It is likely in a culture such as ours, where the focus is on individual characteristics and achievements, a focus that begins during childhood development and early socio-cultural learning, that the search will continue. Perhaps James Dean will continue to be one of those chosen.

ENDNOTES

1 There is no simple method to measure Dean's general popularity today and in the recent past. The following "measures"—"culturomics," data from *People Weekly* and *Forbes* magazines, YouTube, and Google online searches—provide a general indication of his popularity. The 2010 introduction of "culturomics" via the "Books Ngram Viewer" from Google (Michel et al. 2011) provides one way to judge popularity. A run on "James Dean" for the years 1954 to 2005 with "0" smoothing provides interesting results. It shows peaks in the late 1950s to early 1960s, followed by a dip, a second peak in the mid-1970s, then another dip, with the next, and largest, peak in 1991, followed by a steep dip, then another peak in 1995-96, and another dip. After 1977 the dips never returned to the late 1950s peak, perhaps indicative of a continuing minimum level of popularity. The results included books, book chapters, and many magazines. A comparison with Elvis Presley for the same years had Presley always scoring ahead of Dean except for the late 1950s, 1974, and 1991. A return to the Books Ngram Viewer in 2021 revealed the same downward trend with a slight upturn in 2015 (May 30, 2021).

One measure of popularity currently is to search on YouTube for online video contributions (January 23, 2011). A search for "James Dean" produced 5,360 results (compared with "Elvis Presley," which produced 345,000 results). Individually these videos scored from a few hundred to over 129,000 views. Many of the contributions were personal testimonials and tributes, while others were film clips from his movies, TV appearances, and documentaries (often personalized), performers doing songs about or for Dean, and trips to Fairmount and Cholame, Hollywood, Marfa, Texas, and other places associated with his life. Interviews with his family members, those who worked with him, and fans are found as well. Also included with these search results were a few other James Deans, such as James Dean Bradfield. A more recent search for "James Dean" on YouTube (Feb. 21, 2014) resulted in "about 194,000" hits. Many of those hits are misses, (e.g., who is this James Dean Bradfield?) but estimating a 50 percent hit result is still impressive. The types of posted videos are very similar to those film clips from the 2011 search.

If it's photos you want, check out Pinterest, an online source for "image sharing and social media service." A quick check there for James Dean found a seemingly endless collection of Dean photos on "pin boards." Each pin board was posted by an individual and listed the number of followers. This quick check found one board with thirty-two followers and another with over a thousand with a full range between (September 13, 2021).

People Weekly in March 1991 reported that licensing fees from the sale of Dean memorabilia earned between $2 million and $3 million annually for the Dean heirs. More recent reports have come from the annual *Forbes* magazine and Forbes.com listings of earnings of the top dead celebrities. Dean came in at thirteenth in 2001 with $3 million going to James Dean Inc. (a.k.a. the Dean heirs) far behind Presley who netted a first with $35 million. He was out of the top thirteen or so in the following year but is reported at fifteenth in 2003 and 2004 with $5 million, with Presley retaining first place with $40 million both years. For 2005 and 2006 Dean didn't make the reported lists (up to thirteen), while Presley retained first place. In 2007 Dean was back at thirteenth with earnings of $3.5 million. Dean again misses the top thirteen lists in subsequent years. In 2010 Presley was beaten by Michael Jackson. Fame is so fickle.

Returning to the web may reveal something about popularity. Reflecting the same patterns noted above is a Google online search (21 Dec 2010). "James Dean" had "about 3,320,000" hits, "Elvis Presley" gathered "about 27,300,000," and "Jim Morrison" came in with "about 2,940,000." Of course, these results do not distinguish the persons of our interest from others with the same and sometimes similar names. The "official" James Dean site, www.jamesdean.com, indicated some "69,180 people like James Dean" in 2010. By February 22, 2014, it was 1,332,882. And so it goes.

Finally, recorded attendance at the Fairmount Historical Museum provides an additional, and in part local, measure of Dean's popularity. I compiled attendance data for 1990 through 2012 from the Museum, which lists attendance by country. During festival weekends, attendance is highest, and the Museum controls the flow of visitors and attempts to have each visitor sign in with name and address. They also request visitors on other occasions to sign in. During those twenty-two years, 147,316 visitors were recorded, and of those 7,401 were from foreign countries. (However, during the years 2010-2012 total attendance was not recorded, only foreign.) Although this represents a small percentage of the total, it is of interest to note which countries had the largest percentages. Germany, Japan, Canada, Great Britain, Australia, and France in that order were the top six countries and represented nearly 71 percent of the total. The year with the greatest total attendance was 1997 with 10,791 visitors followed by 1998 with 10,075, while the year with the greatest number of foreign visitors was 1992 with 430. After the peak years of 1997-98, attendance shows a pattern of decline. In 2006 the total was 5,157, only half of the peak year. By 2009 the total was 4,075, and for 2013 the total was 3,452. In 2014 there was a total of 3,216 visitors, of which 183 were from other countries. The year with the least number of foreign visitors was 2012 with 37. These trends may reflect contemporaneous economic conditions in the US and in the various represented countries, as well as the web and flow of cultural tastes.

2   It is not the purpose here to rehash the fine points of James Dean's life; there has been enough of that with a multitude of published biographies in book form of varying quality. The purpose of this brief biography of Dean is to cover the major events in his life for the benefit of any reader unfamiliar with it. There are numerous biographies and hagiographies of James Dean. One of the best is David Dalton's *James Dean: The Mutant King* (1974). It has been reprinted many times and has the distinction of being the most frequently read and reread biography of Dean. Deaners regularly cite Dalton's as their favorite book on Dean. The first biography written on Dean by his friend Bill Bast (1956) is a standard reference; it and Dalton's book constitute the Deaner "bibles." Other solid references for important periods in Dean's life include Dennis Stock's *James Dean Revisited* (1978) and Roy Schatt's *James Dean: A Portrait* (1982). *James Dean: Little Boy Lost* (1992), by Joe and Jay Hyams, contains some new information, and Val Holley's *James Dean: The Biography* (1995) is a good source. The biography by Wes D. Gehring (2005) is well researched and an excellent reference, even though it lacks an index.

3   "The Method" refers to the style of acting developed by the Russian actor and director Konstantin Stanislavsky. It is based on the notion of an actor developing a character by drawing upon his or her own life experiences.

4   It should be noted that during this time most of the fan-type magazines worked closely with the Hollywood studios in presenting and maintaining the desired images of their stars in terms of what they believed the fans expected and desired.

5   Even a brief skimming of Tysl's 1965 dissertation will clearly demonstrate the mountainous coverage Dean received.

6   The foundation closed in late 1960 due to a lack of funds and debts. The bright outlook for revenue from such films as *The James Dean Story* never materialized (Lewis 1960, 32).

7   When I began this project there were at least two functioning clubs. One, the "James Dean Fan Club," founded in about 1980, published a newsletter edited by Greg Larbes of Cincinnati, Ohio. It had ceased to exist by January 1990. The other, and the most active, was "We Remember Dean International." It was founded in 1978 by Sylvia Bongiovanni of New York and Bill Lewis of Indiana as the "We Remember Dean" fan club and together they published a newsletter. In 1982 it became "international." The "WRDI Newsletter" ceased publication in 1999, but was soon followed by "The Deanzine," initially edited and published by Magdalin Leonardo, which continues today, with a different editor. Another newsletter in existence during this project, but without an attached club, was "JD Magazine" published during 1993-94.

8   That the Beats adopted Dean as an icon is reflected in their art as seen at an exhibition held at the Whitney Museum of American Art (Phillips 1995, 192ff, 198, 210, 230, 252, 253, 274). See especially the essay by Ray Carney in Phillips (1995, 190ff). Also, see Tysl (1965, 422ff) for a discussion of Dean's relationship to the Beats and Whitmer's comments (1987, 48, 52-53, 62-63, 66ff).

9   The relationship or connection of existentialism to James Dean occurred to me only because a philosophy colleague, Prof. Robert Trundle, made the connection. I discovered, in addition to Dean's impact on him, he was using Dean as an example of an "existential hero" in his class on existentialism (Interview, June 11, 1990). Gilbert in his study of American juvenile delinquency in the 1950s notes the existentialist elements in *Rebel Without a Cause* and its connection to the Beat poets (1986, 187-188).

10 I contacted David Dalton about the source of the quotation. He replied that he believed it was from Natalie Wood and a statement she made during the taping of *James Dean Remembered*, a documentary for ABC (Ramrus 1974). A search of the film failed to find Ms. Wood making any reference to the quotation. However, the quotation was cited by Peter Lawford in his interview with Leonard Rosenman in the same program. Lawford read the quotation from Dalton's book. St. Michael also lists the same quotation and gives the source as an "answer [by Dean] to reporter about his alleged homosexuality" (1989, 62; cf. Humphreys 1990, 55, Schroeder 1994, 42). Typical of these types of books, there are no specific references given. However, there is a sug-

gestion of Dean experimenting with homosexuality in Bill Bast's *James Dean: Portrait of a Friend* (1975, 55-56).

11 There are numerous examples of the work of Curtis Management on behalf of "James Dean Inc." In March 2014 the *Cincinnati Enquirer* featured a piece "James Dean—a rebel after all these years" and details a suit filed by James Dean, Inc. in an Indiana state court against Twitter "alleging that the Twitter handle "@JamesDean" infringes the James Dean trademark and violates the company's right of publicity" (March 16, 2014, G3). The article also refers several times to Dean as a "rebel," helping maintain that image of the actor.

12 The "family" in this case consists of Marcus and his sister, Joan. Initially it also included Dean's father and Marcus's father and mother before their deaths. Marcus remarked (interview May 10, 2007) that his mother only briefly experienced the benefits from the arrangement with Curtis Management. The only heir to James Dean's estate was his father, Winton Dean. Before the arrangement with Curtis, the Dean estate received payments from reruns of his television appearances (Tysl 1965, 542-543).

13 Still the issue continues to surface. In 2013 Wolfe Video released a film titled *A Portrait of James Dean: Joshua Tree, 1951* directed by Matthew Mishory and staring James Preston as Dean. Though a blend of fact and fiction, it presents Dean as being either bisexual or gay.

14 In addition to what I have learned in face-to-face interaction with people in Fairmount, there is also a good amount of print and film material that relate to the issues discussed. For example, for the fiftieth anniversary of Dean's death and a local celebration in June 2005, the "Dean Fest," two newspapers in nearby Marion and Muncie published *James Dean: 50 Years Later* (Cline and Smith 2005). A special DVD was also issued by the same newspapers (Cline and Kiefer 2005). Earlier material such as a 2000 video, *James Dean—Born Cool*, presents local views of Dean (Pietrowski 2000). Also, with the fiftieth anniversary in mind, *James Dean: Forever Young* was premiered at the "Dean Fest" and made available commercially on DVD (Sheridan 2005). Except for the Cline and Kiefer film and Hauge (2000), the other films and videos I have selected to represent local views, Marcus Winslow Jr. was involved, either as a producer or an executive producer. The film by Alan Hauge, *James Dean: American Legend*, reported to be a born-again Christian, had close ties to the Winslow family during the early stages of its production and boasts on the cassette box that it was "produced over an eight-year period with the cooperation of his [Dean's] family and friends." In an interview (May 10,

2007), Marcus Winslow Jr. described himself as a "reluctant producer" given the film's many ups and downs. He was involved in the beginning, but not later and had little to do with the film's final form. Originally intended to be a feature film starring Damien Chapa as Dean, the project deteriorated and was never released commercially. It was sold in Fairmount at various outlets and at many local events. There are also numerous other newspaper stories and clips from other films I have collected that provide excellent coverage of local views of Dean.

15 It is perhaps no coincidence that in 2000 the plinth was removed in the wake of a new monument to veterans. The brick plinth, marked only with James Dean's name, would have been in view from the new monument—to many vets a reminder still of Dean's getting out of military service. Two symbols in endless conflict, it seems.

16 When Dean requested a deferment using the claim of homosexuality is yet another issue open to continued discussion and debate (Holley 1995, 70).

17 It appears the stories will keep coming. After Elizabeth Taylor's death in March 2011, a story began to appear in the press and online that Taylor had revealed Dean's childhood molestation in 1997 to Kevin Sessums but insisted that the story be kept secret until after her death. According to Taylor, during the filming of *Giant,* Dean revealed to her that he had been molested at age eleven by his minister (Finkelstein 2011; MacIntosh 2011).

18 More information on Dean fans generally is found in Chapter 8.

19 I conducted three taped interviews with David Loehr in 1989, 1994, and 2007. Those along with interaction and casual conversations provided a wealth of information on David's life and place among Deaners. Quotations in this segment are from those interviews. In 2021 David published his memoir *That's How Strong My Love Is: From Rock-n-Roll to James Dean.*

20 Eventually, Loehr would collaborate with Dalton and Cayen on "James Dean, American Icon," published in 1984.

21 Much of this story and some of the additional statements from this interview were also published by Phil Zeigler in an issue of the *WRDI Newsletter.*

22 This type of story can be repeated many times over. A similar one is told by Tysl (1965, 558).

23 Dean's place in Beat culture appears assured based on the Whitney Museum of American Art exhibit and catalog (Phillips 1995, 192ff, 198, 210, 230, 252, 253, 274).

24 Enumerations of poems are not in the original and are added here for convenience only.

25 To frame this as only nostalgia is to miss a critical dimension by focusing only on the "outer" and more superficial level of the phenomenon. A mere fan or nostalgia buff may say "Dean was our hero back in the fifties." For a Deaner, this sentiment would have to be put in the present tense.

26 Clearly cases like this go beyond mere identification with Dean and demonstrate an effort to "blend" with him or his image. Deaners are deeper in their relationship with Dean than simple identification. They seek a closeness approaching a kind of "oneness" or being with the "other."

27 Terms used from Peirce's semiotic will be italicized.

28 There are some notable similarities between Peirce's semiotic and Roy D'Andrade's representation of the American folk model of the mind (1995, 162). D'Andrade's "event" equals the *object* in Peirce, "perception" is best equated as the viewer or interpreter, "thought" would equate with the *sign*, and D'Andrade's "feeling," "wish," "interaction," and "act" equates with Peirce's *interpretants*.

29 There are a host of terms developed by Peirce for exploring the semiotic. Terms such as index, icon, symbol, sinsign, qualisign, and legisign are part of his system to name just a few. For this study I have not found use of all aspects of Peirce's system to contribute in any concrete way and will limit my discussion to the basic form.

30 In Peirce's semiotic, James Dean the person is the *object* and a photograph of him is a *sign* and an *icon*. The reaction to this image of him by a viewer creates a *sign* as an *interpretant*. Given that he is no longer living, I find the combined term *sign-object* appropriate usage in this case, i.e., as applied to the photograph and other images, places, and things associated with him.

31 Dean's Porsche 550 Spyder has "a life of its own" as a *sign-object*, being attached not only to Dean himself, but to Porsche AG as well. It has moved beyond being just an example of that model of Porsche. This is demonstrated by the number of detailed replicas made, full-sized and scale models. Additionally, it is difficult to find a book on the history of Porsche that does not mention Dean, his Spyder, and the events of September 30, 1955.

32 Some Deaners and serious fans will attempt to visit all locations associated with Dean and everyone of import who knew or worked with him for the purpose of videotaping and/or conducting interviews (e.g., Rees 1995).

33 Other "famous sons" of Fairmount, such as Jim Davis (creator of *Garfield*) and Phil Jones (a CBS correspondent), are given very little attention in the events of "Museum Days," although in recent years Garfield has been given additional attention as fare for the younger attendees, and his image has appeared on Fairmount's water tower, along with Dean's.

34 My usage of "transformation" is also related to Crocker's (1982, 80ff.), although I do not limit it only to his "outer" form.

35 There are, I believe, strong points of similarity between the Deaners' search for identity and contemporary movements directed toward re-creating or creating ethnic identity. With Deaners it is a matter of creating an identity since they as such do not have one *in ventre*. Suggested issues here include the role of "identity systems" and other concepts as indicated by Spicer (1971), along with Gans' "symbolic ethnicity" (1979).

36 The sponsorship of the "Museum Days" and control over the parade by the Fairmount Historical Museum, the traditional, hometown, local institution, raise the intriguing view of the parade in terms of a symbolic or dialectical opposition to the more image ("Catholic") oriented, newcomer, and "foreign" (New York) James Dean Gallery (cf. Turner and Turner 1982, 215-218).

37 Of course, many visitors, especially regulars, do not pay the admission charge. Also, during Museum Days, strict control over admission is very lax. Consequently, the estimate of 6,000 is probably off by as much as 30 percent. The gallery's owner has told me that business for the gallery increased each year from 1989 until 2005.

38 Stock suggested to me that his photographs from 1955 of Dean in the hometown setting were instrumental in Dean's and Fairmount's continuing appeal despite changes in the broader society, and in his opinion the same degree of attention would not be given to Fairmount, or perhaps, even Dean himself without those photos (interview, Fairmount, Indiana, September 29, 1991). In an interview with Robert Tysl in 1963, Stock referred to his photographic work with Dean in Fairmount as "a real collaboration…in a 'choreographic sense'" (1965, 58). In my interview, Stock said that Dean had "a fixation with the camera…. And the photos he captured of Dean in Fairmount were very carefully crafted and staged."

REFERENCES CITED

Alexander, Paul. 1994. *Boulevard of Broken Dreams: The Life, Times, and Legend of James Dean*. New York, NY: Viking.

Allen, Douglas. 2010. *James Dean: Words and Images*. n. p.

Anderson, Sam. 2010. "The James Franco Project." *New York Magazine*, June 25.

Armstrong, Robert Plant. 1975. *Wellspring: On the Myth and Source of Culture*. Berkeley: University of California Press.

Baker, J. I., ed. 2014. *James Dean: A Rebel's Life in Pictures*. Vol. 14, No. 18. New York: LIFE Books.

Barthes, Roland. 2012. *Mythologies*. Translated by Richard Howard and Annette Lavers. New York: Hill and Wang. First published 1957.

Bast, William. 1956. *James Dean, A Biography*. New York: Ballantine.

Bast, William.1975. *James Dean: Portrait of a Friend*. [Script] Final Draft (revised), Oct 27, 1975. Mimeographed. The Jozak Company.

Bast, William. 1976. *James Dean: Portrait of a Friend*. TV Movie, NBC Television.

Bast, William. 2006. *Surviving James Dean*. Fort Lee, NJ: Barricade Books.

Baylor Religion Survey. 2006. American Piety in the 21st Century: New Insights to the Depth and Complexity of Religion in the US. Waco, TX: Baylor Institute for Studies of Religion, Baylor University.

Beath, Warren. 1986. *The Death of James Dean*. New York: Grove Press, Inc.

Beath, Warren and Paula Wheeldon. 2005. *James Dean in Death: A Popular Encyclopedia of a Celebrity Phenomenon*. Jefferson, NC: McFarland and Company, Inc., Publishers.

Beck, Laura. 2014. "LOL: Justin Bieber Thinks He's James Dean." Cosmopolitan website, March 2014. Accessed March 30, 2022. https://cosmopolitan.com/entertainment/ celebs/news/a22492/justin-bieber-james-dean/.

Bellah, Robert N., Richard Madsen, William M. Sullivan, Ann Swidler, and Steven M. Tipton. 1985. *Habits of the Heart: Individualism and Commitment in American Life*. Berkeley: University of California Press.

Bongiovanni, Sylvia, ed. 1994. *We Remember Dean International* [newsletter], June/July: 18.

Boyer, G. Bruce. 2006. *Rebel Style: Cinematic Heroes of the 1950s*. New York: Assouline Publishing.

Carr, Cynthia. 2006. *Our Town: A Heartland Lynching, a Haunted Town, and the*

Hidden History of White America. New York: Crown Publishers.

Campbell, Colin. 1998. "Cult," *Encyclopedia of Religion and Society*, edited by William H. Swatos, Jr, 122-123. Walnut Creek: AltaMira Press.

Campbell, Joseph. 1968. *The Hero with a Thousand Faces*. Second edition. Princeton, NJ: Princeton University Press.

Castro, Laura L. 1991. "Larger Than Life: James Dean's Death Did a Lot for Indiana." *The Wall Street Journal*, LXXII (October 9): 1, A6.

Christophorus. 2011. "James Byron Dean Forever Young." Issue 349, April/May: 12-13.

Chronicle-Tribune. 1955. "Last Rites for James Dean Held In Fairmount; 3,000 Attend Services." Oct. 9: 1, 2. Marion, IN.

Cline, Mike, and Matt Kiefer. 2005. "Cool: James Dean, 50 Years Later." *The Star Press* and *The Chronicle-Tribune*. DVD. Indiana Films LLP Production. Muncie, IN and Marion, IN.

Cline, Mike and Sherie Smith, 2005. *James Dean: 50 Years Later*. A special publication of *The Chronicle-Tribune* and *The Star Press*, June 3. Marion, IN and Muncie, IN.

Cohan, Steven. 1997. *Masked Men: Masculinity and the Movies in the Fifties*. Bloomington and Indianapolis: Indiana University Press.

Colapietro, Vincent M. 1989. *Peirce's Approach to the Self: A Semiotic Perspective on Human Subjectivity*. Albany: State University of New York Press.

Camus, Albert. 1954. *The Rebel: An Essay on Man in Revolt*. Translated by Anthony Bower. New York: Alfred A. Knopf.

Conley, Dalton. 2009. *Elsewhere, U.S.A.* New York: Pantheon Books.

Cory, James. 1987. "Fairmount: A Fan's Notes." *Painted Bride Quarterly*, 31:30-40.

Cott, Jonathan. 1984. *Dylan*. New York: Dolphin/Doubleday and Company, Inc.

Cotter, Holland. 2009. "Art Review: The van Gogh of the Gross-Out." *The New York Times* (July 23).

Crocker, J. C. 1982. "Ceremonial Masks." In *Celebration: Studies in Festivity and Ritual*, edited by Victor Turner. Washington, DC: Smithsonian Institution Press.

Corbijn, Anton, Director. 2015. "Life." Screenplay by Luke Davies, Producers Iain Canning, *et al.*, edited by Nick Fenton. A Cinedign Release.

Courtney, James. 1990. *James Dean: Back Creek Boy*. Kentwood, MI: The GEM Group.

Dalton, David. 1974. *James Dean: The Mutant King*. San Francisco: Straight Arrow Books.

Dalton, David. 1991. *Mr. Mojo Risin': Jim Morrison, The Last Holy Fool*. New York: St. Martin's Press.

Dalton, David. 2001. "Hail Fellow Mutants!" *James Dean Gallery Newsletter*, 2 (3): 2-3, July.

Dalton, David, ed. 1991. *James Dean Revealed!* New York: Delta Books.

Dalton, David and Ron Cayen. 1984. *James Dean, American Icon*. David Loehr, Archivist. New York: St. Martin's Press.

D'Andrade, Roy. 1995. *The Development of Cognitive Anthropology*. Cambridge: Cambridge University Press.

Dante [Dante Volpe]. 1984. *The Last James Dean Book*. New York: Quill.

Daun, Till. 2015. "The Rebel." *Christophorus* 372, (3): 38-39.

Dawber, Martin. 1988. *Wish You Were Here, Jimmy Dean: James Dean Recalled in Words and Pictures*. London: Columbus Books.

Demerath, N. J. 1974. *A Tottering Transcendence: Civil vs. Cultic Aspects of the Sacred*. Indianapolis: The Bobbs-Merrill Co.

Dinerstein, Joel. 2017. *The Origins of Cool in Postwar America*. Chicago: University of Chicago Press.

Doss, Erika. 1999. *Elvis Culture: Fans, Faith and Image*. Lawrence: University Press of Kansas

Doss, Ericka. 2005. "Popular Culture Canonization: Elvis Presley as Saint and Savior." In *The Making of Saints: Contesting Sacred Ground*, edited by James F. Hopgood, 152-168. Tuscaloosa: The University of Alabama Press.

Driscoll, Sean. 2005a. "A Shy, Quiet Dean made Childhood Friends with Ease." In *James Dean: 50 Years Later*, edited by Mike Cline and Sherie Smith. Special publication of The Chronicle-Tribune and the Star Press. June 3:12. Marion, IN and Muncie, IN.

Driscoll, Sean. 2005b. "The Kid Could Do Anything He Set His Mind To." In *James Dean: 50 Years Later*, edited by Mike Cline and Sherie Smith. Special publication of The Chronicle-Tribune and the Star Press. June 3:13-15. Marion, IN and Muncie, IN.

Driscoll, Sean. 2005c. "Jimmy. Rack. Deaner. But Never James." In *James Dean: 50 Years Later*, edited by Mike Cline and Sherie Smith. Special publication of The Chronicle-Tribune and the Star Press. June 3:17. Marion, IN and Muncie, IN.

Driscoll, Sean. 2005d. "Farm Life Filled Days with Fun, Friends." In *James Dean: 50 Years Later*, edited by Mike Cline and Sherie Smith. Special publication of The Chronicle-Tribune and the Star Press. June 3: 18, 20. Marion, IN and Muncie, IN.

Driscoll, Sean. 2005e. "Class of 1949." In *James Dean: 50 Years Later*, edited by Mike Cline and Sherie Smith. Special publication of The Chronicle-Tribune and the Star Press. June 3: 22-23. Marion, IN and Muncie, IN.

Driscoll, Sean. 2005f. "Managing His Giant Image." In *James Dean: 50 Years Later*, edited by Mike Cline and Sherie Smith. Special publication of The Chronicle-Tribune and the Star Press. June 3: 24-26. Marion, IN and Muncie, IN.

Driscoll, Sean. 2005g. "He Just Had a Charisma." In *James Dean: 50 Years Later*, edited by Mike Cline and Sherie Smith. Special publication of The Chronicle-Tribune and the Star Press. June 3: 28. Marion, IN and Muncie, IN.

Driscoll, Sean. 2005h. "While he was growing up here, he was always on stage." In *James Dean: 50 Years Later*, edited by Mike Cline and Sherie Smith. Special publication of The Chronicle-Tribune and the Star Press. June 3: 38. Marion, IN and Muncie, IN.

Durkheim, Emile. 1915. *The Elementary Forms of the Religious Life*. Translated by J. W. Swain. London: George Allen and Unwin Ltd.

Eade, John and Michael J. Sallnow, eds. 1991. "Introduction." In *Contesting the Sacred: The Anthropology of Christian Pilgrimage*, edited by John Eade and Michael J. Sallnow. London: Routledge.

Eliade, Mircea. 1986. *Symbolism, the Sacred, and the Arts,* edited by Diane Apostolos-Cappadona. New York: Crossroad Publishing Co.

Elman, Di. 1990. *James Dean . . . Just Once More*. Santa Barbara, CA: Dayenu Productions.

Encinas, Lorenzo. 2008. "A su manera, defienden su sitio en la sociedad." *Milenio*. Monterrey, N. L., Mexico. 4 May. Accessed May 5, 2008. https://https://www.milenio.com/monterrey

Eylon, Dafna and Scott T. Allison. 2005. "The 'Frozen in Time' Effect in Evaluations of the Dead." *Personality and Social Psychology Bulletin* 31(12): 1708-1717.

Fairmount News, The. 1955a. "James Dean Killed as Result of California Car Accident." Special Edition: In Memory of James Dean," Vol. LXXX (Oct. 7): 1. Fairmount, IN.

Fairmount News, The. 1955b. "Fairmount Buries James Dean's Body." Vol. LXXX, No. 44 (Oct 13): 1. Fairmount, IN.

Farmer, Brett. 2000. *Spectacular Passions: Cinema, Fantasy, Gay Male Spectatorship*. Durham: Duke University Press.

Feldman, Frayda and Jörg Schellmann, eds. 1989. *Andy Warhol Prints: A Catalogue Raisonné*. Second edition. New York: Ronald Feldman Fine Arts, Inc., Editions Schellmann, and Abbeville Press.

Finkelstein, Mike. 2011. "Elizabeth Taylor's Shocking Secret about James Dean." Pop goes the Week! March 25. Accessed April 4, 2022. https://www.popgoestheweek.com/?s=elizabeth+taylor+and+james+dean/

Fisch, Max H. 1978. "Peirce's General Theory of Signs." In *Sight, Sound and Sense*, edited by Thomas A. Sebeok. Bloomington: Indiana University Press.

Furst, Peter T. 2003. *Visions of a Huichol Shaman*. Philadelphia: University of Pennsylvania Museum of Archaeology and Anthropology.

Gans, Herbert J. 1979. "Symbolic Ethnicity: The Future of Ethnic Groups and Cultures in America." *Ethnic and Racial Studies*, 2 (1): 1-20.

Gehring, Wes D. 2005. *James Dean: Rebel With a Cause*. Indianapolis: Indiana

Historical Society Press.

Gilbert, James. 1986. *A Cycle of Outrage: America's Reaction of the Juvenile Delinquent in the 1950s*. New York: Oxford University Press.

Gilmore, John. 1997. *Live Fast-Die Young: Remembering the Short Life of James Dean*. New York: Thunder's Mouth Press.

Ginsberg, Allen. 1993. *Snapshot Poetics: A Photographic Memoir of the Beat Era*. San Francisco: Chronicle Books.

Golding, Sue.1988. "James Dean: The Almost-Perfect Lesbian Hermaphrodite." In *Sight Specific: Lesbians and Representation*, edited by Lynne Fernie, Dinah Forbes and Joyce Mason. Toronto, Ontario: A Space.

Gowen, Annie. 1996. "Knowing Jimmy." *Chicago* (Feb): 64-69, 86-88.

Hahn, Cynthia. 1990. "Loca Sancta Souvenirs: Sealing the Pilgrim's Experience." In *The Blessings of Pilgrimage*, edited by Robert Ousterhout. Urbana: University of Illinois Press.

Halberstam, David. 1993. *The Fifties*. New York: Villard Books.

Hauge, Alan, Dir. 2000. *James Dean: American Legend*. Produced by Bill Barber, Frank Di Pasouale, and Jennifer Matney. VHS. Tintype Productions and the LaserFilm Co.

Hausknecht, Douglas and Kevin Casper. 1991. "The James Dean Gallery." In *Retailing by Dale M. Lewison*. Fourth ed. New York: Macmillan Publishing Co.

Hayden, Tom. 1988. *Reunion: A Memoir*. New York: Random House.

Heylin, Clinton. 1991. *Bob Dylan: Behind the Shades, a Biography*. New York: Summit Books.

Heylin, Clinton. 1996. *A Life in Stolen Moments: Bob Dylan Day by Day: 1941-1995*. New York: Schirmer Books.

Hobbes, Thomas. 1950. *Leviathan*. New York: E. P. Dutton and Co., Inc. First published 1651.

Hoberman, J. 2006. "The Spirit of '56." *The American Prospect*, 17 (10): 45-47.

Hofstede, David. 1996. *James Dean: A Bio-Bibliography*. Westport, CT: Greenwood Press.

Holley, Val. 1995. *James Dean: The Biography*. New York: St. Martin's Press.

Hoopes, James, ed. 1991. *Peirce on Signs: Writings on Semiotic by Charles Sanders Peirce*. Chapel Hill: The University of North Carolina Press.

Hopgood, James F. 1992. "What Would Durkheim Say About James Dean?" In *Sociology: A Global Perspective* by Joan Ferrante, 411-413. Belmont, CA: Wadsworth Publishing Co.

Hopgood, James F. 1997. "'Back Home in Indiana': The Semiotics of Pilgrimage and Belief in Honor of an American Icon." In *Explorations in Anthropology and Theology*, edited by Frank A. Salamone and Walter R. Adams, 191-207. Lanham,

MD: University Press of America.

Hopgood, James F. 1998a. "Another *Japanese Version*: An American Actor in Japanese Hands." In *The Social Construction of Race and Ethnicity in the United States*, edited by Joan Ferrante and Prince Brown, Jr, first edition, 470-477. New York: Longman.

Hopgood, James F. 1998b. "Inside Passages to the Self: Deaners and Pilgrimage in Fairmount." In *Wish I Were: Felt Pathways of the Self*, edited by Linda Rogers, 101-114. Madison, WI: Atwood Publishing.

Hopgood, James F. 2000. "'Back Home in Indiana': The Semiotics of Pilgrimage and Belief in Honor of an American Icon." In *Anthropology and Theology: Gods, Icons, and God-talk*, edited by Walter R. Adams and Frank A. Salamone: 337-361. Lanham, MA: University Press of America.

Hopgood, James F. 2005a. "Introduction: Saints and Saints in the Making." In *The Making of Saints: Contesting Sacred Ground*, edited by James F. Hopgood, xi-xxi. Tuscaloosa: The University of Alabama Press.

Hopgood, James F. 2005b. "Saints and Stars: Sainthood for the 21st Century." In *The Making of Saints: Contesting Sacred Ground*, edited by James F. Hopgood, 124-142. Tuscaloosa: The University of Alabama Press.

Hopgood, James F., ed. 2005. *The Making of Saints: Contesting Sacred Ground*. Tuscaloosa: The University of Alabama Press.

Howlett, John. 1975. *James Dean: A Biography*. New York: A Fireside Book.

Humphreys, Joseph.1990. *Jimmy Dean on Jimmy Dean*. London: Plexus.

Hyams, Joe and Jay Hyams. 1992. *James Dean: Little Boy Lost*. New York: Warner Books, Inc

Inglis, Fred. 2010. *A Short History of Celebrity*. Princeton, NJ: Princeton University Press.

Innis, Robert E. 2004. "The Tacit Logic of Ritual Embodiments: Rappaport and Polanyi between Thick and Thin." In *Ritual in Its Own Right*, edited by Don Handelman and Galina Lindquist. New York: Berghahn Books.

Jacoby, Susan. 2008. *The Age of American Unreason*. New York: Pantheon Books.

Jezer, Marty. 1982. *The Dark Ages: Life in the United States, 1945-1960*. Boston: South End Press.

Klapp, Orrin E. 1962. *Heroes, Villains, and Fools: The Changing American Character*. Englewood Cliffs, NJ: Prentice-Hall.

Kaye, Elizabeth. 1991. "Nureyev: Dancing in his Own Shadow," *Esquire*, (March): 122-158.

Kendall, Kenneth. 2004. "Kendall on Kendall," *The Deanzine*, Vol. 4, Issue 15 (Spring):8-10.

Kendall Letters. N.d. David Loehr Collection. Fairmount, IN.

Kipp, Rachel. 2005. "The Heart of a Racer Found Friends Nearby," In *James Dean: 50 Years Later*, edited by Mike Cline and Sherie Smith. Special publication of The Chronicle-Tribune and the Star Press. June 3: 31-32. Marion, IN and Muncie, IN.

Klawans, Stuart. 2010. "One From the Heart," *The Nation*, Vol. 290, No. 15 (April 19): 34-36.

Kluckhohn, Clyde. 1960. "Recurrent Themes in Myths and Mythmaking," In *Myth and Mythmaking*, edited by Henry A. Murray. New York: George Braziller.

Kosmin, Barry A., Egon Mayer, and Ariela Keysar. *2001. American Religious Identification Survey, 2001.* Updated December 19, 2001. New York: The Graduate Center of the City University of New York.

La Barre, Weston. 1970. *The Ghost Dance: The Origins of Religion.* New York: Dell Publishing Co.

Langer, Susanne K. 1953. *Feeling and Form: A Theory of Art.* New York: Charles Scribner's Sons.

Lewis, R. O. 1960. "James Dean Foundation Goes Broke," *Chicago Tribune*, Oct. 16: 32.

Lindholm, Charles. 1990. *Charisma.* Cambridge, MA: Basil Blackwell, Inc.

Loehr, David. 2007. "Is James Dean's Popularity Fading?" *James Dean Gallery Newsletter*, 8 (1): 2-3.

Loehr, David. 2021. *That's How Strong My Love Is: From Rock-n-Roll to James Dean.* Longmont, Colorado: Steuben Press.

Loehr, David and Joe Bills. 1999. *The James Dean Collectors Guide.* Gas City, IN: L-W Book Sales.

Kouvaros, George. 2010. *Famous Faces Yet Not Themselves: The Misfits and Icons of Postwar America.* Minneapolis: University of Minnesota Press.

Lutkehaus, Nancy C. 2008. *Margaret Mead: The Making of an American Icon.* Princeton, NJ: Princeton University Press.

MacIntosh, Jeane. 2011. "Elizabeth Taylor reveals James Dean's childhood molestation," *New York Post*, 26 March. Accessed April 4, 2022. https://nypost.com/2011/03/26/elizabeth-taylor-reveals-james-deans-childhood-molestation

Manara, Milo. 1992. *Click 2.* New York: Eurotica.

Marchand, Roland. 1982. "Visions of Classlessness, Quests for Dominion: American Popular Culture, 1945-1960," In *Reshaping America: Society and Institutions, 1945-1960*, edited by Robert A. Bremner and Gary W. Reichard. Columbus: Ohio State University Press.

Marion Leader-Tribune. 1955. "Many Pay Tribute to James Dean," Oct. 7: 1, 8. Marion, IN.

Maquet, Jacques. 1982. "The Symbolic Realm," In *On Symbols in Anthropology: Essays in Honor of Harry Hoijer, 1980*, edited by Jacques Maquet. Malibu, CA: Undena Publications.

May, Christopher. 1977. *James Dean: A Tribute to Rock's Greatest Influence*. New York: Tempest Publications, Inc.

Meroney, John. 2010. "Ronald Reagan and James Dean: Rare Video from 1954," *The Atlantic*. Accessed April 21, 2010. http://www.theatlantic.com/culture/print/2010/04/ronald-reagan-and-james-dean-rare-video-from-1954/39238/.

Michel, Jean-Baptiste, et al. 2011. "Quantitative Analysis of Culture Using Millions of Digitized Books," *Science:* 331, 176-182 (January 14).

Miller, Russell. 1997. *Magnum: Fifty Years at the Front Line of History*. New York: Grove Press.

Mishory, Matthew, director. 2012. *Joshua Tree, 1951: A Portrait of James Dean*. Iconoclastic Features, Jay-X Entertainment, and MGDB Productions.

Morgan, James. 1999. *The Distance to the Moon: A Road Trip in the American Dream*. New York: Riverhead Books.

Morin, Edgar. 2005. *The Stars*. Translated by Richard Howard. Minneapolis: University of Minnesota Press. First published 1957.

Morrissey, Steven. 1983. *James Dean is Not Dead*. Manchester, UK: Babylon Books.

Nagel, Thomas. 1993. "The Mind Wins" [review of *The Rediscovery of the Mind* by John Searle], *The New York Review of Books*, XL (5), (March 4): 37-41.

Neibaur, James L. 1989. *Tough Guy: The American Movie Macho*. Jefferson, NC and London: McFarland and Co., Publisher.

O'Hagan, Andrew. 2013. "Jack Kerouac: Crossing the Line" [review of *On the Road* (a film) and *The Voice is All: The Lonely Victory of Jack Kerouac* by Joyce Johnson] *The New York Review of Books*, March 31: 15-17.

Peirce, Charles Sanders. 1955. *Philosophical Writings of Peirce,* edited by Justus Buchler. New York: Dover Publications, Inc. First published 1940.

Peirce, Charles Sanders. 1992. "Some Consequences of Four Incapacities." In *The Essential Peirce: Selected Philosophical Writings, Volume 1 (1867-1893),* edited by Nathan Houser and Christian Kloesel. Bloomington: Indiana University Press. First published 1868.

Peirce, Charles Sanders. 1998. "Pragmatism." In *The Essential Peirce: Selected Philosophical Writings, Volume 2 (1893-1913),* edited by Peirce Edition Project, 398-433. Bloomington: Indiana University Press. First published 1907.

Pew Research Center. 2010. *Religion Among the Millennials*. Washington, D.C.: Pew Forum on Religion and Public Life.

Phillips, Lisa, *et al.* 1995. *Beat Culture and the New America: 1950-1965*. New York: Whitney Museum of American Art.

Pietrowski, Dennis, director. 2000. *James Dean–Born Cool*. VHS tape. Marcus Winslow, executive producer. Denver Rochon: Whatantics Productions and Flim Flan Films.

Pilcher, Jeffery M. 2001. *Cantinflas and the Chaos of Mexican Modernity*. Wilmington, DE: SR Books.

Pindar. 2007. *The Complete Odes*. Translated by Anthony Verity. Oxford: Oxford University Press.

PRRI Staff. 2021. "The American Religious Landscape in 2020," *PRRI* (July 8, 2021). https://www.prri.org/research/2020-census-of-american-religion/

Raglan, Lord. 1956. *The Hero: A Study in Tradition, Myth and Drama*. New York: Vintage Books. First published 1936.

Ratner-Rosenhagen, Jennifer. 2012. *American Nietzsche: A History of an Icon and His Ideas*. Chicago: University of Chicago Press.

Rees, Robert R. 1995. *James Dean's Trail: One Fan's Journey*. Published by the author, Katy, TX.

Riese, Randall. 1991. *The Unabridged James Dean: His Life and Legacy from A to Z*. Chicago: Contemporary Books.

Rifkin, Jeremy. 2009. *The Empathic Civilization: The Race to Global Consciousness in a World in Crisis*. New York: Jeremy P. Tarcher/Penguin.

Robertson, Jennifer. 1998. *Takarazuka: Sexual Politics and Popular Culture in Modern Japan*. Berkeley: University of California Press.

Roof, Wade Clark. 1999. *Spiritual Marketplace: Baby Boomers and the Remaking of American Religion*. Princeton, NJ: Princeton University Press.

Roth, Beulah and Sanford Roth. 1983. *James Dean*. Corte Madera, CA: Pomegranate Books.

Rowe, Wayne. 2010. *Zen and the Magic of Photography: Learning to See and to Be through Photography*. Santa Barbara, CA: Rocky Nook.

Rubinfien, Leo. 2009. "Another Trip Through 'The Americans.'" *Art in America* (May): 136-145, 170.

Rusiniak, Yvonne Lubov. 1996. *The Red Ribbon: James Dean in Poetry*. Fairmount, IN: Fairmount Historical Museum.

Russo, William. 2003. *The Next James Dean: Clones and Near Misses, 1955-1975*. Bloomington, IN: Xlibris Corporation.

Ryan, Colin. 2010. "Icon Spam," *European Car*, Sept, 98.

Rydell, Mark, director. 2001. *James Dean*. Israel Horovitz, writer. TNT-TV.

Sartre, Jean-Paul. 1948. *The Psychology of the Imagination*. Translated by Philip Mairet. London: Methuen & Co. First published 1946.

Sawka, Hanna Maria. 2011. *Beyond Iconic: Photographer Dennis Stock*. DVD. Port Douglas, QLD, Australia.

Scorsese, Martin. 2013. "The Persisting Vision: Reading the Language of Cinema," *The New York Review of Books*, Aug. 15: 25-27.

Scott, David. 2009. "Semiotics of the National Icon." In *Cultural Icons*, edited by Keyan

G. Tomaselli and David Scott. Walnut Creek, Ca: Left Coast Press.
Searle, John R. 1993. "The Problem of Consciousness," *Social Research*, 60 (1): 3-16.
Schatt, Roy. 1982. *James Dean: A Portrait*. New York: Delilah Books.
Schroeder, Alan. 1994. *James Dean*. New York: Chelsea House Publishers.
Shelton, Robert. 1986. *No Direction Home: The Life and Music of Bob Dylan*. New York: Beech Tree Books.
Sheridan, Michael J., director. 2005. *James Dean: Forever Young*. DVD No. 59726. Martin Sheen, narrator; Michael J. Sheridan and Kevin J. Sheridan, writers. Warner Bros. Video and Screen Icons, Inc.
Shirts, Matthew. 1989. "Socrates, Corinthians, and Democracy," *The Wilson Quarterly*, XIII (2): 119-123.
Singer, Milton. 1980. "Signs of the Self: An Exploration in Semiotic Anthropology," *American Anthropologist*, 82 (3): 485-507.
Singer, Milton. 1984. *Man's Glassy Essence: Explorations in Semiotic Anthropology*. Bloomington: Indiana University Press.
Slee, Jo. 1994. *Into the Art of Morrissey: Peepholism*. London: Sidgwick and Jackson.
Sosis, Richard. 2004. "The Adaptive Value of Religious Ritual," *American Scientist*, 92 (2): 166-172.
Spicer, Edward H. 1971. "Persistent Cultural Systems," *Science*, 174 (4011): 795-800.
Spitz, Bob. 1989. *Dylan: A Biography*. New York: W. W. Norton and Company.
St. Michael, Mick. 1989. *James Dean in His Own Words*. London/New York/Sydney: Omnibus Press.
Stern, Phil. 1993. *Phil Stern's Hollywood: Photographs, 1940-1979*. New York: Alfred A. Knopf.
Sternheimer, Karen. 2011. *Celebrity Culture and the American Dream: Stardom and Social Mobility*. New York: Routledge.
Stock, Dennis. 1978. *James Dean Revisited*. New York: The Viking Press.
Stock, Dennis. 1987. *James Dean Revisited*. San Francisco: Chronicle Books.
Stock, Dennis. 2005. *James Dean: Fifty Years Ago*. New York: Harry N. Abrams, Inc.
Swenson, Greg. 2015. *Recipes for Rebels: In the Kitchen with James Dean*. Rebel Writer Pub.
Tamarin, Jean. 2011. "Nicholas Ray, Auteur." *The Chronicle Review*, Oct, 21: B23.
Truffaut, François. 1978. *The Films in My Life*. Translated by Leonard Mayhew. New York: Simon and Schuster.
Turner, Victor W. 1969. *The Ritual Process: Structure and Anti-Structure*. Chicago: Aldine Publishing Company.
Turner, Victor and Edith Turner. 1975. *Image and Pilgrimage in Christian Culture: Anthropological Perspectives*. New York: Columbia University Press.
Turner, Victor and Edith Turner. 1982. "Religious Celebrations." In *Celebration:*

Studies in Festivity and Ritual, edited by Victor Turner. Washington, DC: Smithsonian Institution Press.

Tysl, Robert Wayne. 1965. Continuity and Evolution in a Public Symbol: An Investigation into the Creation and Communication of the James Dean Image in Mid-Century America. Ph.D. Dissertation, Michigan State University, East Lansing. Ann Arbor: University Microfilms International.

Warner, W. Lloyd. 1959. *The Living and the Dead: A Study of the Symbolic Life of Americans*. Yankee City Series, Vol. 5. New Haven: Yale University Press.

Weber, Max. 1968. *Max Weber: On Charisma and Institution Building*, edited by S. N. Eisenstadt. Chicago: University of Chicago Press.

Whitehead, John W. 2001. *Grasping for the Wind: The Search for Meaning in the 20th Century*. Grand Rapids, MI: Zondervan Publishing House.

Whitmer, Peter O. 1987. *Aquarius Revisited: Seven Who Created the Sixties Counterculture that Changed America*. New York: Macmillian Publishing Co.

Winick, Charles. 1958. *Dictionary of Anthropology*. Ames, Iowa: Littlefield, Adams and Co.

Wittgenstein, Ludwig. 1979. *Remarks on Frazer's Golden Bough*, edited by Rush Rhees. Translated by A. C. Miles. Doncaster: Brynmill Press.

Yahoo! 2005. "Netflix Survey Shows Enduring Popularity of James Dean on 50th Anniversary of His Death." *Yahoo! Finance* (online), Sept 30.

Zalov, Eric. 1999. *Refried Elvis: The Rise of the Mexican Counterculture*. Berkeley: University of California Press.

INDEX

1950s and other eras. *See* America
abstract art, 34, 114
Academy Awards nominations, 27
The Acid Song (Wainwright), 134
acting training
    Actors Studio (Method acting), 23, 26, 27, 33
    Hollywood acting school, 22, 26
Actors Studio (Method acting), 23, 26, 27, 33
adolescence
    and becoming fans/Deaners, 80, 81, 99, 113, 116, 181, 182, 188
    of Dean, 24–25
    and Dean's appeal, 18, 67, 124, 153, 196
    and identity, 64
    and juvenile delinquency concerns, 38, 214n9
    and rebel image appeal, 21, 84, 92–93, 102, 153
    and teenage markets, 11, 24, 28, 29–30
    and teen angst/idol worship, 18, 124, 131
adoration
    and art photography, 5
    and charisma, 193
    and controlling the Dean image, 45–56
    and creative expression/individualism, 105, 121, 127, 131, 203
    and early death/unfulfilled promise, 5, 18, 28, 32, 124, 195, 204
    as hero worship/myth or legend, 20, 202–203
    and interaction between self and *icon*, 109
    and the "next James Dean", 19, 30–31, 32
    of Nietzsche, 197–198
    role of place and community, 69, 109, 204, 206-
    as sacred/secular religion, 12–13, 65, 203, 209
    between secular and sacred (liminal), 14
    the self and the search for meaning, 201–204
    See also art (creative works); charisma of Dean; Deaners, creative pursuits; devotion/love; enchantment; fan clubs
advertisements, 10, 16
aesthetics theory, 154–155
affect
    affect made concrete, 158
    and creative activity, 15, 81
    and inspiration/courage/individualism, 117, 119
    in sacralization of objects, 155–156, 158–159, 190
    and sign-object-interpretant looping, 110–111, 114, 125–126
    See also emotions; transformation

"Albert" (the Professor)
　Dean, desert, Camus thought/meaning interactions of, 116
　Dean, meaning, experience and his inner self, 118–119, 120
　films, desert, politics, philosophy interactions/meaning, 116–118, 120
　impact of Dean on his behavior, 119–120
　and semiotic processes, 115, 120–121
　See also existentialism
Alexander, Paul, 18, 50–52, 77, 202–203
Allen, Douglas (artist), 124–125
Allen, Douglas, (poems and painting), 124–125
aloneness
　being alone with Dean image, 80, 94, 98, 123, 198–199
　as isolation/alienation, 116, 116–117, 119–121
　standing alone as loner/lone-wolf, 20, 55, 101, 117–118, 120, 148, 196
altars/shrines
　James Dean rooms, 69–72, 71, 100, 156–157, 192
　to Nietzsche, 198
　and self/object phenomenon, 104, 130
Altman, Robert and George W. George, 29–30
Amazing Grace, 171, 176, 177
ambiguity, 31, 52, 58, 111, 195
America
　and Deaner identity, 183, 184
　and nostalgia, 196
　secularism of, 12–13
　and *transformation*, 179, 180
America in the 1950s

The Beats/Beat movement, 34–35, 64, 120
blues and jazz, 36
conservatism in, 38–39, 207–208
icons of, 34–39
youth rebellion/alienation, 21, 37–38, 152–154
See also Beats/Beat movement
America
　in the 1950s and 1960s, 4, 11, 24
　in the 1960s, 36–38, 39
　in the 1970s and 1980s, 11, 12
　in the 1990s and American decline, 11–12
American Century, 35, 114
American dream, 42, 45, 48, 60–61
"American Gothic, II", 148
"American Pie" (song), 130–131, 135
"American Roulette" (Robertson), 135
Anderson, IN, 40, 44, 184
Andress, Ursula, 58
Angeli, Pier, 58, 76
Armstrong, Louis, 178, 201
Armstrong, Robert Plant, 154–155
art (creative works)
　and Dean as helper-consoler, 124, 130
　and devotion/love, 15, 128–130
　fetishism, 151–152, 153, 157
　and floral design (Swenson), 149–151
　as *form incarnating feeling* (aesthetics), 153–154
　"Jasper Johns, James Dean with Coca Cola", 5
　of Kenneth Kendall, 137–144, 128
　music and musicians, 130–136
　photography and photographers, 146–149
　plastic arts, 136–137
　public art, 11, 136, 137, 164

and the sacralization of ordinary
 objects, 122, 128, 155, 156–159,
 190
as self-expression, 105, 129, 203, 208
and tattoos, 122, 152–154
transformation into something sacred,
 127–128
in *WRDI* newsletter, 129
The Atlantic, 4
authenticity
of Fairmount, 206
vs. hypocrisy, 20, 35–36, 117
and individuals/individuality, 35–37,
 119, 120
of the Museum's projected image of
 Dean, 42, 48, 49, 61
and "mystique", 35–36
automobiles. *See* cars
awards (Dean's), 27, 30
Back Creek Friends Meeting
and Dean's funeral, 2
memorial service, xvii, 94, 141, 170,
 171, 192
as pilgrimage site, 164, 192–194
as visitor/tourist destination, 163
Winslow family church, 86
Barthes, Roland, 7, 147
Bast, William (Bill)
on Dean's sexuality, 58, 214-215n10
description of Fairmount, 44, 160
and genesis of image, 22
"Bazooka, Nicky", 94, 170, 172–173, 175
The Beach Boys, 135
Beath, Warren, 33, 93, 94
The Beatles, as icons, 15
The Beats/Beat movement
and 1950s culture, 34–35, 64, 120
and Deaners, 64, 80, 95, 120, 154
and the Dean image, 34, 146, 147,
 214nn8,9, 217n23
and Schatt's "Torn Sweater", 146
and Stock's Times Square photo, 147
Becker, Howard, 191
behavior
of Deaners, 119, 121–122, 125, 127–
 128
and emotion, 107
religious/devotional/cultic, 13, 14, 28,
 192
and research methods, xv
and the sacred, 14
in semiotic theory, 112, 114–115,
 121–122, 125
and *transformation*, 156
See also Deaners, creative pursuits;
 emotions; semiotics
Bellah, Robert N., 181, 189, 190
Bieber, Justin, 30
Biograph (Dylan), 132
biographies
of Bob Dylan, 131–132
*Boulevard of Broken Dreams: The Life,
 Times, and Legend of James Dean*
 (Alexander), 17–18, 18, 50–52, 77,
 202–203
Cool: James Dean, 50 Years Later,
 56–57
father-son estrangement theme in, 56
vs. hagiographies vs. hagiology, xiii,
 8, 56, 195
James Dean: A Biography (Bast), 22,
 44, 68, 213n2
James Dean: A Portrait (Schatt), 146,
 213
James Dean: A Rebel's Life in Pictures,
 (Life Books), 148
James Dean: Little Boy Lost (Hyams
 and Hyams), 25, 51, 56, 58, 213n2

James Dean: Portrait of a Friend, 215n10
James Dean (Howlett book), 102
James Dean Revisited (Stock), 146, 185, 213n2
James Dean (Rydell film), 56
The James Dean Story (Altman and George), 29, 31, 72, 214n6
of Jim Morrison (Dalton), 133
Life on Stock-Dean relationship, 23, 148
at memorial/monument to where Dean was born, 6
multitude of, 8, 128, 213n2
referenced at annual memorial service, 171
of Stock (*Beyond Iconic*), 148
Wes D. Gehring, 213n2
See also *James Dean: The Mutant King*
birthday party and weekend (February), 160–161
Blackboard Jungle, 35, 38, 113
blues and jazz (1950s), 36
Bongiovanni, Sylvia, 51, 71, 72
Boulevard of Broken Dreams: The Life, Times, and Legend of James Dean (Alexander), 17–18, 50–52, 77, 202–203
Boyd, Malcolm, 38
"boy next door" image, 25, 42, 45, 196
Brackett, Rogers, 22, 23, 26, 59
Brando, Marlon
　and Actors Studio (Method acting), 23, 34
　ambiguous sexuality/masculinity of, 17
　compared to Dean, 31–32
　as cultural icon, 19, 35, 101, 136
　Dylan song, 132
　and Kendall, 137, 138, 142, 144
　On the Waterfront, 89
　The Wild One, 32, 35, 38
Brookshire, Wilma (Smith), 55
Burghuis, Tom, 86, 99–100, 170, 171, 172*fig.*, 174, 205
busts of Dean
　by Kenneth Kendall, xv, 57, 99, 137–139, 140, 141–142, 161, 163
　and merchandising, 29
Byron, George Gordon, Lord (poet), 24
"Cal Trask", 58, 95
Campbell, Colin, 191
Campbell, Joseph, 7–8, 18
Camus, Albert, xiii, 116, 117, 118, 121
Cantinflas (Mario Fortino Alfonso Moreno Reyes), 31
Canty, Marietta, 72
cars
　in art, 136
　car runs, 33, 162, 192
　car shows, 90, 153, 161, 167, 168–169, 184, 206
　in Dean imagery, 23, 60, 118
　Dean's crash, 10, 18, 19, 113, 135
　"Mercs" and Deaners, 81, 92, 168, 169
　racing, 23, 25, 27–28, 32, 48, 58, 60, 83, 196, 203
　theft, 50
　See also Porsche
Carter, Mildred, 55
Castro, Laura (*Wall Street Journal*), 50
Catcher in the Rye, 35, 37
"Catholic" and Catholicism, 70, 88, 152, 183, 191, 218n36
Caulfield, Holden (character), 37
CBS, *News Sunday Morning*, 54, 62
CBS studios, 22

celebrity, 7–8, 28, 30, 32–33, 38, 142, 198, 202
charisma of Dean
  for Deaners, xiv, 20, 64, 82, 116, 120
  and icon status, xiii, 18
  multifaceted quality of, 207–209
  and the "next" Dean, 30
  "a radiant angel"/big personality, 139–140, 141, 144
  and sacred symbolism (collective charisma), 189–190, 193
  and screen presence, 6–7
child molestation
  of Dean, 216n17
  plaintiff, 53–54
  prosecution of Loehr and Prussack, 40–41, 52–54
Cholame
  crash on September 30, 5, 10, 18–19, 28
  in Elman poetry/writing, 98, 99
  James Dean memorial car runs, 33, 162, 192
  "James Dean Memorial Junction", 162
  monument and events at, 162
  pilgrimages to, 67, 82, 100, 102, 103, 160, 162
  as a sacred place, 157
  in St. Antoine's memoir, 5
  Seita Onishi memorial at, 6, 23, 162
  semiotics of crash-site imagery meaning, 113–115
Christ and Celebrity Gods, 38
The Chronicle of Higher Education, on Nicholas Ray, 4
cigarette imagery, 30, 46, 118, 125, 139, 147, 148, 152, 166
civil religion, 13–14
civil rights movement, 36, 39, 207

Clift, Montgomery, 17, 23, 34
clothing
  and fetishism, 151–152
  licensing and merchandising, 29, 46–47, 212n1
  motorcycle/leather jackets, 70, 71, 82, 94, 97, 138, 165, 172
  as physical transformation, 179
  and "rebel style", 20–21, 35, 101, 168–169, 179
  red jacket, 64, 124, 131, 177
  red jacket, T-shirt, blue jeans and boots as media sign/symbol, 20–21, 148
  and ritual for inspiration, 150–151
  and *transformation*, 180–183
  transformed into the sacred, 157
  white T-shirt and cigarette image, 30
  See also cigarette imagery
CNN, "James Dean: The Man, The Legend" (Larry King), 47
Cohan, Steven, 17
collecting
  and collectibles, 11, 29, 136
  the Dean of Deanabilia (Loehr), 72–74
  Deaner memorabilia, 81, 85–86, 100, 103
  as emotionally dialogical interaction, 15
  and fetishism, 151–153
  of Museum/Gallery, 128
  scrapbooks, 48, 62, 70, 71, 91, 128
collective representations (symbols)
  "collective charisma", 189
  and Fairmount's collective self-image, 57, 61, 206
  sacred vs profane, xiv, 14, 21
commerce and business of Dean image

Curtis Management, xvii, 45–46, 215n11-12
fan clubs, 33
James Dean Inc., 45–47, 212n1, 215n11
licensing and merchandising, 29, 46–47, 212n1
monetary value of memorabilia, 133, 136, 185
and near-by towns, 184–185
"Where Cool Was Born" (tourist marketing), 43–44, 165, 215n14
communitas transformation. See transformation, communitas (community)
community
    and Deaner friendships, 69, 72, 76–79, 85, 86–87, 93, 102, 119
    Deaners moving to Fairmount, 83, 86–87, 181, 182–183
    group solidarity, 69, 193–194, 205–206
    imagined, 199
    See also Fairmount, IN; individualism
consciousness
    and Dean/self metaphorical dialogue, 96, 104–105, 107, 109–110, 115, 130
    in devotee/icon relationship, 108, 120
    group, 38, 199
    and the interpretant, 110
    and introspection as amplifier in object-sign interactions, 115, 126
quale-consciousness, 109
    in religion and the arts, 155–156
conservatism, in 1950s-1960s US culture, 38–39, 207–208
"cool"
    and Dylan's rebel style, 131–132
    and rebel image, 35–36, 84, 153, 154
    in song lyrics, 135, 136
    "Where Cool Was Born" (tourist marketing), 44, 165, 215n14
Cool: James Dean, 50 Years Later, 55, 56
Cory, James, 57
Cotter, Holland, 36
Courtney, James, 124
Cox, Phyllis, 54
"cults"
    "crises", 10
    and cultic (ritualistic) behavior, 28, 192, 197
    vs. Deaners, 187, 191–192
    and Deaners, 191–193, 194, 197
    definition and characteristics, 191–192
    as pejorative, 28, 38, 190
    in print media, 29, 194
    and religiosity of celebrity adoration, 68
    and search for next Dean, 32
Curtis Management Worldwide of Indianapolis, xvii, 45–46, 215n11-12
Dalton, David
    biography of Jim Morrison, 133
    on CNN's "Larry King Live", 47
    interactions with Deaners, 49, 68, 74, 89, 105
    See also James Dean: The Mutant King
D'Andrade, Roy, 217n28
"Daniel Blum Theatre World Award for Most Promising Personalities", 27
Dante [Dante Volpe], 128
Davis, Jim (*Garfield* creator), 47, 163, 218n33
Dawber, Martin, 128, 140
Deacy, Jane (agent), 23

Deaner-fans, becoming/stories
  east coast writer("Frank"), 101–102
  I had a dream ("Jennifer"), 102
  Latin American writer ("Sofia"), 103–104
  little prince (Tom Burghuis), 99–100
  a loner ("Jeff"), 21, 101, 113, 165
  obsessed now mellowed ("Angela"), 103
  and rebel youth culture, 152–154
  west coast woman ("Judy"), 100–101
Deaners, becoming/stories
  to be part of his life ("Oliver"), 87–91, 105
  a budding actor ("Lawrence"), 74–76
  Dalton's Book (Kathie Wilson), 92–94
  Dean of Deanabilia (David Loehr), 72–74
  dreaming of Dean, 102
  existentialist ("Kenrick"), 79–81
  girl on a motorcycle (Di Elman), 97–99
  the James Dean Room (Maxine Rowland), 69–72
  journey of a Deaner ("Vince"), 76–79
  the navy vet (Phil Zeigler), 81–87
  never too young ("Billy"), 81
  passages to the self ("May"), 80, 94–96, 130, 169
  personal/family relationships, 83, 84–86, 87, 91–92, 194
  second generation Deaners, 84–86, 91–92, 181, 182–183
Deaners, characteristics of
  collecting, 67, 81, 85–86, 96, 100, 103
  vs. fans, xv–xvi, 8, 66–67, 81
  four types, 66
  lives intertwined with Dean, 73, 80, 87–91, 95–96, 105
  and obsession, 14–15, 67, 72, 88, 103, 132, 138, 206
  and pain, 35, 64, 87–88, 89, 98, 118, 124
  private devotees, 66, 93, 98, 105, 160, 191, 192, 197, 198, 202
  reading up on Dean, 50–52, 66, 84, 99, 100, 102, 103
  See also individualism
Deaners, creative pursuits
  acting/drama/films, 71–72, 79, 81, 83, 89–90, 100–101
  and arts generally, 73, 81, 88, 103
  Dean as inspiration for, 129–130
  published in *WRDI* newsletter, 123, 125, 129–130
  range and quantity of productions, 127, 128–130
  sculpting, 81, 92
  writing, 90–91, 96, 96–99, 100–101
  See also art (creative works); photography and photographers
Kenneth Kendall, artist
Deaners, group characteristics of
  as a community, 69, 193–194, 205–206
  and Dean clubs, 26, 33, 67, 71, 82
  ideology, 194–196
  "lifestyle enclave" and *communitas*, 181
  and movements, 187, 193–194, 197
  organization, 187–188, 197
  a "quasi group", 187, 199
Dean, James Byron, acting roles
  Family Theater as John the Apostle, 26
  Pepsi-Cola commercial, 25
  See the Jaguar, 26
  The Immoralist, 26, 58
  See also East of Eden; Giant; Rebel without a Cause

Dean, James Byron, as cultural "icon"
  compared to Marilyn Monroe, 24, 32, 107, 132, 136
  compared to other icons, 4, 5, 12, 133
  and "cults", 5, 18, 25–28, 32–33, 124, 195, 204
  and the culture of the 1950s, 5, 12, 34–39, 214n8
  and fetishism, 151–152
  and iconic photos, 23, 147–148
  linked through witnessing, 159
  in Mexican counter-culture, 31–32, 33–34
  and movements, 187, 197
  and Porsche, 18, 23, 29, 113–115, 136, 146, 217n31
  print media's role, 28–29
  problematical use of term, 15–16
  role of his early life and influences, 21–24
  role of tragic death in, 5, 18, 28, 32, 124, 195, 204
  role of TV and film in, 29–30
  and the search for meaning, 201–202, 208
  seeking the "next James Dean" hype, 19, 30–31, 32
  and self/Dean, 104–106
  See also America in the 1950s; Brando, Marlon; devotion/love; images of Dean; Presley, Elvis; semiotics
Dean, James Byron, the "real" person
  career trajectory, 22–24
  childhood and adolescence of, 25, 216n17
  as described by Kendall, 138–140, 142
  vs. film image, 55–56, 59, 66, 92, 100
  vs. the image constructed and reinvented by others, 200, 203, 204
  known facts of his life and death, 24–28
  memories of childhood friends, 54–60
  vs. multivocal sign and symbol, 8, 41, 57, 208–209
  "no death wish", 59–60
  "not estranged from his father", 56–57
  "not gay", 57–59
  "not a rebel", 54–56, 59, 100
  overview of life and death, 24–28
  from speculation to myth, 195
  and *transformation*, 180
Dean, Mildred (mother, née Wilson)
  background and impact on Dean, xvii, 22, 24, 25
  Dean's attachment to, 60, 179
  and Grant Memorial Park (Marion), xv, xvii, 2, 6, 164, 169
  in the mythology of Dean, 7, 19, 24, 60, 178
Dean/self. *See* self/Dean
Dean, Winton (father)
  biographical details, 22, 24, 25
  and Deaners, xvii, 86, 143, 144
  depiction of, 7, 24, 56–57, 60
  and the James Dean estate, 45, 215n12
Deanzine, 68, 86, 152, 183, 214n7
death of Dean
  in Allen art and poetry, 124–125
  and death wish claims, 59–60
  deniers of, 10, 29
  funeral, 1–3
  as journey from celebrity to "icon" status, 5, 18, 28, 32, 124, 195, 204
  "Live fast and die young", 17, 47, 59–60, 143
  in media, 10, 27–29, 59, 130
  personal reactions to, 1–3, 68, 82, 84,

140, 179
posthumous awards, 27, 30
in Roth's "Last Supper", 146
The Death of James Dean, 93
delinquency, 38, 214n9
demographics of Deaners
   Brando vs. Dean fans, 32
   France, 6
   Japan, 6, 9, 30–31, 171, 174, 176, 177, 188, 196
   Mexico, 31–32, 33–34
   older vs. younger generations, 64–65
   other nationalities, 30–31, 104, 171, 174, 188–189, 196
   in the US, 188–189, 212–213n1
   See also Onishi, Seita
DesBarres, Pamela, 68
devotion/love
   and adulation as creation of the sacred, 12–14, 197–198
   cost-benefit, 65
   and creative activity, 15, 128–130
   experienced as inexplicable, 72, 73, 82, 96, 99, 201
   extent and depth of, 6, 66, 205–206
   getting "hooked" by reading Dalton, 72, 74, 81, 83, 88, 93, 149
   and *icon*-devotee dialogue in semiotics, 96, 107, 109–110
   of Jim Morrison, 32
   meaning and semiotics, 14–15
   and Nietzsche, 197–198
   and nostalgia, 196
   and pilgrimages, 33, 160, 178–179
   a private/not group form of, 193–194
   vs. religiosity of Deaners, 8–9, 70, 193
   and the semiotics of pilgrimage, 178–179
   and tattoos, 152, 183
   and the terminology of icons, 15–16
   as worship, 67–68, 104, 209
DeWeerd, James (Rev. Dr.), 2, 25, 42, 58–59
dialogue/conversation, internal, 96, 104–105, 107, 109–110, 115, 130
DiCaprio, Leonardo, 30, 137
The Distance to the Moon, 113–114
documentaries
   ABC's *James Dean Remembered*, 40–41, 214n10
   and family/Museum control of the Dean image, 47
   James Dean, Forever Young: Rebel, Outcast, Hero, Legend, 47
   The James Dean Story, 29, 31, 72, 214n6
Durkheim, Emile, xiv, 14, 189–190
The Eagles, 135
East of Eden
   Academy Awards, 27
   in "American Roulette" (song), 135
   and "boy next door" characterization, 42
   "Cal Trask", 58, 95
   as creative inspiration, 135, 144, 149, 154
   Deaner viewings of, 71, 82, 83, 93, 94–95, 182
   and Dennis Stock, 146
   and draft deferment, 58
   impact on Kendall, 140
   memorabilia, 133
   and Mendocino pilgrimages, 67, 160, 162
   and mirroring, 105, 106
   powerful responses to, 72, 74, 80–81, 82, 87–88, 100, 102, 140, 182
   and rebel image/conflict, 20, 21, 131,

196
release of, 24
eikōn, 15
Eliade, Mircea, 155
Elman, Di (poet), 96, 97–99
emotions
   and accepting the non-rational self, 87–88, 120, 125
   and ambiguous masculinity, 31
   contempt for hypocrisy, 20, 35–36, 117
   and creative acts, 127–128, 155–156
   Dean's mother, 169
   and devotion/worship, 66, 67–68, 201
   dreaming of Dean, 102
   emotional interpretant, 113, 121
   the idea of feeling, 155–156
   in interaction with an *icon*, 15, 108–109, 117
   and meaning in mind-*icon* interaction, 105–106
   and mystique, 35–36
   and pain, 35, 64, 87–88, 89, 98, 118, 124
   in Porsche advertising, 18
   and "quale-consciousness", 109
   reactions to his death, 68, 82
   sensitivity, 17, 35, 74, 100, 103, 113
   and *transformation* through place and pilgrimage, 178–179, 206
   and "witnessing" link, 157–158
   See also devotion/love
enchantment
   and Dean's smile, 118, 124, 139–140, 142, 144
   and entanglement, 14–15
   as a helper in hard times, xvi, 72, 89–90, 93–94, 185, 196, 208
   and hope, 79, 88, 101, 107, 181, 195, 196, 208, 209
   impacts of on Deaner behavior, 13, 65, 67, 101, 139, 144, 202
   and James Dean rooms/walls, 69–72, 71, 100, 130, 156–157, 192
   and obsession, 14–15, 67–68, 72, 88, 91, 96, 103, 131–132, 137–138, 206
   sensitivity/vulnerability, 17, 31, 35, 74, 100, 103, 113, 120
   touching things and places of his, 28, 67–68, 98, 123, 141, 151, 180, 202
   and transcendence, 13, 88, 118, 198, 203, 209
   See also aloneness; charisma of Dean; inspiration; time/timelessness
Encinas, Lorenzo, 33–34
"energy"
   and the Dean phenomenon, 56, 92, 139
   and "mystique", 35
   and the sacralization of objects, 156
entanglement. *See* involvement
Essex, David, 130, 133, 134, 136
eulogies at Dean's funeral, 2, 25, 42, 175
"everywhen", 104, 185–186
existentialism
   and the 1950s, 34
   Camus, xiii, 116, 117, 118, 121
   Dean/Dean image as, 104, 147, 208, 214n9
   of Deaners, 79–81, 106, 117
   and Heidegger, 117
   and projection into an image, 17
   of Stock's photos of Dean, 147
   See also "Albert" the Professor; aloneness; emotions
Eylon, Dafna and Scott T. Allison, 28

Fairmount events
    birthday party and weekend, 160–161
    "Deaner Breakfast Club", 161
    "James Dean Spring Car Show" (June), 161
    Spring Fans Get-Together (May), 161
Fairmount Friends Church, 177
Fairmount High School and Playacres Park, xv, 163, 167, 168, 197
Fairmount Historical Museum (the Museum)
    artifacts, 42, 48, 62, 128
    attendance figures, 212–213n1
    Deaner pilgrimages to, 85
    festival weekends, 212n1
    "James Dean Birthday Weekend" event with Gallery, 61
    "James Dean Exhibit", xv, 47, 48
    as The James Dean Museum (name change), 63
    overview, 48
    personnel's harassment of Gallery owners, 50, 62
    struggle with Gallery to control Dean image, 41–42, 45, 48–50, 60–63, 218n36
    volunteering, 86, 100
    See also Fairmount Museum Days; James Dean Gallery (the Gallery)
Fairmount, IN
    as catalyst for self/Dean transformation, 106, 179–183
    and child molestation prosecution against Gallery owners, 40–41, 52–54
    collective self-image, 57, 61
    commercialization of Dean, 165
    and Deaner creative works, 90–91
    and Deaners as a community, 206–207
    Deaners moving to, 83, 86–87, 181, 182–183
    demographics and history of, 44–45
    in Di Elman poetry, 98
    insiders vs. outsiders, 40–41, 43–44, 50, 57, 61, 205, 214n10
    "it's still America there", 181
    and the journey of a Deaner, 76–79
    as pilgrimage site, 69, 71, 179–180, 185–186
    as Quaker community, 20, 25, 44–45, 88, 165
    Stock's "iconic" photos of, 23, 146
    as typical midwestern small town, 45, 47, 60–61, 75, 196, 206
Fairmount, IN, pilgrimage sites
    annual memorial services, 25, 33, 48, 86, 94, 143, 169–177, 172*fig.*
    Back Creek Friends Meeting, 164, 192–194
    and Dennis Stock photos, 23, 146, 164, 185
    James Dean Memorial Park (Main St.), xv, 137–138, 141, 163, 164*fig.*
    overview, 160–161, 162–165
    See also specific sites and events
Fairmount locals
    childhood memories of Dean, 54–56, 180
    and child molestation case against Loehr and Prussack, 40–41, 52–54
    Dean "just like us" collective self-image, 42–43, 57, 61
    and the "Gallery", 50–51
    and Dean's sexuality, 50–52, 57–61
    and the "Museum", 47–48
    vs. outsiders and "wrong" image of Dean, 40–41, 43–44, 50, 57, 61,

214n10
See also Dean, James Byron, the "real" person
Fairmount Museum Days
  activities and events overview, 166, 167–168
  alternate names for, 9, 163
  and community, 205–207
  in Deaner stories, 76
  Dean Fest (50th anniversary of death), 215n14
  economic and local significance of, 47–48, 162–163, 167–168, 184–185, 218n33,37
  "James Dean Run" and car show, 167, 168
  Museum and Gallery sales during, 185
  parades, 48, 167, 169, 183, 184, 206, 218n36
  as pilgrimage event/experience, 165–169, 183–185, 218n36
  and separations of secular-sacred/"Catholic"-Protestant, 183–184
  symbolic of another time and place, 185–186
  See also Fairmount Historical Museum (the Museum); Fairmount, IND, pilgrimage sites; memorial services, annual in Fairmont
Fairmount's other "famous/favorite sons"
  James Houston, 47
  Jim Davis (Garfield creator), 47, 163, 218n33
  and Museum Days, 166
  Phil Jones (CBS correspondent), 47, 54, 62, 218n33

fan clubs, 26, 33, 67, 71, 82
  Deanzine, 68, 86, 152, 183, 214n7
  See also WRDI
fans/fandom, 13–14, 28, 66–67, 81
  See also Deaner-fans, becoming/stories; Deaners, becoming/stories
Farmer, Brett, 17
father/parent-child conflicts
  and Deaners/fans, 21, 82–83, 87, 95, 101, 154, 194
  in Dean films, 20–21, 95, 117
  in depictions of Dean's father, 7, 24, 56–57, 60
  and Dylan, 131
  See also Dean, Winton (father)
feelings. See emotions
Ferber, Edna, 1
the "Festival". See Fairmount Museum Days
fetishism, 151–152, 153, 157
films
  and emotional connection to Dean, 179
  and the genesis of Dean's image, 24
  James Dean: American Legend (Alan Hauge), 215n14
  Life a biography of Stock-Dean relationship, 23
  as spark to become a Deaner, 67, 81–82
  watching as product of *energetic interpretant*, 113
  See also specific films
"Free, Like James Dean" (Deaner article), 91
funeral of Dean, 1–3, 25, 42, 175
The Gallery. See James Dean Gallery
Gas City, 44, 50, 63, 168, 184
General Electric Theater, 4

George, George W., 29
The Ghost Dance: The Origins of Religion, 10
Giant
   at the Academy Awards, 27, 30
   appeal of Dean's role in, 120
   cast and crew of at funeral, 1
   Deaner reactions to, 83, 84, 118, 120, 182
   and Dean's image and persona, 194–195
   iconic photographs, 23, 148, 149
   Jett Rink (character), 148, 168, 179
   outsider/loner theme in, 120, 148
   and pilgrimage, 70, 82
   striking oil scene, 153
Gilbert, James, 38, 214n9
Gilmore, John, 17
Ginsberg, Alan, 34, 35, 214n8
Ginsberg, Henry, 1
"Girl on a Motorcycle" (poem), 97–98
Google, 211n1
Gorsky, Vladimir, 137
Grant County, IN, and commercialization of Dean, 165
Grant Memorial Park (Mother's gravesite in Marion), xv, xvii, 2, 6, 164, 169
Greenberg, review in *The Nation*, 3
Grindle, Jim, 54–55, 174–175
Habits of the Heart, 190
hagiographies, xiii, 8, 56, 105, 195, 200, 213n2
Halberstam, David, 32, 35
Hall, Anthony Michael, 58
Harvey, Xen (Reverend), 2, 42, 175
Hauge, Alan (*James Dean: American Legend*), 55, 57, 58, 59, 60, 215n14
Hayden, Tom, 37–38, 39
Heckman, Mark (book illustrator), 124

Heidegger, Martin, 117
heroes
   Dean as existentialist hero, 214n9
   Dean image as, 7–8, 17, 18–20, 65, 104
   death and "crises cults", 10
   and modern celebrities, 7–8
   Rev. DeWeerd for Dean, 42
   traits, typology/subtypes, 19–20
   See also adoration; devotion/love; images of Dean
Hinkle, Bob, 171
Hobbes, Thomas, 13
Holley, Val, 213n2
Hollywood
   and celebrity, 7–8, 28, 30, 32–33, 38, 142, 198, 202
   in Deaners' experiences, 71, 89, 90, 92, 129
   in Dean mythology, 7, 19–20, 27–29, 204
   in Dean related art creation, 124, 137, 141–142
   Dean's dislike of it, 26
   at Dean's funeral, 1, 3
   and Dean's sexuality, 58, 61
   Griffith Park and Observatory pilgrimage site, 9, 82, 100, 137, 161–162
   vs. "hometown boy" Dean, 55, 61
   and pulp magazine imagery of Dean, 5, 10, 27–29, 59, 130, 213n4
   and teenage "rebel" films, 30
homosexuality
   and changing times, 11
   of Dean in biographical works, 50–52, 214-215n10
   and Deaners, 80
   and draft deferment, 57, 58, 216n16
   gay rights and Deanerism, 79

vs. girlfriends, 58
and images of Dean, 41, 43–44, 57–59, 61, 79
and the multivocality of Dean as a symbol, 61
and Reverend DeWeerd, 25, 58–59
sexual ambiguity of "macho" film icons, 17–18
and *The Immoralist*, 26
and the Winslow family's projected image of Dean, 41, 47
See also sexuality in Dean image
Hoopes, James, 115
hope, 79, 88, 101, 107, 181, 195, 196, 208, 209
Hope, Wall of, 6
Hopper, Dennis, 4, 30, 154, 171
Houston, James, 47
Howlett, John (biographer), 102
Hunt Funeral Home, 2
Hyams, Joe and Jay, 25, 51, 56, 58, 213n2
hypocrisy, 20, 35–36, 117
Icon Magazine, 15
iconography, 204
iconophilia, 203
identification, 68, 73, 78, 100, 151, 217n26
identity
and adolescence, 64
"American", 183, 184, 188
construction through Dean, 203, 218n35
of "Nicky Bazooka", 172
through pilgrimage, 183
See also self/Dean
ideology/"theology" of Deaners, 190, 193, 194–196
idol, 67, 69, 75, 83, 101, 122, 131

images of Dean
as abandoned by father, 7, 24, 56–57, 60
academic classifications of, 17–20
as anti-establishment rebel, 6, 20–21, 29–30, 39, 59, 67, 196, 215n11
and cars, 18, 27–28, 60, 118, 136
changing over time, 10–12
and cigarettes, 30, 46, 118, 125, 139, 147, 148, 152, 166
and conventionality vs. unconventionality, 18, 35–36, 194, 198
"cool", 35–36, 55, 56, 84, 135–136, 153, 154, 165, 215n14
and creative activity, 129, 131–132, 137
and Deaner ideology, 194–196
and eikōn, 15
Gallery-Museum struggle for control over, xvii, 41–42, 45–50, 60–63, 218n36
genesis of, xiv, 6, 21–24
and hero mythology, 7–8, 17, 18–20, 65, 104
and his struggles, 7, 18, 20, 24, 129, 133, 196, 200, 203, 204, 207–208
as *icon*, *index* and *symbol*, 109
as liminal, 14, 20
"Live fast and die young", 17–18, 47, 59–60, 143
"local boy next door/just like us", 25, 42, 45, 54–56, 60, 196
and look-alikes, xvi, 30, 74, 168–169, 171, 179, 207
many-layered, 20–22, 28, 45
as a modern hero, 7–8, 18–20
and "mystique", 35–36
as outsider/loner, 120, 148, 203
as projections of the self/multifaceted,

244

17, 45, 64, 95, 98, 208–209, 217n26
vs. "reality", 66, 92
and rock and roll, 29, 35
and the sacred, 127, 170, 183, 192, 195
as savior, role model, 64–65, 67, 68, 102, 140, 180
scrapbooks, 48, 62, 70, 71, 91, 128
and semiotics, 108–110, 112–113, 125, 217n30
See also authenticity; Deaners, becoming/stories; Fairmount, IND; Fairmount locals; Kendall, Kenneth, artist; mirroring/identification; motorcycles; semiotics; photography and photographers; Dean, James Byron, as cultural "icon"
imagined community, 199
"Immaculate Heart James Dean Appreciation Society", 26
The Immoralist, 26, 58
immortality, 59, 104, 122, 125, 164, 200
Indian Motorcycle shop, xiv, 163
individualism
 and authenticity, 35, 91, 101, 119, 120
 and Deaner ideology/"theology", 190, 193, 196
 vs. Deaners as a "quasi" group, 69, 193–194, 197, 198–199, 206, 209
 "expressive", 189
 and independent spirits, 19, 83
 interaction with an *icon* (sign-object), 112, 116–117, 120–121
 and rebel charisma, 207–208
 and the sacrality of secular objects, 156–157, 158, 190, 193
 in self and search for meaning, 203, 205, 208–209
 and the semiotics of pilgrimage, 178–183

inspiration
 to be and develop oneself, 154, 202–204, 208
 of being mesmerized, blown-over, 82–83
 for Bob Dylan, 131–132
 Dean as for Deaners, 101, 103, 129–130
 to live authentically/free, 101
 as a role model for creating/living, 68–69, 75, 81, 103, 105, 129–130, 149–151, 196
 and the sacred, 13, 189
interactions
 vs. collective representations, 14, 21, 57, 189, 206
 of devotee with *icon* (symbol), xiv, 15, 106, 178
 emotionally dialogical quality of, 15, 198
 internal dialogues, 96, 104–105, 107, 109–110, 115, 130
 See also "Albert" (the Professor); aloneness
interchange. *See* mirroring/identification
internal conversation/dialogue
 in Deaner self/Dean interactions, 96, 104–105, 107, 109–110, 115, 130
 in Peirce's semiotic theory, 107, 110, 112, 115, 122
 See also self/Dean
interpretants
 and "Albert", 115, 121
 in art and the sacred, 121–122, 125
 and complex of meanings derived from one image, 113–115
 and Dean's sexuality, 41
 and Dean's wrecked Porsche, 114

emotional, energetic, and *logical,* 112–113, 121
  in the Gallery-Museum struggle for control of Dean image, 41
  motifs in poems, 125
  and Peirce vs. Roy D'Andrade, 217n28
  in "rebel" pose poster and Deaner reaction, 112
  and the sign-object, 217n30
  "tone" and "attitude" and behavior, 125
  in the triadic semiotic, 109–111
  in the viewing a wrecked Porsche photo, 114–115
 involvement
  being intertwined with Dean, 73, 80, 87–91, 95–96, 105
  collecting, 67, 81, 85–86, 96, 100, 103, 151–153
  vs. enchantment, 14–15
  moving to Fairmount, 83, 86–87, 181, 182–183
  See also collecting; Deaners, characteristics of; Deaners, creative pursuits; enchantment; Kenneth Kendall, artist; pilgrimages
Isaacs, Marlene, 169
Jackson, Barbara Jane (Middleton), 55
Jackson, Michael, 33, 201, 212n1
Jagger, Mick, 31, 133, 136
James Dean: A Biography (Howlett), 102
James Dean: American Legend (Hauge), 55, 57, 58, 59, 60, 215n14
James Dean: A Tribute to Rock's Greatest Influence (magazine), 130
James Dean: Back Creek Boy (Courtney and Heckman), 124
James Dean: Little Boy Lost, 51, 213n2
  See also Hyams, Joe and Jay

James Dean: The Mutant King
  disapproval of, 52, 70, 100
  on homosexuality and child molestation prosecutions, 40–41, 52
  as the "James Dean bible", 74, 90, 93, 94, 213n2
  as most-read book for Deaners, 77, 80, 100
  reading of excerpts at annual memorial service, 171
  reading and getting "hooked", 72, 74, 77, 81, 83, 88, 93, 149
  and self/Dean mirroring, 72–73, 96, 103, 104–105
James Dean: Portrait of a Friend (Bast), 58
James Dean: Race with Destiny, 143–144
  See also Live Fast, Die Young
"James Dean: The Man, The Legend" (Larry King-CNN), 47
James Dean, A Biography (Bast), 22, 44, 68, 213n2
James Dean—Born Cool, 215n14
"James Dean" (Eagles song), 135
James Dean Festival Weekend. *See* Fairmount Museum Days
James Dean Gallery (the Gallery)
  as base for sociality, 206
  birthday party, 160–161
  and *communitas transformation*, 181, 182, 183
  and Dean-Deaner self-discovery journey, 76–79
  as a Deaner "hangout", 50, 60
  "James Dean Birthday Weekend" event with Museum, 61
  "Kenneth Kendall Room", 128
  as outside/corrupting influence,

40–41, 43–44, 50, 57, 61, 205, 214n10
regulars, 143
retail sales figures for, 185
souvenir bricks and certificate, 163
struggle with Museum over Dean image, 41–44, 45, 48–50, 60–63
James Dean Gallery Newsletter (Loehr), 6–7, 63
James Dean Inc., 45–47, 212n1, 215n11
James Dean Is Not Dead (Morrissey), 133
James Dean...Just Once More (Elman), 97–99
James Dean Memorial Foundation, 33, 214n6
"James Dean Memorial Junction" (Cholame), 162
James Dean Memorial Park, xv, 137–138, 141, 163, 164*fig.*
The James Dean Museum. *See* Fairmount Historical Museum (the Museum)
James Dean Remembered (documentary), 214n10
"James Dean Remembered Fan Club", 183, 189
See also WRDI
James Dean rooms/walls, 69–72, 71, 100, 130, 156–157, 192
James Dean (Rydell film), 56
James Dean stamp, 162, 165
The James Dean Story (Altman and George), 29, 31, 72, 214n6
"James Dean Walking Tour" (Fairmount), 183
"James Dean Walking Tour" (NYC), 73, 93, 153, 161
"Jimmy Dean Days", 48, 163, 166

Jimmy Dean Days. *See* Fairmount Museum Days
Joel, Billy, 133, 136
John, Elton, 133, 136
Johnson, Ray, art exhibit, 5
Johnson, Ray (artist), 5, 136
Jones, Phil (CBS correspondent), 47, 54, 62, 218n33
Joshua Tree, 1951: A Portrait of James Dean, 18
Kahanamoku, Duke Paoa Kahinu Mokoe Hulikohola, as local icon, 15–16
Kazan, Elia, 27, 92
Kendall, Kenneth, artist
  annual Dean birthday party, 141, 192
  and Brando, 142
  bust of Dean at Griffith Park, 161–162
  capturing the "radiant angel", 109, 139, 141, 144
  as a Deaner and Dean celebrity "Jimmy's gift", 141, 142–143
  and Deaners, 103, 181
  Dean life mask, 142
  Dean's impact on, 139–140, 141
  on Dean's sculpting, 142
  on Dean's smile, 139–140, 142, 144
  description of Dean, 138–139
  films and subject matter, 137
  homages to Dean, 141
  meeting with Dean, 137, 138–139, 138–144
  mirroring with Dean, 96
  obsession with Dean, 138
  telling and retelling the first meeting, 138–140, 141
  and "witnessing", 156
Kendall, Kenneth, artworks
  busts of Dean, xv, 57, 137–138, 140,

163, 164*fig.*
"Byron", 144
"The Dead Toreador", 144, 145*fig.*
"Dean as Malcolm", 144
"Giant", 144, 145*fig.*
"Hamlet", 144
"Jacob Wrestles With an Angel", 144
"New York", 144
"The Torn Poster", 144
working method and genre, 144
Kennedy
John F., 39, 71
Robert F., 117, 121
Kerouac, Jack, 34, 35, 37, 38, 64, 133
King, Larry, "James Dean: The Man, The Legend" (CNN), 47
Kinnaman, Mark, xvii, 177, 182–183
Klapp, Orrin E., 18–19
Klawans, Stuart, review in *The Nation*, 3
Kluckhohn, Clyde, 18
Knock on Any Door (Ray), 60
Kovaleski, Jeff, 53
Kruse Museum Complex, 41
La Barre, Weston, 10
Landau, Martin, 47, 148
Langer, Susanne, 127, 155–156
"Late Night with Jimmy Fallon" (NBC), 4
leather jackets, and Deaners, 82
legend, 135, 170, 203, 215n14
and celebrity, 7, 16
and Dean as hero, 18–19
and Dean's life story, 22–24
James Dean: American Legend (Alan Hauge film), 58, 59, 215n14
"James Dean: The Man, The Legend" (Larry King-CNN), 47
James Dean, Forever Young: Rebel, Outcast, Hero, Legend (documentary), 47

in poetry and songs, 122, 123, 135
role of Deaners in creating, 170, 202–203
Lewis, Bill, 71, 214n7
Life, "iconic" Dean images in, 23
Life (film), 23
lifestyle, 7–8, 31, 34, 37, 53, 125, 130, 133, 134, 181, 189
"lifestyle enclave", 181, 189
and personas of famous musicians, 134
"Lifestyles of the Rich and Famous", 8
liminality
of Deaner phenomenon, 193, 203
in Deaner worship, 14
in films, 20
and *transformation*, 178
"Little Bastard", 18, 28
"Little Deuce Coupe", 135
The Little Prince, 99–100, 151, 171, 177
"Live Fast and die young", 47, 59–60
Live Fast-Die Young: Remembering the Short Life of James Dean, 17–18, 143–144
loca sancta souvenirs (medieval), 157
Loehr, David, xvi, xviii, xix
archives, 9, 67–68, 102
author's interviews with, 216n19
candlelight vigil to cemetery event, 177
car theft allegation against, 50
child molestation case against, 40–41, 52–54
child molestation plaintiff, 53–54
collection, 129
"Dean of Deanabilia" and collection, 49, 63, 72–74, 96
Dean events spearheaded by, 161
and Dean's rebel image, 59

on declining popularity of Dean, 6–7, 67
as definitive Deaner, 8
"Gallery" establishment, moves and closure, 41, 43, 49–50, 62–63
individuality vs. group dynamic, 198–199, 205, 206
and "James Dean, American Icon", 216n20
"James Dean Walking Tour" (in NYC), 73, 93, 153, 161
letters from Kendall, 138, 139, 140
Marion monolith memorial design, 6, 165
"mirroring"/identification with Dean, 96
and other Deaners, 69, 76, 77, 81, 153, 182, 183
publishes memoirs, 216n19
seen as outsider/corrupting influence sexuality issue, 43–44, 50, 57, 61
sexuality and anti-gay harassment of, 52–53, 62
loneliness, 29, 80, 98, 104, 116, 119, 120–121
See also aloneness
loners, 20, 55, 101, 117, 118, 120, 148, 196
look-alikes, xvi, 30, 74, 168–169, 171, 179, 207
Lopez, Perry, 175
Los Angeles
as Deaner pilgrimage site (Rebel filming), xvi, 102, 103, 160, 161–162
and Deaners' acting, 72, 137
Dean's life in, 22, 25–26, 73
Kendall's Dean birthday party, 141, 192
murals of Dean in, 137
Lowe, Arthur Jr., 33
Lutkehaus, Nancy C., 15
McLean, Don ("American Pie"), 130–131, 135
Mad magazine, 36
Madonna, 133, 136
magazines
  Automobile, 5
  Christophorus (devoted to Porsche things), 18
  and Dean's icon status, 10, 27–29, 59, 130
  Forbes, 211n1, 212n1
  Life, 23, 28
  Mad, 36
  Motion Picture, Modern Screen, and *Photoplay* (movie star pulp magazine), 28
  People Weekly, 211–212n1
  Saturday Review, 28
  stock photos in, 5
  teen genre, 11
  Time, on Dean teenage craze, 28
magic. *See* enchantment
Man's Glassy Essence (Singer), 178
Marchand, Roland, 21, 35–36
Marfa, Texas, 27
Marion Chronicle-Tribune, 53, 174
Marion, IN
  and the annual Memorial Service, 174, 175
  cemetery, xvii
  and Deaner pilgrimages, 77, 103, 177
  Dean's birth, 24, 165
  economic impact of Fairmount on, 165, 184
  Grant Memorial Park/mother's grave, xv, xvii, 2, 6, 164, 169
  memorial commemorating James

Dean's birth, 5–6
relationships of town and locals to Fairmount, 44, 182, 184, 215n14
Masked Men, 17
"May", 80, 94–96, 130, 169
May, Christopher, 130
Mazzola, Frank, 47, 171
Mead, Margaret, as icon, 15
meaning
  and consciousness in semiotic analysis, 108–109
  and Dean's multivocality as a *sign*, 8, 41, 57, 61
  and emotion/affect, 158, 178
  and Fairmount, xiv, 162, 185–186, 206
  Gallery-Museum struggle for control over, xvii, 41–42, 45–50, 60–63, 218n36
  and the interaction of being, emotion, thought and *sign-object/icon* (the Professor), 120–121
  and liminality, 14
  and the problematic terminology of "icon", 15–16, 24
  and the *Rebel* image, 20–21
  and ritual "witnessing" through objects, 156–157
  of the self and interaction with the *sign-object/icon*, 126, 179, 201–202, 203, 208
  and the semiotics of viewing a wrecked Porsche photo, 113–115
Mellencamp, John Cougar, 133, 136
memorabilia
  business and commercial aspects, 48, 133, 136, 185, 212n1
  collecting by Deaners, xvi, 15, 67, 72–74, 81, 85–86, 100, 101, 102
  and "cult" phenomena, 32
  and Deaner community, 180–181
  and fetishism, 151–152, 157
  in Museum and Gallery collections and gift shops, 48, 49
  and the "Rebel" image, 148–149
  sacralized, 122, 128, 154–155, 156–159, 190
  transformation from ordinary objects to sacred, 122, 128, 154–155, 156–159, 190
  transformed role of in Deaner behavior and ritual, 121–122
memorials
  monolith commemorating Dean's birth (Marion), 5–6
  Seita Onishi's at Cholame crash site, 6
  "Wall of Hope" (Lacoste, France), 6
memorial services, annual in Fairmount
  and Adeline Nall, 99–100, 170
  attendees, speakers, special guests, and emcees, 169–171, 172
  candlelight vigil ritual, 3, 177, 192
  church service format and ritual of, 170, 171
  and *communitas transformation*, 180
  description of 2005 service, 174–175
  format, 170–171
  the Grand Parade, 167, 168–169, 183, 184
  gravesite offerings, 172, 173*fig.*, 176
  "Nicky Bazooka", 170, 172–173, 175
  Phil Zeigler, 171
  procession to grave and rituals, 94, 170, 172, 175, 177, 192, 194, 198
  secular vs. sacred/ "Catholic" vs. Protestant, 183–184
  and Tom Burghuis, 170
Mendocino, 67, 160, 162

merchandising and licensing, 29, 46–47, 211n1
"Mercs" and Deaners, 81, 92, 168, 169
Meroney, John, 4
method acting, 150
methodology, 9–16
millennial generation, and religion, 13
Mineo, Sal, 3, 30
"mirror image", 95, 98
mirroring/identification
   of Dean by Bob Dylan, 131
   defined, 98
   through emotion-mind-icon interaction, 105–106
   in famous songs, 134
   and *James Dean: The Mutant King*, 72–73, 96, 103, 104–105
   mirroring the self in creative expression, 105–106, 175
   and parent-child conflicts, 95
   self/Dean, Dean as role model, 64–65, 67, 68, 102, 180
   the self as Dean and vice versa, 84–85, 94–96, 97–99, 101–102
   and tragedy/trauma, 88–89, 93–94
Mizui, Yasuo (sculptor of "Wall of Hope"), 6
Monroe, Marilyn, 24, 32, 132, 136
Moore, Terry, 58
Morgan, James, 113–114
Morrison, Jim, 32, 133, 133–134, 212n1
motorcycles
   accident, 93–94
   in Dean events, 94, 165, 166, 170, 172
   and Dean image, 32
   and Dean pilgrimage/Fairmount visitor sites, xiv, 48, 55
   Dean's Czech Whizzer, 55
   and Dylan's "chrome horse", 132
   Indian Motorcycle shop, xiv, 163
   motorcycle jackets, 70, 71, 82, 172
   in songs and poetry of Dean, 97–98, 132
   in stories of Dean's life, 55, 60
murals, 11, 130, 137, 164
Museum. *See* Fairmount Historical Museum
Museum Days. *See* Fairmount Museum Days
music and musicians
   Bob Dylan, 130–132
   other famous musicians inspired by Dean, 130, 133
"mystique", 35–36
myth/mythology
   and cultural "icons", 24
   and the Deaner phenomenon, 64–65, 104, 126, 179, 195, 202, 204
   and Dean as modern hero, 7–8, 18–20
   and modern media, 7
   and the search for the "next Dean", 31
Mythologies (Barthes), 7
Nall, Adeline
   death and memorial for, 86, 143
   early influence on Dean, xvi, 22, 25
   and the genesis of the Dean image, 22
   interactions with fans and interviewers, xvii, 85, 99–100, 170, 171
   memorial service emcee, xvii, 86, 170
   role in the community, 33, 205
The Nation, review of *Greenberg*, 3
NBC, "Late Night with Jimmy Fallon", 4
Neibaur, James L., 17
New York City
   Broadway, 26
   and Dean's career, 22, 23
   and "Dean wannabes", 95

"iconic" Stock photographs of Dean in, 23
See also Brackett, Rogers
New York Times, 36
The Next James Dean: Clones and Near Misses, 1955-1975, 30
Nicholas Ray (Raymond Nicholas Kienzle Jr.), in The Chronicle of Higher Education, 4
"Nicky Bazooka", 94, 170, 172–173, 175
Nietzsche, 197–198
nostalgia, and the 1950s, 196
objects
    commercial value of, 46
    considered sacred, 157
    and fetishism, 151–152, 153, 157
    and *form incarnating feeling*, 155
    as links/containers of the sacred, 158
    and meaning through affect made concrete, 158
    postcards, 141, 153
    sacralization of, 122, 128, 154–155, 156–159, 190
    and viewer/possessor as participant, 154–155
    and "witnessing", 156, 157–159
    See also posters
object-sign, 114, 115
object-sign-interpretant triadic interaction processes, 109–112
objects and places, touching his things/being where he had been, 28, 67–68, 98, 123, 141, 151, 180, 202
obsession, 14–15, 67–68, 72, 88, 91, 96, 103, 131–132, 137–138, 206
"130", on Porsche 550 Spyder, 27
Onishi, Seita
    collector of Roth's photographs, 23–24
    memorials to Dean ("Wall of Hope" and Cholame monument), 6, 24, 162
On the Road, 34, 38
On the Waterfront, 89
Park Cemetery (Fairmount), Dean's grave, 183, 192, 194, 198, 205
    and the annual memorial service, 170, 172–173, 175–178, 192
    burial, 2–3, 19
    emotional and sacred connections of, 178–179, 183, 192, 198, 205–206
    in Fairmount tourist marketing, xv
    images and relics of, 71, 157
    Kendall's bronze bust, 57, 137, 140, 163
    location of Deaner Phil Zeigler's ashes, 86
    and pilgrimage rituals and offerings at, 70, 76, 94, 166, 167fig., 170
    pilgrimages to, 76, 84–85, 99, 132
    and Winton Dean, xvii
Payne, David (attorney), 53
Payne, Jerry, 56
Peacock, Joan (née Winslow), xvii, 25, 45, 47, 56, 85, 215n12
Peirce, Charles Sanders, 14, 107–108, 108–115, 121, 125
    See also semiotics
persona
    and Deaner phenomena, 113, 194, 195
    development and transformation of, 8, 21, 22–24, 26, 194–195
    and film vs. person, 196
    as inspiration, 39, 132, 134
    and lifestyle, 134
    and Porsche image, 18
    as rebel, 59
    and rebel image, 19–21, 29–30, 208–209

and self/icon interaction, 109
and social movements, 193
Pew Research Center, 13
photography and photographers
   Dennis Stock, 4–5, 146
   James Dean: A Rebel's Life in Pictures, 148
   Phil Stern, 23, 148
   photos from films, 148, 149
   Roy Schatt, 4–5, 146
   Sanford Roth, 4–5, 146
   and *satori* (enlightenment) concept, 147
photography and photographers, iconic photographs
   "The Crucifixion", 148
   "Last Supper", 146
   "The Loner", 148
   "The Outsider", 148
   "Rebel", 148–149
pilgrimages
   of Dylan to Fairmount, 132
   to Fairmount, 33, 70–71, 84–85, 92, 94, 95, 99, 102, 103
   to Fairmount as *logical interpretant*, 113
   to film sites, 67, 82, 160, 162
   and intermixing of time and space, 98, 179–180, 185–186
   to Kendall's studio, 141
   the memorial service, 33, 169–177
   and Morrissey's "Suedehead", 132–133
   and self/Dean mirroring/transformation, 106
   semiotics of, 14–15, 177–183, 178–183
pilgrimage sites
   Back Creek Friends Meeting, 164, 192–194
   Cholame, 67, 82, 100, 102, 160, 162
   Fairmount High School and Playacres Park, xv, 163, 167, 168, 197
   Griffith Park and Observatory, LA (location of *Rebel* scenes), 9, 82, 100, 137, 161–162
   "James Dean Walk" (NYC), 73, 93, 153, 161
   Los Angeles, xvi, 160, 161, 162
   Marfa, Texas, 27, 67, 82, 148, 160, 162, 211n1
   Marion, 77, 103, 164–165, 177
   Mendocino, CA (Eden filming), 67, 160, 162
   overview of, 160–165
   Park Cemetery, Fairmount, 94, 172
   poetic reactions to, 97–99
   Winslow farm, 70–85, 99, 123–124, 157
Pinterest, 129, 212n1
places and objects, touching his things and places, 28, 67–68, 98, 123, 141, 151, 180, 202
Playacres Park and Fairmount High School, xv, 163, 167, 168, 197
poems
   "Anniversary" (visit to Fairmount), 123, 123–124
   "Collectors Illustrated Poetry", 129
   "Communion" (Dean and the sacred), 124
   "James Dean: Actor" (poems and illustrations), 124
   motifs as *interpretants* in, 122, 125
   "On the Marquee" (Dean as helper), 124
   published in *WRDI* newsletter, 122–123, 125
   The Red Ribbon: James Dean in Poetry (Rusiniak), 123–124
poetry, *sign-object* interaction with

interpretant in, 122, 125
"Pop Art", 5, 136
popularity of Dean over time, 211–212n1
  in decline since 2005, 6–7, 208
  an enduring legacy, 3–7
  generational and technological changes, 11–12
  and second generation Deaners, 12, 81
  vagaries in American popular culture, 204–205
Porsche
  550 Spyder, 18, 27–28, 136, 146, 168, 184, 217n31
  at Deaner events, 168, 184
  image and imagery of, 18, 23, 29, 135, 136, 146, 217n31
  "Little Bastard", 18, 28
  wrecked, semiotics of, 113–115
  See also death of Dean
posters
  as artist creation, 128, 144
  and authenticity, 152
  "Boulevard of Broken Dreams" (Helnwein), 128
  and Deaners, 64, 68, 84, 91, 92–93, 96, 153
  in Museum's collection, 48
  and the proliferation of Dean memorabilia, 11, 29
  and the rebel image, 148, 169
  and the semiotics of viewing, 112–113
  as spark for becoming Deaner, 67, 68, 93
Presley, Elvis
  and the 1950s era, 35, 84
  and Deaners, 84, 113
  Dean's influence on, 130–131, 135
  as icon, xiii, 15, 24, 29, 35
  as the jester in "American Pie", 135
  and Jim Morrison, 133
  and Mexican counter-culture, 31–32
  as myth/icon, 24
  as a "next" Dean or Dean of rock and roll, 30, 32
  popularity compared to Dean, 74, 201, 211–212n1
Prussack, Lenny
  anti-gay harassment of, 52–53, 62
  business "Rebel Rebel", 61
  child molestation prosecution of, 40, 52–54
  as Deaner, xix, 40
  labelled outsider/corrupting influence, 40–41, 43–44
  as Loehr's partner, xviii, 43, 49, 76, 77, 182, 205
  in memorial processions, 177, 192
  "Shirts by Lenny", 63
psychology and psychoanalysis, 36, 130, 134, 152
public art, 11, 136, 137, 164
Public Religion Research Institute, 13
Pulley, Bob, xvii, 8, 55, 59, 171, 174
Quakerism, and Fairmount, 20, 25, 44–45, 88, 165
"quale-consciousness", 109
quasi-movement, 187, 199
quasi-sacred space, 156
Raglan, Lord, 7–8
  hero myth and typology (subtypes), 18–19
Ratner-Rosenhagen, Jennifer, 197–198
Ray, Nick (director), 4, 60, 92, 146
Reagan, Ronald, vs. James Dean, 4, 12
rebel image
  and the 1950s and the Beats, 34–39
  and authenticity, 35–37

and Dean, 20–21, 29–30, 148, 169
vs. kid next door image, 54–56, 59
and rock and roll, 29, 38, 130–131, 133, 134–136, 207
tokens of the type, 21
See also rock and roll
"Rebel Rebel", 61
"rebel style"
and clothing, 20–21, 35, 64, 101, 148, 150, 151, 168–169, 179
influence on Dylan, 131–132
rebel pose, 46, 75, 112, 113, 149, 152
See also clothing
"Rebel without a Band", Dean as a rock star, 90
Rebel Without a Cause
Academy Awards, 27
and Dean's image, 20–21
and desire to possess Dean, 153
existentialist and Beat elements in, 214n9
"favorite" Dean film, 93
iconic photographs from, 148–149
identification with, 102
impact on Jim Morrison, 133
and juvenile delinquency fears, 38, 214n9
in "Little Deuce Coupe", 134
and memorial in Marion, 6
and physical *transformation*, 179
vs. the "real" Dean, 55–56, 59, 100, 182
and rebel style, 101, 131–132, 151
in review of *Greenberg*, 3
semiotics of Deaner reactions to, 112, 117–118
spark to connect with people and things Dean related, 71–72, 81–83, 149
as spark for obsession, 91–92, 103–104
and youth alienation, 37
Recipes for Rebels: In the Kitchen with James Dean, 151
relics, 15, 152
religious belief
combinative in America, 13
and cults, 191–192
of Dean, 42
as innate, 13
See also cults; sacred, the
Remembering James Dean. See Fairmount Museum Days
renewal and transformation, 105–106
research methodology
and the academic literature, 9–10
breadth and depth of material on Dean, 10–11
interviews, xv, xvii
participant-observation and fieldwork, 9–10, 45, 94–95, 143–144
use of "texts", 195
Rifkin, Jeremy, 37
rituals
the "costly signaling theory" of, 193
and cultic behavior, 28, 191–192, 197
and emotion, 179
and fetishism, 152, 157
in the making art, 137, 150–151
public vs. private, 160, 192, 197–199
and the sacralization of objects, 121–122, 128
and the separation of secular and sacred, 183–184
and the suspension of time and place, 104–105, 185–186
and "witnessing", 156, 157–159
See also memorial services, annual in Fairmount

Robertson, Robbie, 133, 135
Robin Hood, 19
Robiscoe, James, 123–124
"Rock On" (song), 134, 136
rock and roll
  and the 1950s, 35
  and Deaners, 64, 85–86, 90, 93, 120
  and the Dean image, 29, 130–131, 133
  and Dean in song lyrics, 134–136
  icons and the construction of icons, 15, 30, 31, 32
  and the rebel image, 38, 207
Rolling Stones, as icons, 15
"Ronald Reagan and James Dean: Rare Video from 1954", 4
Rosenman, Leonard (composer), 59, 214n10
Roth, Sanford (photographer)
  last scene in *Giant*, 146
  and the making of Dean's image, 4–5, 23–24
  and Siamese cat imagery, 132
  "The Last Supper", 146
Rowe, Wayne, 147
Rowland, Maxine, 69–72, 93, 143
Rusiniak, Yvonne Lubov, 123–124
Russell, Jane, 4
Rust, Harrold, 55
Rydell, Mark, 47, 56
sacred, the
  and adoration as a secular religion, 12–13, 65, 203, 209
  and art, 127–128, 132, 137, 155–159
  and collective charisma, 189–190, 193
  and Deaner ideology/"theology", 195
  and fetishism, 151–152, 157
  and images of Dean, 127, 170, 183, 192, 195
  and pilgrimage sites, xiv–xv, 19, 157, 164–165, 178, 183, 185–186
  vs. secular and liminality, xiv, 12–14, 178, 193, 203
  in the semiotics of art, 121–125
  time and space, 186
  the transformation of ordinary objects into, 122, 128, 154–155, 156–159, 190
  See also altars/shrines; rituals; transformation
sacrifice, 152–154, 193–194
Saint Antoine, on Dean's last days, 5
Salinas, 27
Salinger, J.D., *Catcher in the Rye*, 35, 37
Santa Monica, 22, 24, 25, 146
Sartre, Jean-Paul, and projection into an image, 17
Schatt, Roy (photographer), 4–5
  images in poetry book, 125
  James Dean: A Portrait, 146, 213n2
  "The Photographer", 146
  "sweater series", 23
  "The Photographer", 23, 146
  "Torn Sweater", 23, 146, 149, 174
Scorsese, Martin, 204
See the Jaguar (Broadway play), 26
self/Dean
  art "incarnating feeling", 154–155
  being part of Dean's life, 87–91, 104–106
  through creative pursuits/self-expression/blending their lives with his, 105–106
  Deanerism as self-discovery/self-transformation, 64, 65, 94–96
  in Deaner poetry, 97–99, 122–124
  and Dean as icon, 104
  and devotion/adoration, 202–204
  dialogue in poetry, 122–124

and dissolution of self/other, 106
through Fairmount, 209
through family, 105
through films, 105, 106
interactions in poetry, 125
and objects/places, 28, 67–68, 98, 123, 141, 151, 180, 202
as phenomenon, 104–105
renewal and transformation through, 105–106
seeking an older brother, 80
and shrine/altars, 104, 130
and transformation, 105–106, 157–159
See also mirroring/identification
semiotics
amplifiers, 115, 126
and Dean as *index*, *symbol* or sign, 109
definition and use of, 15–16, 112, 178
devotee-object (dyadic) interaction, 107–108
and the Gallery-Museum struggle for control of Dean image, 41
"habit change", 125–126
icon defined as complex symbol, 112
interactions with an *icon* (sign-object), 112, 116–117, 120–121
interpretants, 109–113, 121
meaning as a bundle of responses to a *sign-object* (*icon*), 113–115
the object-*sign-icon* interaction, 108–109, 201
and object-*sign-icon* interaction in Kendall's art, 109, 139, 141
permutations of consciousness in, 108–109, 126
and the sacred, 121–122, 125
and self/Dean *internal conversations*, 96, 107, 109–110, 112, 115, 122
and time, 108, 112, 114
transformative processes, 156–159
triadic interaction processes (object-sign-interpretant), 109–112
viewing a wrecked Porsche photo, 113–115
See also interpretants; sign-objects; signs; transformation
semiotics of pilgrimage
and devotee-*icon/object* vs. devotee-*place* interactions, 178
emotion and *transformation*, 178–181, 206
sexuality in Dean image
and his appeal, 17, 35, 100, 133
and masculinity of icons, 17, 35
and Museum vs. Gallery struggle to control it, 41–43, 47, 60–63
and "mystique", 35–36
and stolen bronze bust, 57, 137, 140
See also homosexuality
Sheen, Martin, 30, 84, 171, 172
Sheridan, Liz, 44, 47, 171
Shirt, Matthew, 10
Shirts by Lenny, 63
shrines/altars
James Dean rooms/walls, 69–72, 71, 100, 130, 156–157, 192
to Nietzsche, 198
and self/object phenomenon, 104
sign-icon, 108
sign-objects
and consciousness, 126
as Dean, things and places of him, 110
as *icon* or *sign-icon*, 108, 112
and *interpretant* interaction, 122, 217n30
and interpreter (devotee), 110–111, 112

linked to *signs* as a bundle, 121
object-sign variant of, 114, 115
signs
  in Peirce's theory, 112, 113, 115, 121
  interacting with self, 112
  as *interpretant*, 217n30
  vs. symbols, objects and icons, 8, 10–12, 201, 217n28-31
Singer, Milton, 14, 107, 109–110, 178
social media
  Google's "Books Ngram Viewer", 211n1
  Instagram, 30
  Milenio, 33–34
  Pinterest, 129, 212n1
soul/souls, 97, 134, 180, 191, 200, 203
Spitz, Bob, 132
sports, Dean's interest in, 25
Sports Car Club races, 27–28
Springsteen, Bruce, 90, 133, 136
Spyder, 135
  See also Porsche
Stark, Jim, Dean character in *Rebel*, 20–21
Stein, Phil, 146
Stevens, George (Director), 27
Stock, Dennis (photographer)
  background, 1, 4–5
  background and significance of, 1, 4–5, 23, 146–147
  Beyond Iconic (documentary film), 148
  Fairmount photos, 23, 146, 164
  Fairmount pilgrimage and *transformation*, 180
  "iconic" photographs, 23, 147–148
  James Dean Revisited, 146
  Life Books/*Life* magazine, 23, 146, 148
  Life (film "biopic"), 148
  and Morrissey, 132–133
  photographs of Fairmount, 132, 164
  satori, *studium* and *punctum* concepts, 147
  Times Square photo in the rain, 23, 147
  "Tintype with Sow", 147–148
  "You Can't Go Home Again", 147
Strasberg, Lee, 26
Students for a Democratic Society (SDS), 37–38, 39
"Style Lyrics" (Swift), 134
"Suedehead" music video (Morrissey), 132
suicide, 29, 60, 87, 88, 191
Surviving James Dean (Bast), 58
Swenson, Greg, 149–151
Swift, Taylor, 134
symbols
  and collective representations, 14
  Dean as "the symbol" for Fairmount, 61
  multivocal, 8, 41, 57, 61
  tattoos, 64, 152–154, 168, 183
Taylor, Elizabeth, 1, 148, 171, 216n17
Taylor, Mark, 195
teenagers. *See* adolescence
temporal transformation, 179
  See also time/timelessness
testimonials and tributes to Dean, on YouTube, 4
"texts", defined, 195
The Hero: A Study in Tradition, Myth, and Dreams, 7
The Hero with a Thousand Faces, 7
theophany, 157
The Ritual Process (Turner), 8, 41, 178, 181, 218n36
time and space, intermixed in pilgrim-

ages, 98, 179–180, 185–186
Times Square photo in the rain, 23, 147
time/timelessness
   in creative works, 97–98, 105–106, 108, 134, 186
   "everywhen" of Dean rituals/myth, 104–105, 185–186
   "frozen in time", 28
   and the self/Dean (part of his life), 104–106
   and that "other time" dialectic, 179, 180, 185, 206–207
   time and space/place, xiii, 186, 202
tough guy/anti-hero image, 17
tragedy, and the making of Dean's image, 24
transcendence, 13, 88, 118, 198, 203, 209
transformation
   and Dean as intermediary of creative expression, 105–106
   of Dean into sign and symbol, 8, 39, 41
   defined, 178
   experiences of Deaners, 102, 125–126
   and the sacralization of ordinary objects, 122, 128, 155, 156–159, 190
   six types of, 179
   as *transformation* in semiotics, 178–181, 206
   the transformative process, 190
   and "witnessing", 156, 157–159
transformation, communitas (community), 180–183
   Deaners moving to Fairmount, 83, 86–87, 181, 182–183
   See also community; James Dean Gallery (the Gallery); memorial services, annual in Fairmount

transformation, existential, 106, 179–180
   See also Deaners, creative pursuits; emotions; mirroring/identification; self/Dean
transformation, journey completion
   defined, 180
   See also Fairmount, IN, pilgrimage sites; pilgrimage sites
transformation, physical, 179
   look-alikes, xvi, 30, 74, 168–169, 171, 179, 207
transformation, tactile
   defined, 179–180
   touching his things/being where he had been, 28, 67–68, 98, 123, 141, 151, 180, 202
   See also collecting; Fairmount, IN
transformation, temporal, 179
   See also myth/mythology; time/timelessness
triadic relation, as result of interaction between person and symbol, 15
Troup, Bobby, 135
Trundle, Robert, 214n9
Turner, Victor, 8, 41, 178, 181, 218n36
TV, CBS *News Sunday Morning*, 54
TV programs, "James Dean: The Man, The Legend" (Larry King-CNN), 47
Twitter, 215n11
   and Curtis Management, 215n11
Tysl, Robert Wayne, 33, 194, 213n5, 214n8, 215n12, 216n22, 218n38
UCLA, 22, 25
The Unabridged James Dean: His Life and Legacy from A to Z, 81
Van Fleet, Jo, 27
videos/DVDs
   James Dean: Forever Young, 215n14

James Dean—Born Cool, 215n14
violence, and "mystique", 35–36
"visual haiku", 147
vulnerability, and Dean appeal, 17, 31, 74, 120
Wainwright, Loudon, III, 134
Wall Street Journal (Castro), 50
Wanless, Stanley (sculptor), 136
Warhol, Andy, 73, 128, 136, 149, 152
Warner Bros., 1, 27, 28, 82, 84, 148–149
Warr, Ann, 85, 142
websites, www.jamesdean.com, 212n1
White, Christine, 171, 174
Whitmore, James, 22, 26
The Wild One (Brando), 32, 35, 38
Winslow family, 24–25, 41, 43–44, 45–47, 53, 180
  Joan (cousin), xvii, 25, 45, 47, 56, 85, 215n12
  Joanne, 85
  Marcus Jr. (cousin "Mark"), 25, 45, 56–57, 59, 62
  Marcus Sr. (uncle), 1, 24
  Ortense (Aunt), 1, 24–25, 70, 85
Winslow farm, 70, 85, 99, 123–124, 157
Wish You Were Here, Jimmy Dean (Dawber), 128, 140
Withers, Jane, 47
"witnessing", 156, 157–159
Wittgenstein, Ludwig, 107, 187
Wood, Natalie, 3, 29, 40–41, 151, 214n10
worship
  of Dean as civil religion, 13
  hanging out at the "Gallery" as possible form of, 60
  as liminal between secular and sacred, 14
WRDI (*We Remember Dean International*) fan club
  on Alexander's *Boulevard of Broken Dreams*, 50–52
  Deaner and fan creations, 123, 125, 129–130
  and Deaners/fans, 71, 99, 188, 216n21
  history, 189, 214n7
  testimonials, 67, 99, 129
youth
  and 1950s-1960s culture, 35–38, 152–154
  and appeal of Dean's rebel image, 21, 81
  and emergence of films and media for teenage market, 24, 28
  "urban tribes" phenomena, 33–34
youth images
  in Bob Dylan's "May you stay forever young", 131
  and Deaner identifications, 96
  "Forever Young", Neil Young song, 96
  James Dean: Forever Young (DVD/Video), 215n14
  James Dean, Forever Young: Rebel, Outcast, Hero, Legend (documentary), 47
  "Live Fast and die young", and family control of image, 47
  Live Fast-Die Young: Remembering the Short Life of James Dean, 17–18
  and timelessness in Fairmount representations, 185
YouTube, 211n1
  and Deaner artworks, 129
  and popularity of Dean over time, 4, 211n1
Zalov, Eric, 31–32, 34
Zeigler, Phil, 216n21
  and the annual *Back Creek Friends*

Meeting memorial service, 171,
    172*fig.*, 174, 175
becoming a Deaner, 81–87
in Fairmount, 143, 182
leather jacket and father, 82
memorabilia collection, 85–86, 86*fig.*
    4.1

Made in the USA
Middletown, DE
27 November 2022